To Shirley,
Thank you so
to your home. It was
great to
meet you!
Best wishes,
Debbie Sands

Tropical Rose

DEBBIE SANDS

CROSSFIELD
PUBLISHING

CROSSFIELD PUBLISHING
www.crossfieldpublishing.com
books@crossfieldpublishing.com
2269 Road 120, R7, St. Marys, Ontario, N4X 1C9, Canada

ISBN 978-1-990326-28-8 (softcover)
ISBN 978-1-990326-38-7 (ePub)

Printed and Bound in Canada.

Editor: Maura Blain Brown
Cover and interior: Magdalene Carson RGD New Leaf Publication Design

ONTARIO ARTS COUNCIL
CONSEIL DES ARTS DE L'ONTARIO
an Ontario government agency
un organisme du gouvernement de l'Ontario

Crossfield is committed to publishing works of quality and integrity.
This is a work of fiction. The characters, scenes and situations are all drawn from the author's imagination. Any resemblance to any persons, living or dead, is entirely coincidental.

Library and Archives Canada Cataloguing in Publication
Title: Tropical rose / Debbie Sands.
Names: Sands, Debbie, 1952- author.
Identifiers: Canadiana (print) 20230528465 | Canadiana (ebook) 20230529267 | ISBN 9781990326288 (softcover) | ISBN 9781990326370 (EPUB)
Subjects: LCGFT: Biographical fiction.
Classification: LCC PS8637.A549 T76 2023 | DDC C813/.6—dc23

In memory of my grandmother,
Cécile Marie Thérèse Robinson

Acknowledgements

This book probably wouldn't have happened without the Covid pandemic as, although I had always wanted to try writing a novel, I couldn't seem to find the time or the commitment to actually sit down and do it! Finally, having time on my hands, I began to think about what I wanted to write about my grandmother's interesting life. There were a few people along the way who helped me, and I would like to acknowledge them here.

First of all, I would like to thank my publisher, Tina Crossfield, for believing in me. Also, my wonderful editors, Isabel Amiento for your encouragement, and Maura Brown for helping me to improve a work in progress. You both were invaluable in making the story better.

I'd like to also thank my family for their support of my writing efforts. My husband, Ed, for reading through the manuscript and helping me with World War 2 history and geographical matters. Also my cousin, Liz, for providing me with some of our grandmother's anecdotes. I wish my mother, Valerie, had still been with us to give me some finer details of some of the biographical details of my grandmother's life. Also, my children, Stephanie and Mike, and my friends, for supporting me throughout my endeavours.

Last, but not least, I'd like to thank my beautiful grandmother, Cecile, for being an inspiration for her resilience, strength, kindness and encouragement of her grandchildren. She was a wonderful lady who had friends and admirers all over the world. I'll always cherish the memories, Grandma!s

Tropical Rose

My grandmother and Uncle Philip

My great grandparents

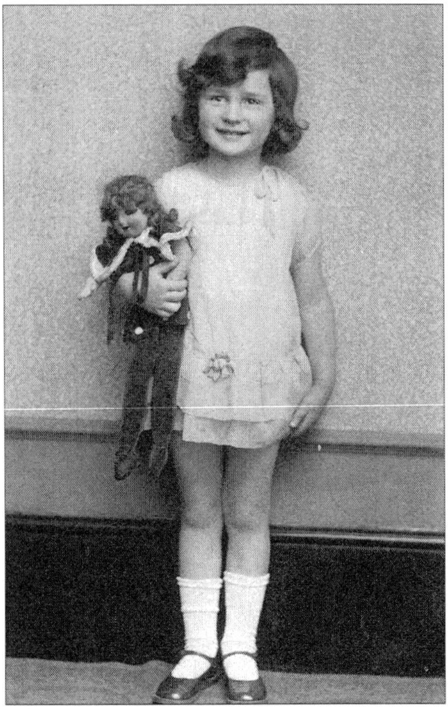

My mother, age 6.

My Auntie Joyce

My grandmother's house in London

My grandmother and her roses

"Come along, Thérèse!" said her mother to the girl. "We still have to check on Georgette's baby, so we'd better hurry if we're to get back in time for luncheon."

Madeleine bid goodbye to Rachelle, and they hurried out of the shack. The full heat and humidity of the day struck them as they began to walk along, and Thérèse immediately felt a light sweat break out on the back of her neck and down her back. Her corset and the ankle-length dress she wore weighed heavily on her, and she wished she could be wearing only her shift to walk the mile-long path back to the Big House. Around them, the palm trees and lush growth beside the plantation seemed to buzz with the heat, as lizards and other creatures scurried about and exotic insects flew from plant to plant.

The tropical climate of Mauritius was not pleasant for walking in the noon-day sun, but Thérèse's mother was committed to her rounds with the sick servants. She loved them all as though they were her children and, even though she had nine children of her own, she never failed to look after the sick and the injured. She had started bringing Thérèse with her on these errands of mercy when she turned twelve, but Thérèse didn't possess the same devotion to the household staff as her mother. She regarded them as rather beneath her, although she always remembered the soft and gentle hands of her "Nana" with fondness. The large, coffee-coloured woman who had looked after Thérèse until she started school had loved her devotedly, and Thérèse had returned her love. However, as time went by and she started to interact with her classmates, the inbred snobbery that most of the plantation owners and their families felt towards their employees started to manifest itself. She began to look down on the servants who ran their home so silently and diligently, although she was always unfailingly polite to them, as she had been taught to be.

After checking on the new mother and her baby, they finally arrived at the Big House, which was the centre of life on the plantation. It was a white, fourteen-room house, with a large hall, a sitting-room and dining room at the front, several bedrooms upstairs and servants' quarters at the back. The busy kitchen, presided over by the East Indian cook, Dhala, led off the dining room. Madeleine's husband, Paul, ran the estate efficiently with the help of his overseer, Ahmed, and the business manager, Charles. Thérèse was somewhat afraid of her father although, as she was his first daughter after five sons, he had a soft spot for her and didn't treat her with the same severity as he did his boys. Her two younger sisters, Angélique and Marie-Anne, were treated with indulgence, but not with the same devotion as was shown to Thérèse. The youngest child, André, was still a toddler and therefore mostly ignored by his father.

"Madeleine, *chérie*, where have you been?" asked Paul, as Thérèse and her mother walked into the cool dining room for lunch. The large fan overhead kept the air circulating, and the heat was not as suffocating as in the rest of the house at this time of day. The other children were already seated there with their father, and they studied their mother and sister as they came in, although didn't greet them.

"Tending to Amélie, then visiting Georgette and the baby," Madeleine replied as she sat at the foot of the table opposite her husband.

"And how is the little one?" he asked, although he didn't really care about the servants' offspring, but rather saw the baby as a future employee of the plantation. Créoles were hard-working and didn't ask for high wages. He wasn't concerned about Amélie, either, and already regarded her as a lost cause. Even if she survived the pneumonia, she probably wouldn't be able to work for several days once she recovered.

"He seems to be thriving, and should grow into a strong youth," replied Madeleine, joining her hands together to say grace, as her husband nodded his head in satisfaction.

Madeleine recited the prayer, and then her family joined her in making the sign of the cross. Everyone looked towards Paul to see when he would start eating before picking up their knives and forks to begin the first course.

"I believe there's a war coming," said Paul, chewing thoughtfully on the mango and arugula salad.

"I sincerely hope not," replied Madeleine nervously. She glanced around the room at her six sons, four of them old enough to sign up for the army. The boys continued eating soundlessly, although Thérèse noticed Rémy and Dominic, the two eldest, exchanging a quick look of excitement.

"If there is," replied Paul, "and I don't doubt it with the way the Kaiser is sabre-rattling these days, then the boys will join the French army. I'm not having them fighting with the bloody British!"

Madeleine pressed her lips together. Her husband had always maintained a staunch dislike of the British rulers of the island, no doubt inherited from his father, who had come to Mauritius in the mid- nineteenth century. Mauritius had been colonized by the French in the eighteenth century, and then was lost to the British in 1810. The British had allowed the French colonists to keep the language they spoke and their legal system, and to decide in which army they would fight in the event of a war involving both countries. To Madeleine, it didn't matter which army her sons were enrolled in, she didn't want to lose a single one of them to the Kaiser and his imperialism. All but one of her children, a stillborn, had survived childhood. It had been her luck that all of them remained healthy, although she knew that an infection or a tropical disease could easily carry them off at any time.

Paul continued to discuss the Kaiser and the impending war that was being talked about in the newspapers. With his contempt for the British rulers of Mauritius, he had always kept the French language and way of life on his estate. The fact that he paid his taxes to the British government irritated him, although he wasn't above accepting subsidies for his sugar cane crops in the event of a drought or flood.

"Kaiser Bill is trying to wrest our colonies from us," mused Paul. "It won't be long before we see his armies landing on the shores of our little island."

"It will never happen," replied Madeleine, more to comfort herself than to disagree with her husband.

Her statement hung in the air, and silence reigned for the rest of the first course, interrupted only by the kitchen servant removing the salad plates. Thérèse noticed that her mother seemed to be in an irritable mood and kept glancing at her husband nervously. She perhaps didn't appreciate his bringing up the subject of war in front of her sons.

After luncheon, the young people went outside to sit on the covered porch and allow their parents the quiet of the afternoon for a siesta. Thérèse sat beside her sister Angélique, while the boys talked animatedly among themselves.

"Do you think Father is right about the war?" asked Dominic.

"Of course he is!" replied Rémy, his eyes shining. "Then you and I, and Philippe and Georges as well, will become soldiers. Isn't that exciting?"

"What will have to happen for Britain and France to declare war on Germany?" Georges asked.

"I've heard that Bismarck said many years ago that the Kaiser would lead Germany to ruin," added Philippe. "He wants to build a navy as strong as the British, and some say that he has succeeded."

"He certainly has ambitions to win Germany a place in the sun," remarked Rémy sardonically.

Thérèse stopped listening to the conversation, entertaining fantasies of handsome young French soldiers arriving on the shores of Mauritius, and dances being held at the Hotel de Ville to celebrate their victories against the enemy. She was aware of a slight feeling of dread, however, that it might be the German army arriving on the island and that her brothers would have to fight them. She imagined each of her tall, strapping brothers in their uniforms, engaged in hand-to-hand combat with their adversaries. She felt a sudden cold flutter down her back as she saw in her mind's eye one of her brothers being struck by a sword.

But then it occurred to her that this war wouldn't be fought with swords, but with guns, and she dismissed the frightening image from her head. The heat was making her sleepy, and she laid her head on her sister's shoulder, closing her eyes and dropping off into a light slumber.

2

Thérèse opened her eyes and looked around her room. In the dawn light, she could just barely make out the shape of the huge wooden dresser with the gilded mirror and porcelain washbasin on it. The thick curtains kept out the light during the night, but a crack in them was allowing a few rays of early morning sun to creep in. She jumped out of bed and slipped out of her nightdress, pulling on her shift and taking a quick drink from the water glass on her bedside table.

She crept to the bedroom door and opened it a crack, making sure that nobody was in the long hallway, not wanting any of the boys or the servants to see her in her shift. When she ascertained that the coast was clear, she crossed the landing and crept soundlessly down the stairs.

Once downstairs, she crossed the front hall and let herself out of the house, closing the door gently behind her. She stepped into the garden and bent over the nearest bougainvillea bush, tipping her face down into the fragrant flowers and allowing the early-morning dew to bathe her face. She did this every day, believing that it would refresh her and keep the skin on her face soft. She had been told this by one of the servants and would continue to do it every day that she lived on the island. She had beautiful skin for the entirety of her life, and always credited "washing" her face in the bougainvillea flowers as a young girl for her soft, ageless skin.

Thérèse walked around the garden a few times, and then returned to the house, creeping slowly back in so as not to disturb anyone. She let herself soundlessly into her room, throwing herself on her bed and falling back into a light sleep until the day servant, Paulette, came to wake her for breakfast.

Her brothers and sisters were already seated at the breakfast table, and Thérèse went to give her mother a kiss on the cheek. She thought her mother looked rather pale and was going to ask her whether she was feeling well when her father entered the room, waving a newspaper.

"Archduke Ferdinand has been assassinated in Sarajevo!" he exclaimed. "They say that a Yugoslavian named Princip is to blame."

"Who's Archduke Ferdinand, Papa?" asked Thérèse.

"He's the heir to the Austro-Hungarian empire," replied Paul. "This will surely upset the powers that be in Europe. I think we've just edged closer to war."

A ripple of excitement ran through Thérèse's brothers.

"Do you think war will be declared, Papa?" asked Rémy, as Dominic looked on happily, hanging on his father's answer.

"It's only a matter of time," said Paul.

Madeleine suddenly stood up, holding her stomach with both hands, and looking very shaky.

"Please, Paul, must we discuss this at breakfast?" she asked, a hand on the back of her chair. Her face had gone from pale to ashen in a matter of moments.

"Are you alright, *Maman*?" Thérèse looked anxiously at her mother, standing up and putting an arm around her mother's waist.

"I'm not feeling well," replied Madeleine, wiping her brow with the back of her hand. She had suddenly broken out in a sweat. "I think I'm going to be sick."

"Thérèse, help your mother to her room," ordered Paul.

Thérèse obeyed her father, guiding her mother gently to the door of the dining room. As they left the room, she heard her brothers eagerly questioning their father about the military and historical situations going on in other countries far removed from their little tropical island. It all seemed miles away from the sugar cane plantations, the lush rain forest and the genteel colonial life in their part of the world.

She assisted her mother into her room and pulled the bell rope for the maidservant to come and help her back to bed. She poured a glass of water from the jug on the nightstand and handed it to her mother, who sat down on the bed and drank it cautiously.

"Do you think you have what Amélie has, *Maman*?" she asked, alarmed. She was aware of the way that illness can be transmitted to those in close contact with people who are ill.

"No, *chérie*, it's something else," her mother responded. She looked up at Thérèse, then decided that the girl was old enough to receive the news. "I think I'm in the family way again."

"Oh, that's wonderful, *Maman*!" Thérèse clapped her hands, but then stopped when she noticed that her mother didn't look happy. She already had nine children, but surely she would happily welcome another little son or daughter? She loved babies and relished the servants' new infants just as much as her own.

Her mother grimaced.

"This is not a good time, with a war possibly coming and your brothers having to join the army," she replied quietly.

"But maybe *Papa* is wrong?" Thérèse suggested. "Surely the murder of this Duke what's-his-name won't cause the European countries to declare war on each other? What difference would it make to them?"

"I don't know, *ma chérie*, but I have a bad feeling about it," said her mother, handing Thérèse her glass of water and lying back on the bed. Thérèse thought she saw tears start into her mother's eyes, and then a soft knock sounded on the door

"Come in, Eugénie," said Thérèse, opening the door to admit her mother's personal maid. "Would you help *Madame* get undressed and into bed, please?"

"Of course, *mademoiselle,*" replied the tall, striking maid. She was about eighteen years old, a pretty Créole who drew many second glances from the male servants in the household. Thérèse had once noticed her father studying the girl rather thoughtfully when she accompanied Madeleine on an errand, but had dismissed the thought at the time.

Eugénie bent solicitously over Madeleine, loosening her robe and murmuring to her quietly. As she quickly slipped out of the room and returned to the dining room, Thérèse thought she noticed her mother wiping her eyes with her handkerchief.

Her father and Rémy were having an animated discussion about the Austro-Hungarian Empire and the tensions escalating between Germany and the other powers of Europe.

"I shall join the French army as soon as war is announced, Papa," said Rémy emphatically.

"Me, too!" echoed Dominic.

"I'm proud of you, my sons," replied Paul, looking fondly from one to the other. "I'm glad that you don't want to join the British."

"Must I join, too, Papa?" asked Philippe, looking slightly terrified. He was the quiet one of the brothers, the one who didn't enjoy sports and riding, preferring to stay in his room reading books or writing poetry. His father had always looked on him rather disdainfully, feeling that he spent his time doing what women do, rather than engaging in manly pastimes. The boy loved animals and was very sensitive.

"Of course, my boy. You're of the right age."

Georges looked happy. "That means I can join the army, as well, Papa? I turn eighteen at the end of the month."

"Yes, you too, my son," replied Paul. He never could remember the birthdates and ages of his numerous progeny. He left it up to his wife to remind him when a birthday or coming of age happened.

Thérèse slipped into a chair beside her sister Marie-Anne and ate her breakfast quickly. Life on the estate had been rather humdrum for the last little while, but it was suddenly becoming more exciting. A new baby in the family, and now her brothers might go off to war. Her fantasy from the day before of French soldiers dancing at the Hotel de Ville popped into her head again, and she couldn't help but feel a warm sensation in the pit of her stomach. Things might liven up around here, and the future looked promising!

3

August 1914

Thérèse was once again accompanying her mother on her rounds through the estate. The afternoon was stiflingly hot and humid, and the only sounds that could be heard were those of birds and creatures in the rain forest. She was tired and getting bored with tramping along the clearing to Georgette's little hut to visit the new baby.

"Will we be done after this, *Maman*?" she asked her mother plaintively.

"Yes, *chérie*," replied her mother. "And then you can go back to the house and ask Dhala to make you some fresh lemonade."

The thought of a cold drink buoyed Thérèse's spirits somewhat, although she felt a pang of guilt that her pregnant mother was probably more tired and hot than she was, and she should be more concerned about her than herself.

"Is it hard being in the family way in this weather, *Maman?*" she asked.

"Yes, it is. But it's what we women have to endure, so there's no point in complaining."

"I hope I never have to be *enceinte,*" Thérèse responded. "It seems as though it would be very uncomfortable."

Her mother laughed lightly as they turned into Georgette's hut, where they found her seated on the floor of the hut with her child. The original settlers of the island had been Dutch, and they brought many slaves from Africa with them to work on the sugar cane and tobacco plantations. The slaves had been freed in the eighteenth century, but many of the French settlers who came to Mauritius later on had taken African mistresses and produced the race of Créoles who now populated the island. Together with the East Indians and Chinese, along with the English and French minorities, the little colony had become quite cosmopolitan. The Créoles hadn't fared as well as the Indians and Chinese who made up the business community, however, and they lived in poverty, working as servants to the whites. The hut was tiny and smelled of the curry that Georgette was cooking for supper.

"How is your handsome little man, Georgette?" asked Madeleine, laying a hand on the infant's head.

"He's growing very well, *madame*," said Georgette. "I'll soon be able to take him into the fields with me."

"Well, I'm glad he's thriving. *Monsieur* will be pleased," said Madeleine. She knew that her husband was always happy to see servants return to their work, as having a full complement of workers meant increased yields of sugar cane. It didn't matter to him if they had to toil with a baby on their backs and stop to feed the child every so often, as long as they were able to produce their quota every day.

"And you are recovered from the delivery? Your bleeding has ceased?"

"Yes, *madame*," the woman said shyly, not looking at her mistress directly. It was generally not considered polite to discuss such things with one's employer, but Madeleine saw herself as a nurse to her servants, and she expected a reply to her question.

"Good. Then you can return to the fields tomorrow," she replied.

Georgette bit her lip but nodded her head. Thérèse thought she might have preferred to stay in her hut for a few more days with her infant, but that was not the life of a servant on the plantations of the island. Madeleine bid her goodbye, and Thérèse followed her mother out of the hut.

They followed the path until they came to the edge of the plantation, and then Thérèse asked her mother whether she could stop and break off a piece of sugar cane for the two of them to chew on during the walk back to the big house. Her mother agreed, and Thérèse ran to the field to find some cane for them. This was her favourite treat, and something she often sneaked out of the house to do on a hot afternoon.

They walked along chewing on the sugary sticks, then finally arrived at the Big House and walked through the door to the lobby. Madeleine murmured something about going upstairs for a nap before dinner when they suddenly heard a commotion coming from the sitting room.

"*Maman, Papa* says that the Allies have declared war on Germany!" Rémy emerged from the sitting room, his face flushed and excited. "Now the boys and I can go and sign up!"

Madeleine put a hand to her mouth.

"That's not good news, Rémy," she said quietly, worry showing on her face. "I don't want you boys to go to war."

For Thérèse's brothers, it was a great honour to be able to serve their homeland in this new war and a privilege to wear the uniform of the French army. Madeleine knew better that many sons didn't return from the battlefield, having lost one brother who fought for the British in the Boer War in South Africa. He had been her favourite brother and, having four sons who were old enough to fight, she knew that there was a very good chance that she would lose at least one of them.

She turned away from her eldest son and pushed open the door of the sitting room, followed closely by her daughter. Paul sat in the great chair, reading the newspaper that announced the start of the war.

"The war has started," Paul declared. "I predicted that it wouldn't be long after the Grand Duke was assassinated. Germany doesn't stand a chance against the Allies. The war will be over by the end of the year."

"I hope you are right, Paul," replied Madeleine. "I don't want any of my sons to be lost in the confrontation."

"They will do their duty, *ma chère,*" he replied, his mouth drawn into a grim line. "I expect my boys to serve France."

His wife turned away so that he couldn't see her face. She had always been easily intimidated by Paul's sternness and had been brought up to be a dutiful wife, but she didn't necessarily believe he was right about everything. Her husband had great devotion to France, but she didn't share his patriotism. Europe was hundreds of miles away from the tiny island where they had grown up, and politics was of no interest to her. Her children's welfare, on the other hand, was of the utmost importance, and she would do whatever it took to protect it. However, she knew that with a declaration of war, her sons would feel a strong obligation to fulfill their military duty and she really didn't have a choice other than to let them go. With her emotions especially sensitive during this pregnancy, she felt tears springing into her eyes and quickly excused herself from the room.

Thérèse watched her hurry upstairs to her bedroom and was puzzled by her mother's behaviour. She felt that it was an honour for her brothers to serve in the French army and that her mother should be proud. But Thérèse adored her beautiful, kind mother and usually took her side in any disagreement, so it didn't occur to her to disapprove of her unhappiness with the situation.

After dinner, the four older boys and Thérèse remained at the table to discuss their signing-up the next morning with their father. Rémy and

Dominic were happy, and Georges seemed infected with their enthusiasm. Philippe remained quiet, but he listened intently to everything that was being said.

"*Papa*, can we go upstairs and lay out our best suits for tomorrow morning?" inquired Rémy.

"Yes, of course," replied his father, beaming.

"Come on, *mes frères*!" called Rémy to the others, "We have to look our best when we go to Port Louis tomorrow, especially if we hope to become officers."

The older three ran up the stairs, two at a time, but Philippe walked more slowly than the others, biting his lip as he went. Thérèse watched him for a moment, then excused herself from the room and followed the boys upstairs.

"Philippe!" she called out softly.

Philippe turned to her, anxiety written all over his face.

"What is it?" he questioned.

"Don't let the others see that you're scared," she replied, coming up to him as he stood awkwardly on the landing. "They'll never leave you alone."

He turned away from her, and she noticed that he was perspiring heavily.

"You'll be a wonderful soldier," she told him. "When the time comes, you'll find the courage to do what you have to, and then you won't be afraid any longer."

"I'm not sure I have the same confidence as you have in me, little sister," he said, avoiding her eyes.

She went to him and hugged him hard. She loved all of her brothers very much, but Philippe, the closest to her in age, had always been her favourite. Vulnerable and sweet, he had never teased her or made her feel foolish. He was always respectful to her, even when their parents weren't in the room, and didn't look down on her as one of a lesser species the way the other boys sometimes did.

"Go and get ready," she whispered. "Don't keep the boys waiting. You don't want them to notice you're worried."

She watched him walk reluctantly up the stairs and suddenly was aware of another cold feeling running down her back just like she had felt before, when the talk of war had begun in their household and their father had announced that his boys would serve in the army. She didn't know what these odd sensations were, but she had a feeling that they were in some way connected to her brother Philippe's dread of going off to war.

4

Her brothers returned that evening from Port Louis, having successfully registered with the French army, but they brought a stranger with them. He was a tall, thin young man, with black hair carefully combed over his rather large scalp and piercing, dark eyes. He wore a small moustache, according to the fashion of the day, but it looked more like down on his upper lip.

Thérèse's father greeted him with affection, hugging him and calling him "*mon neveu*." The young man returned his uncle's hug, then his eyes swept the room and alighted on Thérèse.

"And who do we have here, *Oncle* Paul?" he asked, looking her up and down appreciatively.

"This is my eldest daughter, Thérèse," replied Papa. He turned to his daughter and continued, "Thérèse, this is my nephew, Raoul."

Raoul took her hand and shook it firmly.

"*Enchanté, mademoiselle*," he said, holding her eyes and not releasing her hand immediately. "Why have we not met before, since we are cousins?"

"Second cousins," interjected Paul. "Thérèse has never been off the island, and she wasn't even born the last time you were here with dear Simone."

"I should have been most upset if *Maman* had kept me away from such a charming young woman," replied Raoul, gallantly.

Thérèse eyed him rather suspiciously. He was obviously much older than she was, and she didn't like the expression in his eyes as he gazed at her. However, he was a member of the family, and therefore should be shown politeness.

"*Merci, mon cousin*," she murmured quietly. She avoided his gaze and went to sit on the sofa with her brothers.

"So, how was signing up?" she asked Rémy.

"Wonderful!" he replied enthusiastically. "We met the commanding officer, and we have to return tomorrow to be fitted for our uniforms. We'll probably be shipped out to Europe in about a month from now."

"To Europe?" she asked him incredulously. "But won't you stay here, to guard our little island?"

"Chances are there will never be any fighting here," exclaimed Dominic. "The war is situated mostly in Europe, so we'll be going to France."

Thérèse was taken aback.

"Oh, I shall miss you so much!" She burst out. "What will *Maman* and I, and the other children, do without you here to protect us?" She couldn't imagine life here without her older brothers, exploring the island with them, and all of their adventures in the rain forest. They made her life exciting, in spite of their sometimes patronizing attitudes, and relieved the boredom of everyday domestic chores and accompanying *Maman* on her sick rounds.

"*Papa* and the servants will take care of you, Thérèse," said Georges. "You have nothing to fear here. We'll be the ones seeing the action in Europe and fighting off the Huns!"

The boys immediately began a loud conversation, discussing what it would be like to engage in battle with the enemy. Thérèse glanced over at Philippe, who had remained silent throughout and was biting his lip and looking anxious again.

She shot him a look of sympathy, then noticed her cousin Raoul was once again staring at her. She deliberately looked away and excused herself from the room, feeling his eyes upon her as she went.

Dinner was rather difficult, fraught with sidelong looks from Raoul and her attempts to avoid his eyes. She had been brought up as a very correct young woman and had never been taught how to fend off young men who took an interest in her. She felt that her cousin shouldn't be looking at her in that way, but then remembered that he was only a second cousin, and that Queen Victoria had married all of her children off to their royal cousins throughout the civilized world. In fact, the Kaiser was her nephew, and it seemed strange that he would wage war against his aunt's country. However, it wouldn't be the first time that cousins had taken up arms against one another in the history of the world. The English and the French had been known to do it many times since the days of William the Conqueror.

Thérèse tried to maintain conversations with her two sisters, Angélique and Marie-Anne, during dinner and to avoid Cousin Raoul's gaze. As soon as the three girls were finished eating, she asked Papa for permission to be excused, and the girls stood up and left the dining room.

Once out on the porch, Angélique turned to her.

"I think Cousin Raoul is in love with you, Thérèse," she exclaimed, grabbing her sister's hand excitedly.

Thérèse glowered. "He'd better not be declaring himself to me," she replied in an annoyed tone.

"But he's so handsome!" Marie-Anne interjected. She pretended to swoon against the beam that held up the thatched roof of the porch.

Angélique and Thérèse laughed together.

"He's so old!" replied Thérèse. "And, anyway, he's our cousin and I wouldn't want to marry my cousin."

"You don't have to marry him," said Angélique, coyly, "but you could flirt with him, at least."

"I'll practise on him," answered Thérèse. "But if he tries to kiss me, I'll slap his face!"

"Oh, that's so unkind of you," said Marie-Anne. "I shouldn't mind if he kissed me."

Thérèse and Angélique sized up their thin, rather gangly younger sister and burst into giggles.

"But you're only twelve," announced Angélique, when she had recovered her composure. "*Papa* would be very angry with him if he kissed you and would probably send you away to a convent. At least Thérèse is old enough to be courted."

"Old enough or not," said Thérèse. "I won't allow any old men to kiss me. I prefer young men just a little older than myself, and I don't like men with oily hair and moustaches."

"But *Papa* has oily hair and a moustache," replied Marie-Anne.

"My point precisely," said Thérèse wryly. "I don't want to marry someone who looks like *Papa."*

The three girls giggled again and then became immersed in a conversation about the young men on the island, and who Thérèse should consider as a suitor some day. She frankly felt that there was no one on the island who took her fancy. It was her firm belief that there was someone else far more interesting waiting for her in the future.

5

Thérèse opened her eyes the next morning, jumped out of bed, pulling a wrap around her, and stole down the stairs. She hurried out into the garden, taking in the scent of the magnolias and appreciating the lush green of the vegetation. Dawn was just breaking, and hummingbirds were hovering over the flowers. She walked over to the flowerbed to begin her daily ritual of washing her face in the early morning dew.

She straightened up once she had wet her face and decided on a little walk down the path from the house to the bottom of the garden. She felt the dew slowly drying on her skin and being absorbed by her face. It immediately made her feel so much more awake.

She loved the early morning hours before anyone stirred. Her life in the Big House had always included many family members and servants, so she enjoyed the solitude of her pre-breakfast outings. It wasn't easy to find time alone when you had nine brothers and sisters, and the house would be filled with the cries of a newborn baby before too long. She always enjoyed the babies and helped her mother and the nannies to take care of them, but it certainly didn't make for a quiet life.

She was lost in her reverie when she suddenly heard a twig snap behind her, followed by rapid footsteps. She turned to see her cousin Raoul hurrying towards her.

"Thérèse!" he called out warmly, almost running up to her and then grabbing one of her hands in both of his.

"What are you doing out here, cousin?" she asked, shaking off his hand. "You frightened me!"

"I always go for a ride before breakfast", he replied. "Would you like to join me?"

She indicated her wrap. "I'm hardly dressed for the occasion," she said drily.

He had the good sense to look confused, and she noticed the colour heightening his cheeks.

"You are right," he answered, looking her up and down. "But, perhaps after breakfast, then, would you accompany me?"

"I have to go with *Maman* to visit one of the servants who is unwell," she said quickly, hoping that her mother would indeed have a sick employee to visit. *Maman* did so fairly often, but there was no predicting when one of her kind errands would take place. She might have to persuade *Maman* to send her into town with one of her brothers to pick up supplies instead.

Her cousin gazed at her, seeming to be at a loss for words, and Thérèse almost felt sorry for him for a brief moment. But then she remembered her conversation with her sisters from the night before and started making excuses.

"I must go back to the house," she told Raoul. "Our servant, Paulette, will be upset if she doesn't find me in my bed when she comes to wake me up."

"Yes, yes, of course," he stuttered, standing aside to let her pass. She quickly started up the path, not looking back as she reached the house, where she quietly let herself in and went up the stairs.

Once back in her room, she laid on her bed and wondered briefly what it would be like if Raoul tried to kiss her. She wasn't so sure now that she'd slap his face if he tried. It might be an interesting experiment! She felt a strange, warm sensation in the lower part of her abdomen, but tried to ignore it and reminded herself of how much older he was than she. He must be at least twenty-five. He would be in his thirties by the time she'd be considered an adult, and she couldn't imagine being married to such an old man. Dismissing the thought, she turned over on her side and fell into an uneasy sleep, dreaming of riding horses with old men and walking down the aisle of an empty church in a wedding dress.

The next week went by quickly. Cousin Raoul had come to the town to register for the French army and, like Thérèse's brothers, he also had to be fitted with a uniform and then wait to receive his orders from the commanding officer.

Her brothers seemed to like him, and always took him with them on their various expeditions around the island. Thérèse would go with her mother on her sick visits every chance she could and would hide in her room when her brothers came home. However, she couldn't avoid her cousin completely. Whenever he met her in the house or garden, or sitting at the table during meals, he would steal surreptitious looks at her. There was no mistaking his interest in her, and her sisters teased her about it constantly. She shook it off and tried to ignore him, but she felt his persistent eyes on her all the time. It was difficult to escape him in the busy household, especially as her mother insisted that the family spend as much time together as possible before the boys went off to war.

The day when they were to leave was getting closer. They had received letters from the army base stating that they would sail to Le Havre, in France, on September 1. Thérèse noticed that her mother became sadder and quieter as the time came closer for them to leave, and she also observed the subdued look on Philippe's face. He was the only one of her brothers not to comment on how much he was looking forward to going to war.

One evening, shortly before their departure, Thérèse's father announced at dinner that he thought the family should host a *soirée* before the young men went off to war, to honour them and show the island's pride in their devotion to duty.

Madeleine looked tired when her husband made the suggestion, but said that she would instruct the head groom to ride around the neighbourhood and invite all of their neighbours. She would confer with Dhala, the cook, about a feast that would be prepared for the occasion.

"We must have musicians, too," said Paul. "I will play my violin, and we must ask our neighbour Charles d'Oubouret whom he would suggest we hire to play with me."

"You are going to play for an entire evening, Paul?" asked her mother.

"Well, I'm sure that my wife won't dance with me, in her condition," replied Paul, his eyes twinkling.

"Perhaps one or two dances," she said with a small smile.

"In that case, maybe Charles himself will relieve me of playing the violin for some of the time, or perhaps he can suggest someone who will."

"No doubt someone can," remarked Madeleine. She then began

to discuss suitable foods for the occasion, with some input from her children.

Thérèse soon found herself lost in a daydream about the party. There would be many handsome young men in uniform there, and she would certainly be allowed to dance with them as long as there were grownups in the room who could chaperone the young ladies. There would be other young girls from the neighbourhood, but Thérèse knew by now that she was among the prettiest and most vivacious of them all. She smiled to herself as she imagined young men lining up to dance with her and saw herself finally choosing the most dashing one to be her partner. As she continued her daydream, she felt eyes upon her from across the table, and once again saw Cousin Raoul staring at her. She immediately started to feel discomfited and looked over at her parents.

"May I be excused, *Maman* and *Papa*?" she asked. "I'm feeling rather tired."

"But it's so early yet, *chérie*," replied her mother. "It's not like you to retire at this hour."

Before she could answer, her father shot her a wry glance.

"Perhaps it's because Thérèse gets up so early to go out into the garden," he said.

Thérèse felt hot colour immediately springing into her cheeks and creeping up her neck. She was completely unaware that her father had seen her flitting around the garden at dawn and hoped he didn't think she was up to no good. Worse still, what if he'd seen her with Raoul that day? It wasn't as if she'd asked her cousin to run up to her and start holding her hand. She vaguely remembered that she had pulled it away from him as quickly as she could.

She escaped up the stairs without a backward glance at either her father or her cousin.

6

The next few days passed by in a flurry of activity, as the household prepared for the farewell party for the departing soldiers. With the help of her cook and the rest of the kitchen staff, Madeleine had organized a huge feast. Many loaves and cakes were baked, fruits and vegetables picked from the estate's vast gardens, and meat ordered by the wagonload for the main courses. The pastry chefs prepared beautiful desserts as the day drew closer, and Thérèse could feel her mouth watering when she heard what they were making.

"*Mille feuilles*, chocolate *éclairs* and *petit-suisses*," said Dhala, when Thérèse asked about the desserts. As a result of growing up on a sugar cane plantation, Thérèse had always had a sweet tooth and this was something that would stay with her throughout her life.

There was an air of controlled excitement around the house as the big day approached, and Thérèse enlisted her mother's help to find a suitable dress in her closet.

"You should wear your white lace *de Bruxelles* dress with the white kid leather boots, *ma petite*," advised her mother. "Wear your hair up, and the gold earrings from your grandmother. You'll be the belle of the ball."

Thérèse smiled happily, but her mother's face looked perplexed.

"Goodness knows what I shall wear," she added. "None of my clothes from last year's parties fit me any more."

"Perhaps Eugénie can let one of them out for you, *Maman*?" Thérèse suggested. Her mother appeared lost in thought. She never appeared happy these days and seemed to be having more difficulties with this pregnancy than any of her earlier ones. Thérèse supposed the fact of her sons going off to war was lingering in the back of her mind, and she wondered for the hundredth time why her mother didn't feel the same pride in her boys that the other mothers in the neighbourhood displayed.

"They'll be home by Christmas, *Maman*, you'll see," she whispered, giving her mother a hug.

Her mother looked at her with surprise.

"How did you know what I was thinking about, Thérèse?" she asked.

"Oh, sometimes I get a feeling about what people are thinking," her daughter replied. "It just pops into my head."

"My mother was like that," Madeleine said. "Perhaps you have inherited her gift?"

Thérèse smiled to herself and shrugged her shoulders lightly. She had noticed that she often had feelings about certain things before they happened. Her ability to feel people's thoughts had often taken her by surprise, especially when they confirmed what she had sensed. It made her stop and consider why she had had those cold feelings about Philippe joining the army, but she didn't want to dwell on that thought.

"Why don't you go and find Eugénie now and ask her whether she can let one of your dresses out for you for the party?" she suggested to her mother, by way of changing the subject.

Her mother nodded and left the room. Thérèse entertained herself by pulling out more of her dresses and comparing them with the white one her mother had picked out. There was no doubt about it: with her dark hair and eyes, the white one looked the best on her.

The evening of the party finally came around, and there was great anticipation in the household. The servants had been decorating the hall, the sitting room and the dining room with flowers all day, and the rooms looked beautiful. One corner of the hall had been set aside for the musicians, and a large area was available for dancing. All of the wood furniture had been polished until it shone, the carpets beaten to remove the dust, and the windows cleaned with vinegar until they squeaked. The three sisters were getting very excited about the prospect of being asked to dance by the soldiers. Thérèse knew that she was a good dancer, so she fully expected her dance card to be full.

The party was due to start at six o'clock so, a couple of hours before, she and her sisters went up to their rooms and donned their party dresses. Thérèse was in white lace, Angélique in pale blue silk and Marie-Anne in green linen. They all shared a resemblance to their mother, but Thérèse was more slender than Angélique, and Marie-Anne was just a thin little girl who hadn't started to develop into a young woman yet. Smiling to herself, Thérèse was sure that she, as the eldest, would be quite sought-after as a dance partner.

After the young girls had dressed and brushed their hair until it shone, they went back downstairs to await the start of the party. The servants bustled to and fro, putting the final touches to the food and decorations, then waited for *Madame* to give her approval. Appearing disinterested, Madeleine agreed to everything, and then went to the sitting room to await the first guests.

They started to trickle in a little after six. Thérèse examined the faces of all the young soldiers and heirs of the local estates to see if they would make suitable dance partners. She knew that, with her white dress and kid boots, she looked quite stunning and wouldn't be sitting in her chair for long.

And she was right. Throughout the evening, young men lined up to request her as a partner, and she enjoyed their attentions. She was even happy to dance with Raoul, as he was a practised dancer and very skillful in propelling her in different directions, therefore avoiding a collision with the other dancers.

At about nine o'clock, thirsty and hot from the dancing, Thérèse went out to the dining room to find a cool beverage and help herself to some fruit from the buffet. Ignoring the other guests gathered around the table, she slipped out onto the verandah to enjoy the fresh air. As she was stood alone, enjoying the night air and the fresh papaya slices, she felt someone seize her arm. She turned to see Raoul.

"Cousin Thérèse!" he said, leaning in towards her so that she could feel his hot breath on her cheek. "I'm so glad I found you alone. I've been wanting to speak with you."

"But we cannot be out here alone, Raoul," she replied alarmed. "I have no chaperone! It's unacceptable for a young woman to be alone with a man at any time."

"I know," he said, staring deeply into her eyes. "But I've consulted your father, and he agreed to allow me to speak to you unaccompanied tonight."

Thérèse let out a little gasp and then felt great annoyance at her father. *Papa* knew the rules of etiquette and had no business agreeing to let Raoul be alone with her. She'd been so worried that he had seen her with Raoul the morning her cousin had come upon her walking in the garden, and now she learned that he was encouraging it. She would have to tell her mother about this breach in good manners and social mores.

She had no idea why Raoul wanted to be alone with her with her father's permission, and so was further shocked when he grabbed her other arm and drew her close to him.

"Thérèse," he murmured quietly, and so close that she could smell the alcohol on his breath. "You must know, you must have guessed, that I am in love with you."

"In . . . in . . . love?" she stammered, consternation showing on her face. "But you're my cousin! We've only just met!"

"Second cousin," he replied, trying to draw her even closer. "And I didn't need long to know how I felt about you. I fell in love with you the minute I saw you! You're the most beautiful girl I've ever seen, and the kindest, and . . . . – "

His voice trailed off, and suddenly he was on his knees in front of her, holding tightly onto her hand.

"Cousin Thérèse," he said, gazing up at her enraptured. "Will you marry me?"

Thérèse felt terrified. What was she supposed to say? She didn't want to marry her cousin, especially one who was so much older. She hesitated to reply, and the seconds ticked uncomfortably by. The expression on Raoul's face slowly changed from ardent to desperate, and she found the courage to face him squarely.

"No, Raoul, I can't marry you," she said quietly. "You're my cousin! Besides," and here she paused for a few moments, "I don't love you."

Raoul looked devastated. Standing up, he seized her by the shoulders.

"But I love you so much!" he stammered. "I'll teach you to love me. You will love me in time, I promise you."

He lowered his face to hers and began to roughly kiss her on the mouth. She recoiled in horror.

"No, no . . . , " she tried to struggle out of his arms, but he held her firmly pinned. "Let me go! Let me go, Raoul."

After a moment, he relinquished his grip on her and stepped back to examine her face.

"Very well," he said, quietly. "So I can't hope that you might change your mind?"

"No! I'm going back inside."

She could feel tears starting into her eyes as she entered the dining room, looking around wildly for her mother. Madeleine was nowhere in sight, so she turned and left the room, heading up the stairs to her bedroom. There, she flung herself on the bed, feeling hot and cold by turns.

Thoughts raced through her head. How dare Raoul ask her to marry him? She was only sixteen, and certainly didn't want to tie herself to an older man, a soldier who was heading off to war and might never come back. And her mother needed her here to help look after the younger ones and to assist her when she gave birth. How could *Papa* have helped Raoul in his ridiculous marriage proposal? She felt anger towards him, just as much as she had towards her cousin.

After Thérèse had calmed down a little, she decided to collect herself and go back down to the party. She would ignore Raoul as best she could and dance with as many of the other soldiers as would ask her. Also, at the first opportunity, she would find her mother and tell her what had happened on the verandah.

She let herself quietly out of her room and started down the corridor. In the darkness, she could hear whispering and she tried to make out the identity of the two people standing outside Papa's bedroom. There was a man and a woman standing close to one another, the man's hand on the woman's arm. As Thérèse drew closer, she could hear what the man was saying in an impassioned whisper,

"Please, Eugénie, don't keep me waiting any longer. I've waited so long for you, and you know that I want you." It was *Papa's* voice.

Eugénie! What was she doing up here with *Papa?* She should be downstairs, helping with the guests at the party, not lingering here with Thérèse's father. Thérèse felt anger rising within her, despite her fear of her father.

"*Non, Monsieur,*" replied Eugénie, trying to turn away from him. "I cannot do this, even though I want to. I cannot betray *Madame.* She has been so good to me."

"She does not need to know, it will be between you and me," *Papa* answered, trying to put his other arm around Eugénie.

So Thérèse wasn't the only one being unwillingly importuned tonight! No wonder *Papa* had given permission to Raoul to be alone with her. He was trying to find time to be alone with his wife's maidservant.

"*Papa,* Eugénie, what are you doing up here?" Thérèse suddenly demanded, startling them both.

They sprang apart. *Papa* stammered excuses, while Eugénie looked dismayed, her head hanging in shame.

"Go downstairs and find *Maman,* Eugénie," Thérèse told her haughtily. The servant hesitated, and Thérèse turned back to her father. "And, *Papa,*

I want to know what business you had telling Raoul that he could be alone with me tonight?"

Papa returned his daughter's stare, seeming to be completely recovered from being caught with the maidservant, then gestured to Eugénie to obey Thérèse. He turned back to his daughter.

"He wants to marry you, Thérèse," he replied. "And I thought he deserved a chance to propose on the eve of setting sail for war."

"You should have told me first!" She stamped her foot. "And what are your doing up here with the servant?"

"That does not concern you, *ma fille*," he replied sternly, as Eugénie began to descend the stairs. "Why don't you go back down to the party?"

"I will in my own time," she said angrily. "I'm very disappointed in you, *Papa*!"

"Do not speak to me that way, Thérèse," he admonished her coldly.

Somewhat cowed, she turned and stomped away from him, following Eugénie down the stairs. She realized that her father had an interest in the pretty Créole girl, and had sensed it when she observed him staring at Eugénie several months ago. It was no secret that colonial men often made advances to the servant girls, and sometimes ended up with mistresses for many years, fathering children who remained on the estate as servants. It was an easy, but wrong, way of ensuring free labour, and also a way of finding consolation when a wife tired of her husband's attentions, or ceased to be attractive to him. The mistresses often outlived the plantation owners' wives and remained with their lovers until the end of their lives.

Quietly simmering, Thérèse agreed to dance with the first available soldier to ask her, trying to throw herself into the party and barely speaking to anyone until she had calmed down somewhat.

Many years later, she reflected back on that evening, and realized the implications of what had been happening. It seemed that women were just playthings in the hands of men, to be passed from one to another with no questions asked, and that angered her. Her father could arrogantly grant her cousin's request to marry her, without even telling his daughter what was happening, and then turn around and proposition his young and attractive servant girl without any thought to his wife, or the servant's feelings.

She would remember that night for many years to come.

7

November 1916

As it turned out, the war that was supposed to be over by Christmas ended up being nothing of the kind. The German army was very well prepared for the confrontation, and their soldiers were extremely well trained.

This was turning out to be a war like no other. It was fought mostly in the trenches of Europe, and the soldiers existed in conditions of mud, filth, rats and lice, while being subjected to every kind of weather. They lived underground in long, narrow corridors, where there was scarcely room to move, and the temperature was either freezing cold or insufferably hot, depending on the time of year. Horrendous injuries occurred on the battlefield, and mass casualties happened on both sides. The conditions of army hospitals were deplorable, and many patients didn't survive the ministrations of the doctors and nurses, who were dealing with acute shortages of medical supplies. To make matters worse, the enemy was employing mustard gas in the trenches, and many soldiers died a horrible, agonizing death. Young men who had been wounded were returning to their homes irreversibly damaged by their injuries, but also by the terrible sights they had witnessed. The term "shell-shocked" was starting to be used, but it really didn't adequately describe the horrific mental anguish these men endured after what they had seen and experienced.

Thérèse would never forget the day the first telegram arrived from France. Her brothers had been fighting in Verdun during the Battle of the Somme, which had gone on for five months. They wrote often of the cold and hardships they endured and wished so much that they could come home to their warm tropical island. Their youthful enthusiasm at the prospect of going to war two years earlier had been replaced by a hard bitterness towards their government for the sacrifices that they were required to make on a daily basis. However, they had been raised with a strong sense of duty and would do what was expected of them.

Thérèse and her mother had been in the sitting-room in the late afternoon, a sense of companionship surrounding them as they worked. Madeleine had volunteered to sew garments for the army and had easily enlisted her daughters to help her. Her youngest child, a boy named Aristide after his grandfather, was having a nap in his little bed in the upstairs nursery as she and Thérèse were working in silence. The other two girls had gone to request some biscuits from the maids in the kitchen, their sewing left idle on the sofa. A knock came suddenly at the sitting-room door.

"*Entrez*!" called Madeleine, looking up from her work. She turned to Thérèse. "Who do you think it could be?"

"I don't know," Thérèse stared at the door as her mother turned the knob, opened it, and let in a telegram boy, who handed the document to her mother. An uneasy feeling enveloped her.

"Telegram*, madame*!" he announced, stating the obvious.

"Thank you," she replied. "Wait a moment."

She went over to the little bureau in the corner of the room and extracted a small purse from one of the drawers. She took out ten *centimes* and handed them to the young man, who smiled and nodded his head in acknowledgement. He left the room and Madeleine quietly closed the door after him.

"What can this be?" she asked her daughter, who shrugged and replied reluctantly,

"Open it."

Madeleine went back to the bureau and took out a paper knife. She quickly slit open the envelope and read the contents of the telegram, then suddenly let out a loud cry.

"*Oh, mon Dieu*!" she exclaimed, clasping her hands to her chest and dropping the envelope to the floor.

"What is it, *Maman*?" asked Thérèse. When her mother didn't answer, she quickly put down her sewing and ran over to her. Madeleine let out another stifled cry, stumbled forward and burst into huge, racking sobs.

"My son, my son . . . " she gasped out, as Thérèse hastily seized her in her arms to stop her from falling to the floor. She half-carried her mother to the sofa and eased her gently down, before picking up the document that had fallen to the floor.

She only glimpsed the words, "Regret to inform you . . . . . your son, Philippe Joseph . . . . at Verdun, the first day of November . . . " but she knew immediately what had happened. Those cold feelings that she had always had about Philippe going to war, and his own dread of becoming a soldier, had been nothing but premonitions of what was to happen.

Her sweet, sensitive brother had died, as they both knew he would, on the battlefield only one week ago. She briefly wondered why she hadn't felt it at the time that it happened, but then her own grief and the inconsolable sobbing of her mother took all of her attention.

"Oh, my God, oh, my God, oh, my God!" she repeated over and over. "*Maman*, what are we to do?"

Her mother was able to gasp out, "Go and let *Papa* know." Her sobs became louder and she clung to Thérèse, not letting her leave to call her father.

The door opened and Angélique and Marie-Anne came in, biscuits in their hands and laughter on their lips. As soon as they saw Thérèse and their mother in their grim embrace, however, their expressions turned to concern.

"What's the matter?" asked Angélique, going to Thérèse.

"It's . . . Philippe . . . he's been . . . k-killed!" stammered out Thérèse. Both girls immediately burst into loud, uncontrollable crying, and Thérèse stood up and seized Angélique by the arm.

"Here," she said to her, as tears streamed down her own face. "Stay with *Maman*. I'm going to find *Papa*."

Angélique sat down on the couch heavily and took her mother in her arms, while her older sister left them together and went out of the room. She ran up the stairs, almost tripping due to the tears that fell ceaselessly and almost blinded her.

"Where is *Papa*?" she asked the nanny in little Aristide's room. The young Créole girl stood up, looking questioningly at Thérèse's face and streaming eyes.

"Are you alright, *mademoiselle*?" she queried.

"No!" sputtered out Thérèse. "Just tell me where he is, if you know."

"I think he's in his room," replied the young girl.

Thérèse turned and went down the corridor, stopping outside her father's door and hesitating before she knocked. She had never really forgiven her father for the night that Raoul proposed to her and she had found him with her mother's maidservant. She also knew that her mother held him responsible for sending her sons off to war, and that this would be another nail in the coffin of their marriage.

"*Papa!*" she called out. "*Papa*!"

Her father must have been asleep, as he answered her in a rather muffled voice.

"What is it, *chérie*?" he asked, using his favourite endearment for the daughter he suspected was still harbouring rancour against him after two years.

"It's Philippe! He's been killed in the war!"

There was some scuffling inside the room, before he appeared in the doorway.

"What? What did you say?" He looked her up and down in bewilderment. His hair was ruffled, and he was wearing his dressing-gown. His face appeared somewhat red, but Thérèse wasn't focusing on that. Her concern was for her mother.

Overwhelmed with fresh anguish, she looked at her father and repeated what she had said through streaming tears. He stared at her for several moments, as though he couldn't comprehend what she had told him, then finally found words.

"Where . . . where's your mother?" he stuttered.

"Downstairs, in the sitting-room," she replied.

"I must go to her," he said, pulling the door of the bedroom to and starting down the stairs. Thérèse followed him down, almost missing a stair at the top as she felt her way down, unable to see through her tears. She failed to see Eugénie slipping quietly out of the room after she and her father went down the hall.

In the sitting room, Paul took his wife in his arms, and she clung to him for dear life. Any anger that she felt towards him for encouraging her boy to do his duty in going to war had disappeared, and she took some comfort in her husband's arms.

The two younger girls were hugging each other tightly, crying loudly, and saying their brother's name over and over. Thérèse went to her parents and put an arm around each of them, her grief for her childhood playmate and sibling unbearable. It was a terrible blow to their family to lose one of its young members, even though many other families on the island had endured the same losses, and it was to be expected that a young soldier fighting in an enormous conflict like this "Great War" might not come back.

That day remained burned in Thérèse's memory for the rest of her life. It was her first experience of death, other than her mother's stillborn baby, but there would be many more to come. She was to experience two world wars and many losses. Some she could feel in her soul before they even happened, and others that were terrible shocks, but the learning of them never got any easier.

8

Shortly after the death of Philippe, two of Thérèse's brothers, Rémy and Georges, returned home for a short leave from the fighting on the front. Christmas was approaching, but Thérèse didn't expect the family to celebrate it this year, due to the loss of her favourite brother. Yet although the house was still in deep mourning for Philippe, the brothers' return on furlough offered some relief.

Madeleine had kept to her room ever since learning of her third son's death, so Thérèse's days were no longer punctuated with visits to the homes of sick servants. She sometimes used to go for walks in the morning before the heat became unbearable, but it was lonely going by herself, so she would soon return to the house. She spent a lot of her time reminiscing with her sisters about their sweet, deceased brother, and speculating on how much longer the war could continue. Thousands of lives had been lost on both sides due to this terrible conflict, and many young men never returned to their homes and families.

Rémy and Georges were welcomed home warmly by the family, and Madeleine even emerged from her room to hug them and cling to them, tears coursing down her face. Paul, who had been very subdued ever since the telegram announcing Philippe's death had arrived, came to shake his sons' hands and put a firm hand on each of their shoulders.

"I'm proud of you, my sons," he exclaimed, kissing both of them on each cheek in the French fashion. "You must tell me all of your stories from the battlefield."

"I'm sure they don't want to talk about that, Paul," Madeleine stepped in quickly. "They've come home to get away from all that."

The boys quickly assured their father that they would be happy to discuss their war adventures with him, making Thérèse think that they were still proud to be soldiers even though they must have seen many horrors during their time in the army. She knew also that, although they were probably traumatized by what they had seen, they would never admit it to their father.

Her mother wiped her eyes with her handkerchief and told the boys that she would be returning to her bedroom and would see them both at supper. Rémy turned to his father.

"Is *Maman* alright?" he asked.

"She's suffering greatly with the death of Philippe," replied Paul, then added after some hesitation, "and she's in the family way again."

This was the first time that Thérèse had learned of her mother's new pregnancy, but it made sense now. Madeleine wasn't just staying in her room all the time because she was in deep mourning. She was feeling physically ill, as well. Thérèse felt a renewed pity for her mother. She knew how sick Madeleine became during the first few months of a pregnancy, and it once again occurred to her how difficult the role of a wife and mother was. This would be Madeleine's eleventh child, and perhaps would help to take her mind off the loss of Philippe. It would never replace him in her mother's heart, though she knew each child was precious in its own right.

The following morning, Rémy and Georges talked about going into Port Louis to buy some food and supplies for the upcoming Christmas season. Jumping at the opportunity to get out of the house, Thérèse asked her brothers if she could go with them. The trip would be a welcome relief from the still-oppressive atmosphere in the house, although the arrival of the brothers had helped to alleviate the sadness somewhat.

"We have to go to the army base, as well, Thérèse," said Rémy, doubtfully.

"Thérèse can stay in the wagon," suggested Georges.

"Yes, that's true," replied Rémy. "If you don't mind being by yourself for a few minutes, little sister."

"No, of course I don't mind," Thérèse replied. "I can amuse myself for a short while."

It was agreed that the boys would take her with them and that she would keep an eye on the supplies while they were in the base with the commanding officer. Anything would be better than staying in this sombre and sad house for another day.

They set off a couple of hours later, Thérèse dressed in an orange cotton dress that highlighted her dark colouring and deep brown eyes. The heat of the morning was already rising, but she knew that she would be fairly comfortable in cotton. A cloche hat, in the new style of the day, shaded her head from the sun, and she knew she looked quite fetching.

The journey to Port Louis was long and dusty, but they eventually arrived in the port city, which was bustling with activity. The smell of the ocean pervaded the air, but Thérèse enjoyed it after the long ride. It also helped to mask the other odours of the narrow streets, rotting litter strewn about and fish being sold in the market stalls. The street vendors called out their wares, and their customers went about their business with hurried purpose.

Thérèse's brothers tipped their hats to various acquaintances as they drove the horse and cart through the busy streets of the city. They stopped at some of the market stalls along the way and purchased rice, meat and special cakes, baked especially for the upcoming festive season. Normally, this would have been the task of Dhala and her kitchen staff, but the boys were happy to do an everyday activity like visiting the market before the spectre of returning to army life and the front in Europe. Thérèse helped them select some of the items, then placed them in her shopping basket.

They finally arrived at the French Army base, and Rémy halted the wagon.

"Now, are you sure you'll be alright, Thérèse?" he inquired, looking at his sister with concern.

"Yes, I'm almost eighteen. I can look after myself," she replied, happy to just watch people coming and going outside the base. Who knew, there might be a good-looking French soldier who would catch her eye before she quickly looked away, showing the expected modesty. The boys both smiled at her, then turned and ran up the steps of the island army headquarters. Thérèse gazed up at the mountain that was visible from the port city, *Montagne des Signeaux.*

The minutes ticked by, and Thérèse was starting to feel rather bored. Her brothers were taking a lot longer than she had thought they would, and she was beginning to feel hungry. She was thinking seriously of getting down from the wagon and finding a street vendor who could sell her a pastry, or perhaps some fruit, to help calm the pangs of hunger. In the midst of these thoughts, she spotted a young soldier wearing the uniform of the British army. He was hurrying down the street and checking his watch. As he came closer, she noticed that he was quite tall, with a thatch of blond hair under his uniform cap. His eyes, as he came to a stop in front of the wagon, were blue, although one eye seemed a bit larger than the other, which gave him a slightly odd appearance. He was slender, and wore an indecisive look on his face, as though he couldn't decide on whether he should address her.

"Can I help you with anything, *mademoiselle*?" he finally asked, tipping his cap politely. "Are you waiting for someone, or do you need a message delivered to someone inside?"

His French was strongly accented with his English mother tongue, but he was fairly fluent. She was immediately captivated by the smile he gave her at the end of his request. Who was this young British soldier, she wondered?

"No, thank you. I'm waiting for my brothers. They're inside, speaking with the commanding officer."

"Are they supply officers?" he asked, holding her gaze directly.

"No, soldiers on furlough. They'll be returning to the front just after Christmas."

The young soldier smiled again. "Why don't you tell me their names, and I'll let them know if I see them inside that their sister is waiting patiently for them?"

Thérèse returned his smile as she gave her brothers' names to the British soldier and he bowed to her, bidding her good morning. She watched him run up the steps to the base, two at a time, and wondered again who this interesting young man was. Her father had nothing but contempt for the British, but she had never felt any animosity towards the most recent colonialists of the island. Her mother had, in fact, met a few English ladies when she would go to Port Louis to purchase fabric for clothing for the children, and had told her daughter that she found them quite charming and polite.

Her brothers emerged from the base a few minutes later, offering their apologies for keeping her waiting so long.

"Did the young Englishman tell you I was waiting?" she inquired.

"Yes," replied Georges, then smiled at her. "I think you made quite a conquest there, Thérèse. He was most impressed with your patience."

"Indeed!" confirmed Rémy. "And he complimented us on having such a beautiful sister."

Thérèse blushed and started fiddling with the folds of her dress.

"I wouldn't be surprised if he asked *Papa* to allow him to call on our little sister," teased Georges.

"I'm not little!" she rounded on her brother, annoyed with his patronizing attitude, but secretly pleased that the young soldier had commented on her appearance to her brothers. Rémy and Georges both laughed and climbed into the wagon, saying that they, too, were starting to feel hungry and it was perhaps time to return home for luncheon. All the way back to the estate, Thérèse mused on the young British soldier and had an instinctive feeling that she would see him again soon.

9

For the rest of that week, Thérèse found herself thinking of the young British soldier. He kept popping into her mind, no matter what she was doing, and she couldn't seem to dismiss him. He was the last thing on her mind when she went to sleep at night, and he came into her head as soon as she jumped up in the morning to go down to the garden.

She began to fantasize about meeting him again one day and imagined what she would say to him. Of course, she knew that was impossible, as he would have to ask her father's permission to meet her, and they would have to be chaperoned. Many different scenarios kept running through her head, and one day she realized that she didn't even know his name. She would ask Rémy or Georges. He may have introduced himself to them when he delivered her message to them inside the army base.

As luck would have it, just one week after their encounter, her brother

Rémy took her aside after lunch and whispered, out of earshot of *Papa*, that he had something to tell her. She looked at him questioningly, and he said, "Let's go outside."

She nodded and followed him out on to the verandah.

"Do you remember the British soldier who came to find us at army headquarters to tell us that you were waiting for us?" he asked, a conspiratorial smile on his face.

Thérèse's heart suddenly sped up and she blushed as she replied.

"Yes?" she asked, breathlessly.

"He caught up with me the other evening when I was at the hotel having a drink with the officers. He asked about being formally introduced to you one of these days."

Thérèse's breath caught in her throat.

"Really?" she gasped, grabbing Rémy's hand.

"He's quite struck with you. I told him Georges and I could arrange it somehow," he replied.

"But he would have to have *Papa's* permission. I can't be without a chaperone," she stammered.

Rémy smiled again. "Don't worry, Georges and I will arrange it. You can accompany us into town again one day, and we'll make sure we bump into him at a pre-arranged spot. That shouldn't be too hard to do."

Thérèse impulsively threw her arms around Rémy.

"Thank you so much, dear brother!" she cried. "I'll never forget this!"

He laughed conspiratorially and squeezed her hand.

"So you'd be interested in meeting him too, would you?" he asked, smiling, then added, "Just be ready to go at a moment's notice. I have to find him and let him know first, then we'll just casually suggest that you accompany us the next time we go for supplies."

Rémy dropped a quick kiss on her cheek, then walked out into the garden to smoke a cigarette. Thérèse hugged herself and skipped back into the house. All that afternoon, she couldn't help but break out into little snatches of song, and she let her fantasies about the young British soldier run away with her. At one point, she even foresaw herself married to him, and the two of them travelling on a boat across the ocean. She suddenly realized that this was the first time she'd felt truly happy since poor Philippe had been killed.

About a week later, once again at breakfast with the family, Rémy turned to his mother.

"*Maman,*" he said, looking forthrightly at her. "I would like to buy some cakes to eat in the afternoon when we have our tea. Georges and I will be leaving to go back to the front soon, so it would be wonderful to have some cakes we have chosen for ourselves."

How clever Rémy was, thought Thérèse. She knew that her mother would be unable to deny her eldest son's request, since he had reminded her that her sons would soon be going back to war.

"Yes, of course, *chéri,*" Madeleine hastened to reply. "I would be very pleased if you would pick up some other things we need, as well."

Rémy looked as if he was hesitating. "Well, we might need Thérèse's help for that," he said. "Georges and I aren't very good at picking things out by ourselves."

"Yes," Thérèse interjected quickly. "I can help them, *Maman*. Besides, it would be nice to go for an outing, since you're not well enough to go anywhere at the moment." She knew her mother would not be up to sitting in the bumpy wagon in her condition, so this would be an ideal opportunity for her to go with the boys.

"Very well," her mother nodded her head graciously. "Unless *Papa* has any objections . . '?"

Her father shook his head, not looking up from his newspaper, and Thérèse quietly smiled to herself. If only *Papa* knew what she and the boys were up to, he would certainly object. She felt again that warm feeling in the pit of her stomach that lately had been accompanying her thoughts of the young British soldier. She didn't know what it was but was certain she would soon find out.

Before they left, Thérèse had changed out of her morning robe and put on a pretty pale grey silk dress with a matching hat. She had brushed her hair till it shone, and pinched her cheeks and lips until they were bright red. She knew that the silk dress would be warm in the tropical heat of the day, but she had to look her best for the young soldier. She contemplated putting gloves on as well, but decided that it would just be too hot and, anyway, she didn't want him to suspect that she had dressed up especially for him. Seeming too eager would not be appropriate behaviour for a young lady, and she couldn't let him think that she had hopes of their encounter.

She ran down the stairs to her two brothers, who were waiting for her at the bottom.

"*Très jolie!*" murmured Georges when he saw her coming, and Rémy put his lips together in a silent whistle.

"Our English friend will be very impressed," he commented, offering his arm to Thérèse.

She took it, and they walked together out of the house and towards the stables where the horse and wagon were waiting for them. The morning was already stifling, and Thérèse thought she would soon regret her decision to wear silk. The cicadas were buzzing in a loud chorus, and there was a haze over the grounds as the temperature climbed. The sun beat down mercilessly on the lush palm trees and bushes of the garden, but Thérèse didn't even stop to look around her. She was getting too excited about the prospect of seeing the young soldier again.

When they arrived at the stables, Rémy helped her up into the wagon and gave her the list of supplies their mother had asked them to buy.

"Where will we see him?" Thérèse whispered, eagerly.

"He's going to meet us at the market," Rémy replied.

"That way, it will look like we just casually came across him," explained Georges.

Thérèse smiled to herself. This had become quite a plot between her and her brothers to keep their parents from finding out that she had gone to meet a young man, and not just to help the Rémy and Georges with their errands. She hoped and prayed that none of their neighbours would see them when they met up with the soldier. There would be a lot of trouble if *Papa* so much as suspected that this had all been arranged.

The wagon ride to Port Louis was as hot and tedious as it always was, and Thérèse felt the back of her dress sticking to her as she sat there. She wished she had remembered to bring a fan with her, but she had been too excited and anxious about choosing just the right dress and making sure that her hair was just right to even think about it. She would be more prepared next time. If there was a next time.

They finally reached the port city, and the wagon horse picked his way through the dusty streets, guided by Rémy's expert hands. By now,

Thérèse had butterflies in her stomach and was trying to pass the time by thinking up different ways to greet the young man.

"Enchantée, monsieur," shaking his hand, or *"C'est un plaisir,"* bobbing her head, or "Good morning" in her accented English (two of the dozen or so words that she knew). She was still pondering this when the wagon came to a halt and her brothers clambered down.

Georges reached up and held out his hand to her, then lifted her down by the waist. She was now trembling slightly but kept her head down so that her brothers wouldn't see the excitement and anticipation on her face. They made their way quickly down the market street, Rémy and Georges keeping an eye out for a stall that would have some of the cakes they were looking for. Thérèse scanned the street for any sight of the soldier in his green uniform. Suddenly, she heard a voice.

"Capitaine Lemieux, how nice to see you and your brother!"

He was coming towards them on the street, making his way quite rapidly considering how hot it was. Thérèse felt her heart speed up and begin thumping in her chest. She felt so breathless that she was afraid she might faint, so she concentrated on standing upright and pretending to look very nonchalantly at the young soldier as he approached them.

"And who do we have here?" he asked, turning to Thérèse.

"This is our sister," Rémy replied. "Her name is Thérèse."

She had forgotten how tall he was. As he stretched out his hand to her, she completely misplaced all of the greetings she had been practising in her head on the way there. Instead, she stood there dumbfounded as he took her hand in his and shook it.

She finally found her voice and murmured, *"Enchantée,"* bobbing a little curtsy to him, then feeling foolish and straightening up. She heard Georges almost snicker behind her, and was annoyed for a brief moment, until the young soldier addressed her.

"Captain Emmett Richardson, at your service," he said in his heavily accented French, bowing from the waist. "I'm so pleased to meet you."

"L – likewise," Thérèse stammered, staring into his face and once again noticing that one of his eyes appeared to be bigger than the other. She hadn't noticed the first time she saw him that he wore gold rimmed glasses, but that that didn't take away from his appeal. He had a kind face and was quite good looking, in her estimation. That had certainly been her first impression of him, and the subject of all of her thoughts and fantasies over the past week. Her musings were interrupted by a cough from Rémy.

"Well, Emmett," her brother remarked. "Georges and I have some marketing to do, so we will leave you temporarily in charge of our sister."

"It would be my honour," Emmett nodded his head.

Thérèse almost gasped. She hadn't realized that her brothers intended to leave her alone with the soldier. *Papa* would be even more angry if he found out! Her father certainly wouldn't approve of her being alone with a young man he didn't know.

Emmett extended an arm to her.

"*Mademoiselle*?" he looked at her expectantly. She hesitated for a moment, then took his arm and they proceeded to walk away from her brothers, down the busy market street with people of many backgrounds going about their business.

"Where are you from?" she asked him.

"Well, England, of course," he replied. "That is to say . . . from the north of England. Yorkshire."

"Yorkshire?" she questioned, looking at him in a puzzled way. "I've never heard of it. I only know of London, and perhaps Hampshire." An English lady had come calling on her mother once and had said that she was from Hampshire.

"Oh, it's a long way from there," he explained. "And generally quite a bit colder. I live in London now, though . . . or rather, I did before the war."

"What are you doing in Mauritius?" she asked him. "The war is being fought in Europe and Russia. Shouldn't you be there?"

He turned to look at her as they strolled along. He hesitated briefly, then spoke directly to her.

"You may have noticed that I have a glass eye," he said, holding her gaze. "I lost my eye when I was a child, due to an infection. It means that I cannot fight on the battlefield as I only have half of my vision. But I have a good education in accounting and ledgers, so the army put me in charge of supplies over here. It was my excellent fortune to be sent away from the front, which I hear is miserable, to a beautiful island with the prettiest ladies in the world."

Thérèse blushed. The poor young man! Her pity for his affliction only added to the pleasure she felt at the compliment he had just paid her. She liked him even more than she had before. Her heart had stopped beating so fast by now, and she had begun feeling a little calmer until she realized that she should react appropriately to his attentions. She turned away from him, at which he immediately became flustered.

"Oh, I'm sorry, *Mademoiselle* Thérèse, I hope I haven't embarrassed you!" he hastened to apologize.

She didn't want to let on that she was pleased, but then thought better of appearing affronted and turned to him with a demure smile on her lips.

"No, of course not," she answered. "It's true that we have the most beautiful Créole women here."

"I didn't mean the Créoles," he said. She smiled at him again and realized that she was by now starting to feel more comfortable in his presence.

They continued down the road, chatting about his life as the quarter-master at the British army base. He explained that his position required him to keep careful count of everything that was stored at the base and to order new supplies whenever they were needed. To date, he had never allowed anything to run short, even though it took several weeks for items to be shipped out from England.

They soon reached the end of the market before turning back and retracing their steps to where they had first met. Thérèse caught sight of her brothers at a neighbouring stall, and wished that they had gone further afield, so that she and the young captain could prolong their meeting. But Emmett tightened his hold on her arm and whispered in her ear, "May I see you again, *Mademoiselle* Thérèse? I would sincerely like to call on you some time in the next week. Do you think it would be possible?"

She hesitated. She knew how her father felt about British soldiers. What would he think of a young man coming to call on her who haled from the hated country that, in his opinion, had stolen Mauritius away from the French? Well, she would just have to think of a way to persuade him. She was a clever girl and would doubtless come up with a plan.

"Yes, you may," she replied. "But you'll have to speak to my father first."

He was about to speak again, but Rémy and Georges were coming towards them. Perhaps they could help convince *Papa* that this young man should be allowed to court their sister. As he handed her off to her brothers with another quick bow from the waist, Thérèse knew that they had to think of something. Captain Richardson had suddenly become very important to her, and she knew beyond the shade of a doubt that he was going to mean something very significant in her future.

As she retreated, she stole a quick glance behind her. He was standing in the middle of the street, gazing after her as she walked beside her brothers, an expression on his face like that of a puppy looking at a beloved master. She turned back and happily put her arms through each of her brothers', continuing to walk along with a spring in her step. He had found her beautiful and was going to ask *Papa*'s permission to see her again. But she kept her excitement carefully concealed, feigning an interest in her brothers' chatter as they continued down the road.

10

The day arrived when Rémy and Georges were to return to the front. Thérèse had been watching her mother closely, knowing that she was dreading this day. *Maman* had mostly been keeping to her room since her pregnancy was announced, but she had now started to come downstairs again so that she could spend the last few days with her sons.

Thérèse knew that her mother feared this day, anxious that she would lose another son to the war. This dreadful conflict had taken millions of lives, and many families had lost more than one of their sons. It would not be unusual for another member of their family to lose his life. It was a prospect that Madeleine refused to even consider, however. *Papa* seemed unconcerned, but Thérèse knew that he had other things on his mind. On her way to the garden one morning, she had seen Eugénie sneaking out of her father's bedroom. Since the time two years ago when she had caught *Papa* with Eugénie, Thérèse had assumed that nothing had come of his flirtation with her. But catching sight of the beautiful

Créole again confirmed her suspicion that *Papa* was having an affair with the servant girl. Denied access to his wife's bedroom due to her pregnancy, he had sought comfort elsewhere.

The thought of it sickened Thérèse. In spite of the number of children her mother had borne, she didn't like to think of the physical aspect of her parents' marriage. Her mother had taught her several years ago about what happened between a man and his wife, and Thérèse had also observed the animals on the estate during the mating season. Obviously, like many other plantation owners before him, *Papa* was taking advantage of the easy access to the female servants that his position afforded him. Thérèse was confused about the Créoles on the island. They allowed themselves to be abused by the rich and influential ruling class, and she couldn't understand why a healthy and good-looking young woman like Eugénie would suffer the attentions of an ageing and selfish man like *Papa*. It was only much later on in her life that she realized that the female servants on the estate didn't have much choice in the matter.

At breakfast that morning, everyone was quiet and subdued. Her mother's eyes were red and swollen looking, as though she had been crying during the night. No one said very much, and breakfast was eaten in relative silence. *Papa* was reading the paper and commenting on the advance of the Allies on the front, but no one acknowledged his pronouncements.

Finally, Rémy stood up.

"Ready, old man?" he shot a questioning glance at his brother.

"Yes, just about," replied Georges. "You go on up and I'll join you in a few minutes."

Rémy nodded and left the room. Meanwhile, Georges turned to his father.

"*Papa*," he said. "If I don't survive this war, you'll make sure that I'm buried in France, won't you?"

Maman let out a little cry and jumped up from the table.

"Oh, Georges, how can you talk about such a thing?"

"Well, *Maman*," he replied. "You can't bring my body back here, as the journey's too long, and I don't want to be buried in any country in Europe other than France." He turned to his father. "You'll make the arrangements, won't you, *Papa*?"

"Don't worry, my son," *Papa* answered. "Your wishes will be respected."

Maman left the room hurriedly. *Papa* watched her leave, and Thérèse was aware of cold shivers suddenly running down her back. "Oh, no!" she thought, with dread. "I hope we're not going to lose Georges, as well!"

Thérèse knew her mother would barely survive the loss of another child. She would have to remain a strong and dutiful daughter and help her through the difficult times.

Later, she remembered the young British soldier. He had said that he wanted to see her again and she had told him that he would have to ask her father's permission. If this happened soon and he started seriously courting her, could she stay by her mother's side if Emmett asked her to marry him and wanted to take her to England after the war? Perhaps she could convince him to stay on the island with her. There could be worse things for a young Englishman than staying on a beautiful tropical island and helping her father run his sugar cane estate. But then she realized that her thoughts were getting ahead of her, and she stopped herself from fantasizing.

The departure of Rémy and Georges caused a heavy feeling of sadness in the house for several days. *Maman* took all her meals in her room, *Papa* busied himself with the affairs of the plantation and Thérèse and the younger children tried to occupy themselves with reading and walking about the estate. The monsoon season was beginning, when torrential rains fell from darkened skies for an hour every morning, followed by oppressive, steamy heat all afternoon and another downpour in the early evening. The family timed their outings to coincide with the afternoon respite from the rains, but Thérèse could hardly bear the humid, stifling air and kept her expeditions short.

One morning, her father, looking serious, called her into his study.

"Thérèse, how do you know this young man, Emmett Richardson?" he asked her.

Thérèse jumped, feeling a hot flush on her cheeks. Oh, no, why did Emmett wait until after her brothers had left to ask her father's permission to see her? They would have been her allies and helped her to persuade her father to agree.

"He's a friend of Rémy and Georges," she stuttered, massaging the truth a little and trying not to give away her sudden excitement at the mention of his name. "They introduced me to him at the market, the last time we went shopping for supplies."

Her father frowned, shuffling through the papers on his desk.

"Well, he has expressed an interest in calling on you," he said slowly.

Her heart jumped. So he *had* followed through on his intention of seeing her again! She looked her father squarely in the eye, although she was clasping and unclasping her hands nervously behind her back.

"Oh, that's wonderful, *Papa*," she exclaimed. "Are you going to say yes? May I see him again?"

Her father came around the desk and drew himself up to his full height, looking sternly at her as he spoke.

"Thérèse," he said. "You know how I feel about the British. Why would you think that I would allow one of their soldiers to call upon my daughter? You're just a child, and he has no right to even think about spending any time with you."

Thérèse felt as though her father had slapped her across the face. Confusion and disappointment raced through her as she challenged him.

"But you married *Maman* when she was sixteen!" she replied, her voice rising. "And Emmett, er, I mean Captain Richardson, is an honourable gentleman with excellent manners."

"Thérèse . . . ," he admonished, speaking above her head. "I make the decisions regarding the company you keep and who will be allowed to court you. Besides, you should respect what I say and not argue with me when I tell you what you are to do. I will not permit this English soldier to spend time with you, and I shall tell him so today."

Panic gripped Thérèse. She knew that Emmett was meant to play an important role in her future, and she was not going to allow her father to stand in her way. She had always been a strong and determined girl, and she now pulled on all of her reserves to confront him. Her heart beating furiously, she stood up tall and looked her father in the eye.

"*Papa*," she said. "Captain Richardson is a respectable soldier with a good living and there's no reason why I shouldn't spend time getting to know him better. You're allowing your prejudices against the British to stand in the way of your good judgment."

Her father looked shocked at his daughter's vehemence. She'd never challenged him so directly before. This was his favourite daughter, but he wouldn't put up with her questioning his authority.

"You know perfectly well that's not true," he replied. "You're too young to have a soldier from another country call on you. They are far too untrustworthy when they're away from home."

"You don't know that about Captain Richardson, *Papa*", she raised her voice as she spoke. "You should spend a little time with him and get to know him better before you judge his character. At least let me see him in the company of a chaperone."

"My mind is made up, Thérèse," countered her father, abruptly dismissing her and going back around his desk.

Thérèse leaned forward and put her hands on the desk, locking her eyes with his, her brain grasping at a straw that had been formulating in the back of her mind since her father had announced his intention to refuse Emmett's request. It was now or never, so she jumped in with both feet.

"*Papa,*" she said firmly. "If you refuse to allow me to see Emmett, I will tell *Maman* about the affair you're having with Eugénie."

There, the words were out of her mouth! She instantly regretted them and was searching for a way to start backtracking from her outburst as she considered her father's shocked expression. But he reacted quickly to her boldness.

"How can you say such a thing to me, Thérèse?" he demanded, his voice faltering. The expression on his face confirmed his guilt and encouraged her to stand firm.

"I've seen her sneaking out of your room at least twice, and I know what's going on between the two of you." His facial expression gave her the strength to continue with her ultimatum. "If you refuse to allow me to go for walks with Captain Richardson in the company of a chaperone, I will tell *Maman* what you are up to."

"How could you do that to your mother at this difficult time in her life? She'll be devastated! How can you be so selfish?"

"How can *you* be so selfish, *Papa*?" she asked, using every ounce of determination to stick to her point. "She's been a devoted and faithful wife to you, and this is how you repay her?"

Thérèse was taken aback at her own bravado. She had known that her father might not give her permission to see Emmett again, but she hadn't expected to be so resolved to carry out her threat and was surprised at her own strength to confront him. A sudden thought came into her head that she would be hurting her mother terribly with this information. However, as for her father, he seemed bowled over by her challenge to his parental role. He hesitated before replying, leaning on the back of his chair for support.

"Would you really do it, Thérèse?" he asked quietly, never once trying to deny what he had been up to ever since the war had broken out. This affair was not a new thing for him, and he didn't want to jeopardize it in any way.

She couldn't back down now. She spoke firmly so that he wouldn't doubt her resolve.

"Yes," she answered.

Sighing, her father sank into his chair, looking up at her with a defeated expression.

"Very well," he replied. "You have my permission. But remember, you must be discreet and behave properly at all times when you're in the presence of this young man. And you must always have a chaperone."

Knowing that she had won, and feeling a glowing sensation starting in her insides, Thérèse thanked her father and left his study. She skipped along the hall and couldn't help but clap her hands and let out a little squeak of triumph.

Eugénie was coming the other way down the hall and stopped to ask if everything was alright with her.

"Oh, something wonderful has just happened," Thérèse replied, clasping her hands to her heart.

"Is there anything I can do for you, *mademoiselle*?" the maid asked.

"No, there's nothing further you can do, Eugénie," Thérèse told her. "You don't know it, but you've done it already!"

Eugénie stood watching Thérèse in a puzzled way as she continued on down the hall, then shrugged her shoulders and headed for the kitchen, leaving Thérèse chuckling to herself. She had scored a point over her father by using his weakness against himself, and Eugénie would probably never know about it. But, better than that, she had cleared the way to being able to spend time with her soldier.

11

A few days later, in between the monsoon showers of the morning and afternoon, Thérèse and her sisters were sitting on the verandah fanning themselves and found themselves unable to face the thought of going for a walk . It was hot on the verandah, but even hotter inside the house. Mugginess hung in the air, and soon the heavy moisture would be translated into pouring, belting rain that would send everyone outside running for cover. Thérèse disliked this season on the island the most, but knew it was essential for the plants and forests if they were to survive the baking sun and hot temperatures for the rest of the year.

She and Angélique were discussing the advantages of the new lisle stockings over cotton ones, how they flattered the legs more, and looked more becoming with the new, above-the-ankle dresses and skirts that women had begun to adopt since the outbreak of war.

The verandah door opened abruptly and their mother unexpectedly appeared.

"*Maman*, you are up," commented Marie-Anne.

"Yes, *ma fille*," replied Madeleine. "I'm starting to feel a little better." She smiled benevolently at Thérèse. "And I have some news."

Thérèse looked expectantly at her mother, as her heart skipped a few beats. She knew what *Maman* was going to say.

"*Papa* told me that a young English soldier asked permission to call upon you this week," smiled Madeleine.

Thérèse felt the colour rush into her cheeks.

"This week?" she asked, clapping her hands excitedly. "Oh, that's wonderful!"

Her mother teasingly wagged her finger.

"But you must have a chaperone," she stated firmly.

"Oh, please let it be me!" begged Angélique. "I'll make sure that everything is appropriate and done as it should be."

"What about me?" pleaded Marie-Anne. "I'd make sure of that, too."

"You're too young," frowned Madeleine at her youngest daughter. She turned to Angélique. "Yes, I think you would be a splendid chaperone, *chérie*."

Marie-Anne pouted, but Thérèse, her mother and Angélique ignored her. Angélique was older, and also a very serious girl. However, Thérèse knew that she could persuade her sister to allow her to spend some time alone with Emmett. She grew more and more excited at the thought of the meeting between them. The next thing would be to decide what to wear, and whether to wear a hat, or to leave her hair uncovered in all its shining, brushed-a-hundred-times-a-day glory.

"When am I allowed to see him, *Maman*?" she asked, happily.

"The day after tomorrow," replied Madeleine. "He will come by in the morning, before it gets too hot. About ten o'clock."

"How will I sleep tomorrow night?" thought Thérèse. "How will I even sleep tonight? That's only two days away." The thought of seeing him again was making her feel weak and shaky.

Thérèse felt her hands trembling and her heart beating very quickly as her mother smiled and went back inside. Her sisters immediately fell to questioning her about the young soldier. What did he look like, how she had met him, how he had dared to ask *Papa*'s permission and, most puzzling of all, how had *Papa* ever agreed to allow her to see a British soldier? Since their father despised the English, it was quite a mystery to them. Thérèse smiled to herself. Her father had easily succumbed to her "persuasion," but she told her sisters that it was because *Papa* could deny her nothing. She was, after all, the eldest daughter of the family and his favourite. Her sisters scolded her laughingly about that, but she decided not to let on to them the real reason. They didn't need to know about *Papa*'s indelicacy.

The night before her rendezvous with her soldier, Thérèse spent two hours in her bedroom with Angélique, trying to decide what gown to wear while going for her walk with her suitor. They had about a dozen dresses, skirts and blouses laid out on her bed and were holding them up one at a time, matching the skirts with the various lace blouses. Angélique favoured her white dress, which presented the look of innocence, but Thérèse preferred the bolder colours, red, blue or canary yellow. They accented her dark hair and eyes, while making the skin of her face look luminescent. She thought she looked rather pale in the white dress, but Angélique reminded her how popular she had been in her white dress at the dance the night before her brothers left for war.

Thérèse tossed the dress she was holding on the bed in frustration.

"Oh, I just can't decide what looks best," she moaned. "I feel so confused!"

"It doesn't matter what you wear, Thérèse," replied Angélique calmly. "Do you think he's going to care? He'll be too busy looking into your eyes to even notice what you're wearing."

"You've read too many romance novels, *ma soeur*," Thérèse admonished her.

"No, it's true," protested Angélique. "Men don't care what you're wearing. They're only interested in your face and wondering when they can kiss you."

Thérèse giggled, and a momentary flash went through her mind of Cousin Raoul kissing her. She wondered briefly where he was in the war at this moment. She dismissed the thought and turned again to the matter in hand.

"Well," she said. "Whether he notices or not, I still have to be happy with myself and look my best."

"I'm sure you'll have no trouble with that, dear sister," Angélique replied. She picked up a green cotton gown with a low waist and ankle-length skirt.

"How about this one? You look fetching in it."

"No, I don't really like green all that much. The soldiers wear green uniforms. He won't want to be reminded of that."

"You're right," mused Angélique. "Well, I think you'd better go with the white silk. You obviously can't make up your mind about colours."

Thérèse pulled off the blue dress she was trying on and picked up the white silk. She fingered the fabric idly, thinking that silk would definitely give the impression of affluence and good taste, and she thought that would impress the young man. Then she remembered that she didn't really know his background. Perhaps he came from a wealthy family, as well? His father could own cotton mills in Yorkshire, for all she knew. She had done some reading about Yorkshire after she had met him in the market the other day and knew that cotton was the county's primary industry.

"Yes", she told Angélique. "When in doubt, white is the best choice."

Angélique nodded. "You should wear your new hat, as well, to keep the sun off your face."

"Yes, I think so," Thérèse replied.

The problem solved, the two girls started hanging up the articles of clothing that were strewn all over the bed, chattering excitedly about where the young soldier would take Thérèse and what they would talk about.

That night, when she went to bed, Thérèse laid with her eyes open for several hours, wishing that sleep would come so that she wouldn't look worn out for her soldier the next day. However, it seemed that no sooner had she closed her eyes than she was opening them again as she glimpsed the dawn through a slit in the lace curtains around her window.

She jumped out of bed excitedly. Today was the day! She pulled on her day gown and raced silently down the stairs and out the front door to start her early morning ritual of bathing her face in the tropical flowers. There was an eerie silence everywhere, and she realized that not even the birds were calling to her.

"Hmm, I wonder why it's so quiet this morning?" she mused, kneeling down in front of the bougainvillea plants.

Her ablutions finished, she got up and started her stroll around the garden. She thought she heard a macaw calling out as she walked around, but it still seemed quiet in the dawn light. She didn't give it any more thought, as her thoughts once again turned to Emmett and wondering what they would talk about during their walk.

The morning seemed to tick by interminably as she went through the motions of eating her breakfast, then going up to her room with Angélique to change into her white dress. She had told Eugénie the night before that she didn't want her to attend her this morning, as her sister would be accompanying her. She was glad that she didn't have to face her father's mistress on the day that her young suitor was courting her for the first time. The innocence of her rendezvous with him contrasted sharply with the clandestine meetings of the housemaid and her father, and she dismissed the thought of it with some disgust. Even though it was a common practice among the colonialists, she couldn't forgive her father for betraying her mother in such an indiscreet way.

When Angélique knocked quietly on her door, Thérèse called out to her to come in as she paced around the room in her shift.

"Help me put the dress on first, Angélique, then you can fix my hair."

Angélique nodded and came in, closing the door gently behind her. The dress taken care of, she started to brush Thérèse's hair before rolling it into a chignon at the base of her neck.

"That should hold when you put your hat on," she told Thérèse.

Thérèse smiled and jumped up, hugging her sister.

"Thank you so much, Angélique," she said. "Don't follow us too closely, but I will tell you everything we talk about this afternoon, I promise."

Angélique put her hands on her sister's cheeks. "You look so beautiful, Thérèse, and so happy. I envy you."

"Oh, you'll have a suitor of your own before long. Maybe I'll ask Captain Richardson if he has a friend he could introduce to you."

"Oh, no, I want a French soldier" replied Angélique firmly. "I don't want to have to learn English, or to go and live in England. It's cold and wet there."

"Well, it's hot and wet here!" pronounced Thérèse. A thought suddenly occurred to her. "I hope the monsoon doesn't start while we're out."

"Me, too," said Angélique. "I think we're going out early enough."

The morning couldn't pass by quickly enough for Thérèse. Finally, a quarter to ten rolled around and she and Angélique were seated on the bench in the front hall of the house, waiting for Emmett to arrive. At five to ten, *Papa* appeared from his study.

"You're ready to go, are you?" he asked, rather pointlessly, since it was obvious they were.

"Yes, *Papa*," replied Thérèse.

"Remember what I said," he addressed Thérèse. "Propriety and decorum."

Thérèse looked at him sourly. What a hypocrite! As if he behaved with decorum. She stared her father down, and he turned to his other daughter.

"I'm counting on you to make sure of that, Angélique," he said, rather sternly.

"Yes, *Papa"* she answered.

They were interrupted by a knock on the front door. Thérèse and her sister jumped up, but *Papa* held out an arm.

"Let Henri answer it," he instructed, indicating the butler, who had silently appeared out of nowhere.

"Sit down, girls."

The girls sat down obediently, and Thérèse was immediately aware that her heart had speeded up again and was thumping in her chest. Henri opened the door, and there *he* was.

"Captain Emmett Richardson," he told Henri, who then turned and announced Emmett's arrival to Paul and his daughters.

Thérèse and her sister again got to their feet as Emmett bowed and then shook hands with her father.

"I am here to escort *Mademoiselle* Thérèse on a walk around the estate," he told *Papa,* who was sizing him up as he watched him with a hawkish expression. Emmett, however, didn't allow himself to be deterred. He turned to Thérèse and proffered his arm.

"*Mademoiselle*?" he asked, shyly.

Thérèse stepped forward, introducing her sister as her chaperone.

"Angélique," she inquired, "Are you ready?"

Angélique nodded her head in the affirmative and went to stand behind the captain and Thérèse.

"Remember what I said, Angélique," said her father, ignoring Thérèse and her escort. Thérèse could feel his disapproving eyes burning into her back as she stepped through the doorway and down the steps of the house. Captain Richardson turned politely to Angélique.

"Are you alright with a fairly long walk, *Mademoiselle* Lemieux?" he asked.

"Yes, of course," she replied. "I will be about twenty paces behind you, and I promise that I won't listen to your conversation."

Thérèse smiled gratefully at her sister, then took a firmer grip on Emmett's arm as they started to walk through the garden. She turned her gaze to her companion, trying to hide her sudden shyness and trembling hands. Her heart continued to thump at an alarming pace as she wondered what they would talk about. Emmett, too, must have been feeling rather shy, but he eventually turned to her to remark,

"The weather's fine for this time of year."

She almost burst out laughing. Trust an Englishman to talk about the weather! Thérèse had heard they were very preoccupied with the weather in their country, mostly because it was often cold and wet.

"Yes, it's a pleasant morning, but the monsoon will start fairly soon," she replied. Actually, she was already beginning to feel the sweat trickling down her back because of the heat and mugginess, but that wasn't going to prevent her from enjoying every minute she could with this young man.

"How long have you been in Mauritius?" she inquired.

"Two years," he replied.

"And you're a captain already?"

"Yes," he explained. "As I told you the other day, the army felt that my skills with ledgers and accounting were sufficient to put me in charge of the supplies at the base. That position comes with an automatic promotion to captain."

"Well, that's wonderful," she said. "That will serve you very well when you return to your country."

"Yes, but I don't look forward to going back there, after being here for two years. The island is so beautiful, and I've enjoyed my time here. I think I'll find Europe very much changed when I return."

"Certainly, France and the continent will be changed after this awful war. But I don't imagine Britain will be all that different. After all, it hasn't seen the armed conflict that other parts of the world have suffered."

"It would have, if the Kaiser had his way."

"Yes but, fortunately, because of the concentrated efforts of the Allies, the world no longer has to fear that."

He stopped walking suddenly and gazed into Thérèse's face. She noticed her sister behind them also stop walking and stand still, fidgeting with her gloves.

"You, *mademoiselle*, are extremely intelligent! There are not very many young ladies in this part of the world who pay much attention to what is going on in this conflict, unless it affects them directly."

"Well, I listen to *Papa* discussing what's in the newspaper with my mother. She's an educated lady who's very interested in politics. We're encouraged to enter into the discussions, and my father always insisted that we girls went to school for as long as the boys."

"Brains, as well as beauty," Emmett exclaimed in an amazed tone, causing her to blush. This young man certainly knew how to compliment a girl! They resumed walking, and she glanced back to make sure her sister was still following them.

"If you don't want to go back to England, why not stay here?" she questioned him. "After all, the army will probably be here for a while once the war ends, or you could inquire about working for one of the plantation companies. You speak French quite well."

"I'm the only living nephew of an elderly aunt," he answered her. "She depends on me to look after her in her old age, and I can't abandon her. She raised me, with her husband."

Thérèse was impressed. Not only attractive and good at what he did, but he was kind. Those were all qualities that she'd always dreamed of finding in a suitor, and she gripped his arm a little tighter.

"You are so loyal, Captain Richardson," she said.

"I'm very loyal, *mademoiselle*," he answered earnestly. "You will find out that it's one of my strongest attributes."

"Please call me Thérèse," she replied, looking up into his face.

"Only if you will call me Emmett."

"Alright."

Having come to the end of the garden, they opened the gate to walk along the path that led down to the sugar cane fields. Emmett gallantly held the gate open and waited for Angélique to catch up to them. She went through, smiling at him as she did, then waited once again for them to get quite far ahead of her before resuming her pace.

They continued on down the path, not paying any attention to the big black cloud that was slowly advancing in their direction. Emmett told Thérèse about his childhood growing up in Yorkshire with his strict aunt and uncle. His parents had been unable to take care of him when he was a young child and had sent him to his father's older sister and her husband. He'd never been told why his parents couldn't care for him, but they had both died by the time he was in his teens, so he never really got to know them. He was brought up strictly in the Methodist faith and was expected to work very hard at school and to perform any chores around the house and garden that his uncle expected of him. This he did without complaint and was rewarded with the affection of his elderly relatives. He had matriculated successfully from school and worked for one year as an accountant at a local bank when the war broke out. Seeing this as a way to escape his gloomy home life and travel the world, he signed up as soon as the war broke out. He was twenty-one years old now and had thought about a possible career in the civil service when he returned home.

Thérèse listened to him telling his story and wondered what kind of parents would ship their child off to an older sibling rather than keeping him with them and raising him themselves. Her large, close-knit family all loved being together, and she couldn't imagine not living in the same household as her mother and brothers and sisters. *Papa* she was no longer as sure about, but she still couldn't imagine not being raised by him with his exacting standards. She felt pity for this pleasant young man and found that she liked him more and more, the better she got to know him. She could add admiration and sympathy to her list of feelings towards him now.

Her sister suddenly interrupted them by calling her name. Thérèse turned around and looked at her questioningly. Angélique was pointing up at the huge, black cloud that was almost upon them. No wonder it had been so quiet this morning. The birds and animals were anticipating the oncoming storm.

"We'd better turn back!" she called out. "The monsoon is closing in fast."

"Oh, dear," said Thérèse, turning to her companion. "We must return to the house, Emmett. If we don't get back very soon, we'll be drenched."

"But we've barely started walking!" he stammered. "We've hardly had any time to get to know each other."

"We won't be able to hear each other over the rain, anyway," she replied. "We must go back. Perhaps you can come again tomorrow?"

He reluctantly turned around, pulling her with him, and they hurried back to where her sister was waiting. They ran faster as the girls' alarm grew at the size of the cloud that was bearing down on them. The wind had got up now, and Thérèse could feel the storm almost upon them. As they half-ran along the path, she felt a large rain drop land on her head, followed swiftly by a couple more. She turned to Angélique.

"It's starting already," she said. "We're going to have to run!"

Emmett gallantly stopped and started to take off his jacket.

"No, no," Thérèse said. "You'll be drenched. Keep your jacket on. Angélique and I at least have our hats."

"But that won't protect you from the rain."

"Nothing will."

In just one minute, the large raindrops had become a heavy downpour and the wind had started blowing mercilessly. Emmett offered his other arm to Angélique and the three of them ran down the path, which was slowly turning to mud. They went as fast as they could, but the two girls were soon out of breath and panting hard. The young soldier was able to maintain a steady pace, however, probably due to his army training, and he pulled them along with him.

They reached the house about ten minutes later, completely soaked to the skin. Running up the garden path and into the house, they arrived soggy and exhausted, their clothes dripping onto the carpet in the hallway. The girls giggled as they looked each other over in their bedraggled states, but Emmett's face showed only consternation. Henri and Eugénie hurried to help them. Henri removed Emmett's wet jacket and cap, and Eugénie helped to take off the girls' hats.

"Come upstairs, *mesdemoiselles,*" she urged, quietly. "We must get you out of these wet clothes."

Before Thérèse could turn away, Emmett caught her by the arm. Lifting her right hand to his lips, he gave it a quick kiss. The servants looked alarmed, but Thérèse smiled up at him.

"*Au revoir, monsieur,*" she murmured softly. Pulling her hand gently away, she turned around and started up the wide stairwell in the wake of her sister and the maid.

"*Mademoiselle Thérèse*!" Emmett called out to her as she went up. "May I see you tomorrow?"

She stopped to look at him over her shoulder.

"Ask *Papa,*" she replied, before turning around again and making her way up to the top of the stairs.

She didn't think her father would refuse his request.

It was about three days later that Thérèse was told that Emmett would be calling on her again the next day. They had been the three longest days of her life. She wished she hadn't dismissed Emmett so cavalierly, but she knew that, without *Papa's* permission, she wouldn't be able to see the young soldier. The first day, she eagerly anticipated being told that he would come the next day but, when that day came and went and no word came, she started to fret a little. The second day, she again woke up feeling excited and convinced that she would hear from him, but nothing. By lunch time of that day, she was pacing around the estate, once again risking getting soaked by the monsoon, but unable to keep her feverish anticipation in check.

After luncheon, she was sitting at the table with her mother, wringing her hands in her lap. Her mother, noticing her agitation, turned to her and asked,

"What's the matter, Thérèse, *chérie*?"

Since they were alone in the room, Thérèse felt that it was safe to confide in her mother.

"*Maman*, why hasn't Captain Richardson asked to see me again?"

Her mother sighed, then frowned.

"Is he so important to you, *ma fille?*" she asked, looking earnestly at her daughter.

"Oh yes, *Maman*," Thérèse replied. "I like him so much . . . *Maman*, why does my heart beat so hard when I see him, or even think of him?"

Madeleine's gaze changed to a warm, protective expression.

"Why, you are in love, my little one!" she said softly. "My daughter has lost her heart to an English soldier."

Thérèse blushed, but then looked squarely at her mother.

"Yes, *Maman*, I think you are right," she replied. "I've never felt this way about anyone, and I think Captain Richardson is going to be very important to my future."

"Normally, I wouldn't pay much attention to a young girl speaking that way," Madeleine said. "But I know that you may have your grandmother's gift for knowing things that are going to happen, so I'll take what you say seriously. I'll have to urge *Papa* to agree to this young man's request."

Thérèse jumped up from the table and rushed to her mother. "You mean, he's asked to see me and *Papa* has refused?" she demanded.

"Well, not exactly refused," demurred her mother. "More put off giving him a reply."

"How could *Papa*, just because he's British?" Thérèse stamped her foot. "He's a respected captain in the army and comes from a good family in England!"

"Yes, yes, I know, *ma chérie,* now calm down," answered her mother. "It's not easy to get *Papa* to change his prejudices."

"I know, but . . . ," Thérèse broke off in frustration. She looked helplessly at her mother.

"Don't worry, *ma petite,* I'll speak to *Papa,"* said Madeleine. "Be patient and remember to always show your father respect. It's what every parent deserves from their child."

There was a warning tone in Madeleine's voice, and Thérèse knew that it was serious. Perhaps *Papa* had deliberately withheld his consent for her to see Emmett again because of her threats to expose his affair with Eugénie? It may have been his way of getting back at her, to make her suffer with anticipation. But how did Madeleine know about her manipulation of her father? Surely he hadn't talked to her mother about it? Thérèse knew that she had better tread carefully in the future and not antagonize him too much. Showing too much disrespect to him could cause her to lose her mother as an ally, so she must be more circumspect.

"I will, *Maman,"* she said softly. "I do respect *Papa,* I just don't understand his contempt of the British. I promise to speak to him more politely, as long as he lets me see my soldier."

Madeleine smiled, aware of just how determined her daughter could be. "I know you will, *chérie,"* she replied.

The next day, Thérèse learned that Emmett was once again coming to call on her. She was certain that her mother had used her powers of persuasion and was on her side.

The morning of his visit, after another all but sleepless night, Thérèse was once again sitting with her sister on the front hall bench waiting for Emmett to arrive. She wrung her hands nervously, unsure about the blue cotton dress she had chosen for her outing. She had twice proven to herself that silk was too hot and uncomfortable for walking, but the blue looked so plain. She knew that her hat was very becoming, though, and Angélique had done her hair perfectly yet again.

"I'm so nervous!" she whispered in her sister's ear. "I feel so certain about Emmett, but I get so shaky when I think of him."

"L'amour, ma chère," Angélique replied. "It does strange things to

people, especially when it's new."

Thérèse wondered how her younger sister knew so much about love, when she had never experienced it for herself. It must be because Angélique was a great reader of nineteenth-century romance novels.

"I suppose you're right."

Her musings were interrupted by a knock at the front door. She watched Henri go to open it with what seemed like agonizing slowness, and then the door was open and Emmett was standing there. She tried to contain herself from jumping up too quickly and going to him, but it was difficult. She felt herself shake hands with him and trying not to look into those irregular blue eyes, but it wasn't possible.

"Good morning, Captain Richardson," she said softly.

"Good morning, *mademoiselle*," he replied, holding her hand for an extra second or two. It felt warm and firm in his, which was moist and shaking. "Shall we go? Are you ready, *mademoiselle* Angélique?"

Angélique agreed, and the three of them nodded goodbye to Henri as they left the house.

"I hope it's not going to start raining again today," said Thérèse as they walked down the path. The garden seemed full of life this morning, with the birds calling to each other and lizards scurrying in the hot morning sun.

"The sky looks clear," replied Emmett, scanning the horizon, "but we don't want to get soaked like we did last time."

"No, we certainly don't," she said. "By the way, about that last time. I'm sorry that *Papa* deliberated for so long before allowing you to accompany me again."

"Oh, that's fine," he said. "I had lots to do at the base anyway, so the time flew by."

Thérèse felt some annoyance. She had been counting the hours and getting frantic at the time that she'd been forced to wait to see him, and he hadn't even noticed because he had a lot to do. Oh, well, she supposed, a soldier is always kept busy during the day, while the life of a young gentlewoman could be very tedious. Although she despised boredom, she didn't think she'd be very happy as a soldier.

He suddenly looked over at her, a chastened look on his face.

"That's not strictly true, Thérèse," he said quietly, looking anxiously into her eyes. "I could hardly wait to see you again."

So he had felt the same way! Thérèse smiled happily. "Me, either," she replied.

They gazed at each other for moment, then she put her arm through his and he squeezed her hand firmly.

"You are even more beautiful after four days away from you than the first day I saw you," he said gallantly.

"You know how to flatter me," she answered.

"It's not flattery," he said urgently. "I've never met anyone like you. Beautiful, intelligent and interested in everything. You're so unlike the English country girls that I've met, or even the city girls from York."

"Well, I'm French," she replied. "Even though Mauritius is run by the British, we're French first and foremost. That will always be very important to me."

"Would you ever consider leaving the island?" He gazed intently at her as he spoke.

Her heart skipped one or two beats.

"What do you mean?" she asked.

He started to stammer.

"Well . . . er, I mean . . . . if someone were to ask you . . . . to. . . " he stopped for a moment, staring at her diffidently.

"Are you asking me to, *monsieur*?" She looked coyly at him, holding her breath as she waited for his answer.

He put his arm around her waist and pulled her to him. Thérèse glanced nervously back at her sister, who was trying to seem as though she weren't watching them, but was nonetheless looking out at them from under her hat. She stopped walking, giving them the space to remain unheard.

"I can think of nothing else but you, Thérèse!" he murmured, putting his cheek against hers. "I've never felt this way before."

"Neither have I," she said breathlessly. "You're all I think about! I don't know why you have this effect on me."

"I think I love you," he murmured against her ear.

She put her hand to his cheek.

"I think I love you, too," she said. "My heart beats so whenever I see you, even though we've only met a few times."

"When the heart knows, it knows," he replied. "Do you believe in love at first sight?"

"Of course, I do," she replied, looking up at him adoringly. *Maman* had said that she was in love and she believed it. What else could make her think continually of him and even manipulate her father into allowing her to see him? The emotions that were running through her right now were dizzying and powerful. She felt sure that this was love.

He glanced back at Angélique, and Thérèse gave her a little wave, followed by a dismissive gesture. Angélique obediently turned around and stood with her back to them. Thérèse looked up at Emmett once again, as he slowly pulled her towards him.

He kissed her softly. His lips were so much more gentle than those of her Cousin Raoul, her only experience of being kissed by a man. Raoul had been rough, urgent, where this man was humble and respectful in his embrace. Thérèse felt herself melting into him and his kiss, and she put her arms around his waist as he pulled her closer to him. She started to feel that warm, tingling feeling in her stomach again and finally realized what it was. It was the beginnings of passion, the stirring of desire. His kiss became firmer, and he finally crushed her to him. She eagerly responded to him and felt her breathing start to speed up.

All of a sudden, she heard a voice calling in the distance.

"*Mademoiselle* Thérèse! *Mademoiselle* Angélique!"

She dropped her arms and jumped back as he let her go. She saw Angélique turn back to her, then look beyond her to a figure that was hurrying towards them. It was Eugénie, and she seemed agitated. Thérèse and Emmett stood awkwardly, more embarrassed at having been caught in an embrace than curious as to why the young woman had come to find them so urgently.

"What is it, Eugénie?" Thérèse asked as she came to a standstill in front of them. She noticed that the young woman seemed flustered but felt annoyed at her for interrupting their precious moment.

"There has been a telegram, *mademoiselle*," she replied, still out of breath and gripping her side from running. "*Monsieur* Georges . . . your mother . . . she said to come back to the house at once."

Angélique had by then caught up to them. She and Thérèse exchanged glances, as Thérèse felt a horrible, sinking feeling go through her. The last time a telegram had arrived at the house, it had been to announce the death of her brother Philippe.

"Is my brother alright, Eugénie?" she asked, searching the girl's face. Her expression only confirmed what Thérèse dreaded to hear.

"Is he . . . ?" she broke off, unable to say the words.

Eugénie nodded, then caught her lip between her teeth and started to cry softly.

"Oh, *mon Dieu*!" Thérèse replied. She turned and seized Angélique's hand. "Angélique, we must go immediately to *Maman*." She looked at Emmett, who had been staring at her with a concerned look on his face.

"Emmett . . . Captain Richardson . . . I'm sorry," she said, laying her hand on his arm. "I have to go, I'm afraid my mother needs us at this moment."

He nodded. "Of course, I understand," he said.

As the girls hurried away with Eugénie, she heard him call out,

"If there's anything I can do to be of service to your family, please let me know."

Thérèse nodded as the tears streamed down her face, blinding her. Another brother lost to this horrible war! She had known it, had felt it in her gut the last time she saw him. Oh, why, did she have to have this terrible gift? She would have given anything not to have known, or to at least have been given more time before tragedy struck again.

12

Arriving at the house, the girls could hear their mother crying upstairs in her room. Her father's voice could be heard softly consoling her, but it only seemed to make her cry more loudly.

Thérèse and her sister bounded up the stairs, two at a time, and ran to their mother. She was standing in the middle of the room, tearing at her face and hair, which stood wildly out from her head and shoulders as she repeatedly struck herself. Her father stood in a corner, at a loss as to what to say or do but trying to make soothing sounds.

"Two of my boys! Gone, gone, to this bloody war! And you, *mon mari*, so proud to have them go to war in the French army! If they'd been with the British army, perhaps they would still be alive!"

"No, no, *ma chérie*," countered their father, tears coursing down his cheeks. "It's all the same, the armies are Allies, they're all fighting on the same fields."

"Oh, my boys, my boys, I never should have let you return when you were here with us! I should have hidden you here on the estate and kept you safe!" Madeleine sobbed.

Thérèse went to her mother and folded her in her arms, trying to smooth her wild hair with calming strokes.

"*Maman, Maman*," she murmured, her own voice choking. "They were only doing their duty. They did what they had to do to defend us all."

Her mother's sobs increased, but at least she didn't voice any more accusations. She allowed Thérèse to hold her and eventually lay her down on the big bed, with Angélique's help. The two girls sat down on either side of their mother, holding her hands and crying with her, trying to comfort her.

Paul patted both of his daughters' heads awkwardly, then left the room.

"I wonder if he's going to Eugénie?" thought Thérèse bitterly as she made soothing sounds to her mother. For one moment, she was annoyed that this announcement had come when she was walking with Emmett. She couldn't seem to have any time with him without something happening. Then she dismissed the thought guiltily as she pondered her brother Georges and how he had helped her to meet Emmett in the first place and, with Rémy, had arranged for her to be alone with her suitor.

"I'm so sorry, Georges," she thought. "You will never be able to experience love, as I have. I'm so sorry for my selfish thoughts."

A desolate feeling washed over her as she contemplated the life that Georges might have had. She watched her mother mourning another one of her sons who had been torn from her by war, a war that she hated and had dreaded from the start.

A letter arrived from France two weeks later, from one of Georges' superior officers, with the news that he had not been killed in action but rather had died of pneumonia after catching an infection in the trenches. That meant that there would be no hero's burial for Georges, but the army wanted to honour his request to be buried in France. The officer asked that Paul send money to Georges' unit so that a casket and a proper funeral could be paid for.

"We won't be able to even visit his grave," said Madeleine bitterly. After several days of crying sporadically and refusing to eat, she had finally agreed to come downstairs and be with the family again. Her pregnancy was now quite advanced, and she moved very slowly. Thérèse was somewhat surprised that her labour hadn't been triggered prematurely by the violence of her emotions.

"We can't really visit Philippe's grave, either," Thérèse pointed out. He had died on a battlefield and was probably buried in an unmarked grave at Verdun.

This caused Madeleine to start sobbing again, and Thérèse felt regret immediately for the words that had come out of her mouth. Her young sister Marie-Anne patted her mother's hand soothingly, which seemed to help a little.

Thérèse had asked whether she would be allowed to see Emmett again, as she felt that he could be a great comfort to her. Paul had refused her request, however, and so she was forced to stay in the house and only contemplate his declaration of love for her and the kiss that had been exchanged between them. Then she felt guilty for having such thoughts at a difficult time and felt disloyal to her brother for even thinking of her own happiness. She was caught between two strong feelings, both great sadness and intense happiness, and would lie awake at night thinking of her soldier. Would he forget her now that she wasn't allowed to see him during the mourning period? Would another girl catch his eye? She remembered him telling her that he was very loyal, and so hoped that he would be as good as his word. She knew she wouldn't forget him, especially as she still had the feeling that he was going to mean something very special to her.

The weeks passed by. Georges' funeral was paid for, and another letter confirming his burial was sent to her parents by the senior officer. The mourning period of three months was observed by the family, all appropriately dressed in black to mark the death of their loved one. Six weeks after the tragic event, Madeleine went into labour and was delivered of a tiny, healthy girl, whom she named "Celeste" (heavenly) in honour of Georges, who most certainly had gone to heaven for his sacrifice for his home. Masses were said at church for his soul every day, and also for the health of the little girl. As tiny as she was, she was a fighter and cried lustily, showing off a strong pair of lungs. As her mother was still weak, Thérèse and her sisters took turns caring for her.

Her father was mostly uninterested in another daughter, since he already had three, and stayed away from his wife. Thérèse suspected bitterly that he was spending as much time as possible with Eugénie, as the young servant was often missing from the house and not present when she was needed. Fortunately, since Madeleine had taught all of her daughters the rudiments of nursing, she wasn't short of caring people to look after her and the infant. The girls took turns sleeping in their mother's room and feeding the baby with goat's milk from a bottle, as Madeleine's milk dried up fairly quickly after the birth.

As soon as the mourning period was over, Thérèse sought out her father to request permission to start walking with Emmett again. As much as she missed her deceased brother, she couldn't help thinking about the young British captain who had captured her heart. She missed him terribly and longed to see him again.

"*Papa,*" she began determinedly, when her father admitted her to his study. "I would like to ask to be allowed to see the young English soldier whom I had been walking with before Georges' passing."

At the reminder of the loss of his son, her father winced visibly.

"*Chérie,* don't ask me about this now," he replied. "We have only just lost your brother, and I cannot think of your entertaining a young man at this time."

"*Papa,* I only ask to be allowed to walk with Captain Richardson again. He has declared himself to me, and I want to see him very much."

"Thérèse, this is not the time to talk about this, please don't bother me about it now." Her father's voice was shaking.

"*Papa,* I know you're grieving Philippe and Georges, but this is my life too, and I don't want to lose a chance to be with this young man. He's very important to me," she replied.

"But he's an Englishman!" burst out *Papa,* in spite of himself.

"Is that why you won't let me see him?" she asked.

When he didn't reply, but only turned away and busied himself with some papers on his desk, she drew herself up to her full height and spoke firmly to him.

"*Papa*, remember what I said to you when you forbade me to see Emmett the first time?" she asked.

Her father didn't look at her, but started rattling through one of the drawers in his desk, as though he'd forgotten something urgent and needed to locate it right away.

"I know about you and Eugénie, *Papa*, and I wouldn't hesitate to tell *Maman*, if you persist in not letting me see him."

Her father still didn't look up and tried to appear engrossed in some papers on the desk.

"Do you doubt me, *Papa*?" she faced him squarely.

Paul turned his full attention to her. "Really, Thérèse? You would do that at a time like this?"

"You know I would, *Papa*,'" she said, refusing to back down.

He turned away from her, angrily throwing the papers on the floor and then bending down and busying himself picking them up again.

"What if I deny it?" he asked her, still picking up papers and not meeting her eye.

"You can try, if you like," she said. "But I'm sure that *Maman* would believe me, and that Eugénie wouldn't dare to lie to me if I asked her."

He continued to avoid her eyes, and a full minute went by slowly and uncomfortably. Finally, he let out a sigh and straightened up, laying the papers right side up on the desk again.

"Very well," he said, in a defeated tone. "I shall let the young officer know that he may start courting you again."

"Have you heard from him since the news of Georges' death?" she inquired, a suspicion growing in her mind.

"Only almost every week!" he replied, exasperated.

"What?" demanded Thérèse, angrily. "You mean, he's been asking to see me and you didn't even tell me?"

Fury at her father coursed through her body. How could he have kept Emmett from her, especially when he had offered support to her family during their time of grief?

"Well, you were busy taking care of your mother, and I didn't think you would want to be bothered by him," Paul spluttered, once again not looking at her.

"Oh, *Papa,* how could you?" she asked bitterly. "He told me that he would do anything he could to help our family, and you wouldn't even let me see him, even for a minute?"

Her father didn't reply, although he did look awkward for a moment.

"I had more important things to think about, Thérèse," he finally replied haltingly. "I had your mother to think about, and the baby, and I was grieving your brother . . . "

"The girls and I looked after *Maman* and the baby, and you did nothing," she exclaimed. "Nothing! And you're proud that you've given two sons to the war. You're regarded as a father of heroes in the community."

Her father hung his head shamefacedly, then looked up his eldest daughter.

"You're very determined, Thérèse," he said quietly. "I would not want to oppose you once your mind is made up. Very well. Let Henri know that Captain Richardson has permission to call on you again."

Thérèse smiled triumphantly. She had won!

"Thank you, *Papa,*" she smiled at him, then went around the desk and placed a perfunctory kiss on his cheek. "I'll tell Henri immediately."

She went quickly out of her father's office, closing the door quietly behind her, then went downstairs to inform the butler of the change in his instructions.

13

Emmett came to call on Thérèse two days later. She was dressed in a white hat and a yellow kimono-style dress, which was all the rage in Paris at the moment. She had purchased it just before Georges' untimely death but had been unable to wear it yet, due to the obligatory three months of mourning.

She and Angélique whispered to one another as they sat on the bench waiting for his arrival. Both girls were very happy to be able to get out of the house and escape the oppressive sense of sorrow that pervaded the mansion. After all, they were sixteen and seventeen years old and, although they missed their brother terribly, life had to go on, and love was always an interesting diversion.

"Make sure you give me some time alone with him, Angélique," admonished Thérèse.

"Don't worry, I know what to do," replied Angélique. "I'll make sure my back is turned if he tries to embrace you again."

They giggled, then quickly changed their expressions to one of seriousness as a knock was heard at the front door. Henri opened it, then bowed to the young Englishman standing on the other side.

"I'm here for *Mademoiselle* Thérèse." Emmett's voice sounded rather nervous.

"Please come in, *monsieur,*" replied Henri, ushering him in.

As soon as Emmett caught Thérèse's eye, his serious expression changed to one of relief.

"How wonderful to see you again, *mademoiselle,*" he said, lifting his cap to her. He then glanced at her sister, "*Mademoiselle* Angélique."

Angélique bowed her head to him, then gathered up her gloves and they all filed out of the house.

"Go ahead," Angélique whispered to them. "I'll give you a head start, then catch up with you a little later."

Thérèse smiled at her and squeezed her hand in gratitude. Emmett offered his arm, and the two of them set off at a brisk pace.

"I've been so anxious to see you, Thérèse," he said urgently. "Your father didn't seem to want to encourage me to come calling."

"He just wanted to observe the period of mourning," replied Thérèse, by way of excuse for her father's behaviour. "Although he could have let me see you in church, or even invited you to the house for tea. That wouldn't have been inappropriate."

"I don't think he likes me very much," Emmett said, giving her arm a squeeze.

"Don't worry, it's just that he doesn't like the British," she answered him. She added, "I can handle Papa."

"Really? He doesn't like the British?" he asked, searching her face with an astonished expression.

"No, but that's because he wants us to remain French, and he doesn't like the fact that the British rule Mauritius."

"Well, it's lucky for me that they do, otherwise I would never have been able to come to this beautiful island, and," he leaned in to whisper in her ear, "I would never have met you."

She smiled up at him.

"I'm so glad that you did," she said, gazing into his unusual eyes.

There was an awkward silence then he turned to her again, looking at her earnestly.

"I've thought of you every day," he said in a hushed tone.

"I've thought of you, too," she replied.

She turned around and looked for her sister. Angélique was nowhere to be seen, so she quickly turned back to Emmett.

"Kiss me," she said urgently. "Kiss me like you did last time. Quickly, before my sister catches up to us!"

He obliged, taking her in his arms and pulling her towards him. This time, his lips were firmer and more demanding. She leaned into him and responded eagerly, feeling her body starting to melt and the tingling sensation returning. She suddenly broke the kiss and looked intently at him.

"Oh, Emmett, I've missed you so," she breathed.

"I've missed you too. I can't even begin to describe how hard it's been. I thought perhaps you didn't want to see me . . . "

"Nothing could be further from the truth! I thought you'd changed your mind about me."

"Never! Never," he murmured against her ear. "I've never met such a wonderful girl or felt this way."

"Neither have I." Perhaps she was being indiscreet in admitting this, but her feelings for him were so strong at this moment that she was barely thinking about what she was saying.

"Oh, Thérèse, I love you." He began to kiss her again and, before very long, they were both holding each other passionately and their breath was coming faster. She felt him put his hands firmly around her waist and she crushed her body against him. She knew this was immodest, but she couldn't help herself, until her strict upbringing reasserted itself. She broke away from him and they stood looking at one another, their breath coming in gasps.

"*Mademoiselle* . . . Thérèse," he asked, earnestly looking into her eyes. "Will you marry me?"

"Oh yes, yes," she replied fervently. Although they had only known each other for a few weeks, she knew that this was right, just as she had always felt that this young man was going to be a part of her future.

He glanced around for her sister, who was still out of sight, and then said,

"Let me do this properly." He dropped to one knee, took one of her hands in his and gazed at her with an adoring expression.

"Thérèse, will you do me the honour of becoming my wife?"

"Of course, I will," she replied eagerly. "But you'll have to ask *Papa*'s permission, and that's not going to be easy."

He rose and put his arm around her waist, kissing her tenderly on the lips.

"I'm sure you can persuade him to agree," he whispered.

"Yes, yes, I can," she said. "He will object, but I'll think of something. Leave it with me."

"I'll call round and ask to see him tomorrow morning," he announced.

"Hmmm, you'd better give me a few more days than that," she answered. "I'll talk to *Maman* first and see if I can get her on our side. I've told you that *Papa* doesn't like the British, and we'll have to be very careful how we go about this."

"Why? Why doesn't he like us? The French are our allies, and we're fighting this war together," he demanded.

"Well, the English took this island away from the French," she started, then added mischievously, "And don't try to tell me that the English love the French. Our two nations have been at loggerheads for centuries!"

He laughed and pulled her close to him again. They snuggled into one another, and he kissed and teased her ear with his lips. Thérèse felt delicious sensations run up and down her spine, and that irresistible sensation starting again in her insides. She closed her eyes and gave herself up to it, until she heard a cough behind them.

"I think we should turn back, Thérèse," announced Angélique, smiling widely at her sister. "It's getting awfully hot, and I think it may rain again."

Thérèse nodded at Angélique, conscious of the lack of decorum that she and Emmett were displaying. She wondered whether her sister had guessed at what had just happened and was anxious to get all of the details. Emmett bowed to Angélique and held out an arm to her. With a young woman on either arm, he turned around and they started to walk back the way they had come. Thérèse found his hand and tucked hers into it, so that he had to hold her arm at his waist. She saw Angélique catch a quick glance at their intertwined hands, and she shot Thérèse a glance as soon as she could catch her eye. Thérèse grinned at her, and her sister gave her a happy smile.

They continued their walk along the path beside the lush rain forest, hearing the birds calling to one another and being very careful where they walked. The pathway was often covered with tangled vines, and it would be easy to lose one's way, but the two girls were very familiar with their route and had no trouble arriving back at the Big House several minutes later.

When they reached the steps of the verandah, Emmett turned to Thérèse and faced her, still holding her hand in his.

"*Au revoir, mademoiselle,*" he said, bowing over her hand. "I will call on you again in . . . shall we say, a week?" he asked, looking up at her intently.

"Yes," she replied, smiling at him. "I will try to get a message to you regarding the matter we discussed."

He straightened up, nodded in Angélique's direction, then glanced back once more at Thérèse.

"*A bientôt, mesdemoiselles,*" he said, turning on his heel and walking back down the steps.

As soon as he was out of sight, Angélique grabbed her hand.

"What was that about, Thérèse?" she demanded in a low voice, in case anyone came through the front door at that very moment.

"Oh, Angélique, he wants to marry me," Thérèse gasped excitedly. "I can't believe that this is happening so quickly. I must get *Maman* to help me convince *Papa* to say yes!"

"Oh, my goodness," replied her sister. "I don't think he'll ever consent! You know how he feels."

"Yes, but you'd think he'd like to get one of his daughters married off and no longer his responsibility."

Angélique bit her lip and considered this as they walked into the house. After Henri helped them take off their jackets, Thérèse told her sister that she wanted to go and find their mother as soon as possible.

14

"Where's *Maman,* Eugénie?" Thérèse demanded, as she ran up the stairs. Eugénie was coming down them with a large pile of linens in her arms.

"In her room, *mademoiselle,*" replied the young woman, her eyes downcast. Thérèse couldn't be sure whether her father had told Eugénie that she had discovered their secret, so she continued to act as though there was nothing hidden between them.

Thérèse continued up the stairs and then along the corridor to her mother's beautifully furnished and spacious bedroom. Knocking on the door, she waited to be admitted.

"*Entrez,*" her mother called out, and Thérèse let herself in quietly.

Her mother sat in the corner of her room in a large chair, her youngest child asleep in her arms.

"*Maman,*" said Thérèse excitedly, "You'll never guess what happened!"

"Well, of course, *ma chérie,*" replied her mother, smiling and sitting up a little, shifting the little one in her arms. "I cannot guess unless you give me a hint."

"Well, you doubtless know that I went for a walk this morning with Captain Richardson, the young English soldier who has been courting me?" she asked.

"Yes, *Papa* said something about it yesterday. I gather he had been asking to see you during the period of mourning for your dear brother, but *Papa* has refused until now."

Thérèse frowned. "Yes, I think that's what happened." She sat on the bed and regarded her mother earnestly.

"*Maman,* this morning he proposed to me, and I said yes."

Her mother let out a little cry, then soothed the sleeping child in her arms as she had stirred at the sudden movement.

"Oh, *chérie* that's wonderful news." She was smiling from ear to ear. "I know you're in love with him, so what could be better?"

"But he's English, *Maman,*" Thérèse answered. "*Papa* will never approve."

Her mother looked conspiratorial. She reached out and patted her daughter's arm.

"Don't worry, *ma belle,"* she said. "I will talk to your father. He may not like the British, but he can never refuse me anything and he wouldn't want to break his daughter's heart."

Thérèse let out a little laugh. In a society in which women had practically no power, she knew that her mother could twist her father around her little finger if she wanted something, having always been a good wife who ran his home and estate efficiently, and always made sure he had his comforts. Thérèse wondered with a passing unease whether her mother guessed at her father's affair.

"Thank you, *Maman*!" She leapt off the bed to give her mother a grateful kiss on the cheek. "You've made me so happy. If *Papa* will consent to my marriage with Captain Richardson, I'll be the happiest girl in the world."

Thérèse bounded out of the room, and her mother watched her go. She hoped that her daughter would be happy with this man, but she wasn't sure Thérèse realized how hard a life could be in a cold, damp country with no servants to help with the daily household work, and no warm, loving family to turn to in difficult times. However, she knew Thérèse to be a strong and resilient young woman, and that she would cope with the hardships, as she herself had done as a young bride.

Two long days went by, and Thérèse tried to contain herself as she waited for her father to give his approval of Captain Richardson's asking for his daughter's hand in marriage. She thought she would burst with the excitement and anxiety of waiting and, as she had confided in her next-oldest sister, the two girls tried to encourage each other in being patient. Finally, on the third day, Henri, the butler, approached Thérèse shortly after breakfast.

"*Mademoiselle,"* he bowed politely. "Your father would like to see you in his study."

Thérèse clapped her hands excitedly as she and Angélique exchanged looks.

"Finally," breathed Angélique, seizing her sister's hand and squeezing it.

As Thérèse left the room, she realized that her hands were shaking and she was starting to perspire. She took the stairs two at a time, arriving outside her father's study with her heart in her mouth.

"Come in," called her father. She opened the door and walked up to the big walnut-wood desk which was covered with papers.

"Ah, Thérèse, good," said her father, looking at her intently. After an awkward silence, he started shuffling the papers on the desk, then looked up at her again.

"So, I understand you would like to marry the English captain who has been paying his respects to you?" he asked, awkwardly.

"Yes, *Papa*," she replied, clasping her hands together to stop them from trembling visibly. Why was she so nervous? Her father wouldn't dare to refuse her in this, she was sure.

"And do you believe you love him?" he asked, once again looking away from her.

"Oh, yes, *Papa*," she replied fervently. "More than anybody in the world!"

Her father frowned. Doubtless he didn't like to hear that she could love someone more than her parents and family members.

"And he loves me, too," she added. "We would be so happy if you would give your consent."

Her father started absentmindedly chewing on his moustache.

"Now, you know how I feel about the British, Thérèse," he said slowly. "And do you really think you could be happy on that cold, wet island?"

"I wouldn't mind the cold, *Papa*," she answered. "We'd have our love and that's all that matters."

"You can't live on love alone," he replied, now looking her squarely in the eye. "There are bills to pay and children to raise. You'll have no friends or family to help you in that country if things go wrong."

"Nothing will go wrong, *Papa*!" she said firmly. "Captain Richardson will make a good living as an accountant and I'm sure I'll make friends there."

"You don't even speak English!" he reminded her.

"No, but I can learn, and Emmett will help me. He speaks French and he can translate for me . . ."

"He won't always be with you, *ma chère*, and it can be very lonely for a young woman, left alone to raise children while her husband is at work."

She caught her father's eye and held his gaze firmly.

"Well, you would know, *Papa*," she said, with a meaningful look.

Her father sighed, then shrugged his shoulders. "Yes, I do, Thérèse," he replied. "And I'm sure that, if I don't do as you want, you will be quick to remind me of my obligations."

Thérèse's heart sped up. Her father didn't need to be reminded of what she knew, and he would have to give his consent even though he didn't want to.

He sighed again, then came around the side of the desk to stand in front of her.

"Very well, Thérèse, you may marry him," he said quietly. She was just about to throw her arms around his neck and thank him, when he added, "But he has to raise any children from the marriage in the Catholic faith. Is he a member of the Church of England?"

Her heart sank. She hadn't thought of that! Surely Emmett wouldn't mind agreeing to raise any children they might have in her faith, if he really wanted to marry her? She hoped that his religion wasn't a priority for him. She would have to prepare him ahead of time for this unexpected condition of their marriage.

"I expect so, *Papa,* but I don't think that would be a problem for him," she replied.

"Very well, then," he rejoined. "But you must wait until the end of the war before you can be married."

Thérèse nodded, then hugged her father somewhat hesitantly. "May I tell him that he can approach you to ask for my hand in marriage, *Papa*?" she asked.

"Yes, you may," said her father, returning to his desk chair and sitting down, giving his attention to the ledgers in front of him.

"Oh, thank you, *Papa,*" she said fervently. "You won't regret your decision, I promise."

He nodded absently.

"I'll tell him that he can ask for an appointment with you tomorrow," she said haltingly.

"Yes, you can do that," he replied.

Thérèse left his study, feeling anxious about what Emmett would have to say about giving up his religion in order to marry her. She knew that she would never give up her faith, so she could imagine how hard it might be for him to do the same. She prayed that it wouldn't be a problem for their marriage.

She went downstairs and sought out Henri, after stopping to write a quick letter to Emmett at the writing desk that was kept in the parlour.

"Dearest Emmett," she wrote. "My father is willing to consider your suit of marriage. You may make an appointment to see him tomorrow. All my love, Thérèse."

"Give this to Captain Richardson at the British army base, Henri," she instructed the butler, putting the folded piece of paper into an envelope and pressing it into his hand.

"Yes, *mademoiselle,*" Henri relied, bowing slightly. He turned and left the room, looking for his suit jacket before making arrangements to take the horse and cart into Port Louis to carry out the errand.

Thérèse returned upstairs, looking for her sisters to share the news with them. Now they must await Emmett's request for permission to marry her, and then they could proceed with an engagement. Her heart pounded again at the thought of a wedding and becoming Emmett's wife. She only hoped that the war would not continue much longer. She had heard *Papa* tell her mother at the breakfast table that the Allies were defeating the German army on all fronts and that he felt it couldn't be very much longer. How nice it would be to have her surviving brothers at her wedding. She felt that her heart would literally burst with happiness.

15

The following day dawned hot and sticky, as usual, and Thérèse could already feel the heat rising as she went out into the garden to perform her morning ritual of bathing her face in the flowers. A white tern flew across the path as she returned to the house, and she hoped it was a good omen.

Breakfast seemed interminable, and she barely joined in the conversation that was going around the table about the movement of troops in Europe. Her mother seemed distracted, as well, and she wondered whether she was also feeling anxious about the young English soldier's visit to the house. She had heard that Emmett would be coming this morning at ten o'clock, and she kept glancing at the clock, willing the time to pass by faster.

After breakfast, she sought out Angélique and the two of them sat outside on the verandah, in spite of the heat, and tried to while away the time until Emmett's approach. They discussed styles of wedding dresses and how many bridesmaids Thérèse should have. They were in the midst of considering colours for the dresses that the three attendants would wear. Angélique, Marie-Anne, and their cousin, Solange were to be bridesmaids and their little sister, Celeste, could be the flower girl. Suddenly, Thérèse heard a horse and wagon coming up the main path to the estate. She grabbed her sister's hand.

"He's coming, Angélique!" she whispered excitedly. "Emmett's here."

They both jumped up as the wagon rounded the path and started advancing towards the house. She could see Emmett sitting at the reins in his dress uniform, and she considered how handsome he looked. Her heart filled with love for him, and she could barely stop herself from running towards him.

Instead, she got up and walked slowly towards him as he dismounted from the wagon and tied the horse up to the fence post at the side of the house. He doffed his cap to the two girls, then went to Thérèse and took her hand in his.

"Good morning, *mademoiselle* Thérèse," he said quietly, looking into her eyes, before bowing his head to her sister, "*Mademoiselle* Angélique."

Angélique smiled at him. "*Bonjour, monsieur,*" she replied.

Emmett let go of Thérèse's hand, and all three of them turned towards the house.

"You received my message, and you're here for your appointment with *Papa*?" Thérèse queried, looking up at him. He nodded in affirmation.

Thérèse thought he looked rather nervous, which didn't really surprise her much. *Papa* could be very intimidating, and he hadn't exactly encouraged them up until now.

"Well, good luck," she whispered, standing on tiptoe to reach his ear. "Angélique and I will wait for you here afterwards."

He nodded again, then went up the steps to the front door of the house, raising his hand to knock. Thérèse and her sister returned to the verandah and sat down to await the outcome of the interview.

Half an hour later, Emmett returned, his face flushed and shiny. Thérèse knew it was hot in the house, but she was sure that her father had grilled Emmett on many points and couldn't blame him for being overheated.

She tucked her arm in his and said,

"Come back in the house with us and we'll find some *limonade* to sip on," she said. "We need to talk about *Papa's* answer to you. Maybe *Maman* will even invite you to lunch."

"I have to return to the base immediately," he replied. "But a cool drink would be most appreciated."

The three of them went into the house, and Angélique disappeared to the kitchen to request the lemonade from Dhala, the cook. Thérèse excitedly turned to Emmett, gripping his arm.

"What did he say? What did Papa say to you?" she demanded breathlessly,

Emmett wiped his brow with his hand and tucked his cap under his arm.

"Well, I requested your hand in marriage, and he said that he would consider it, but only if I promised that any children we may have will be baptized in the Catholic faith," he answered.

Is that all?" Thérèse asked. "He didn't ask you to renounce your own faith?"

"No, but I suppose that that comes along with it," he replied.

"Not necessarily, but would you be willing to do that?"

"Of course," he looked earnestly into her eyes. "Anything for you! Church has never been all that important to me anyway."

"Alright," she nodded, her eyes shining. "But would you be willing to be married by a Catholic priest?" she pushed further.

"Yes, as long as we get married at the army base," he smiled.

"Oh, Emmett, that's wonderful! I would be honoured to get married at the base." She threw herself into his arms, after making sure that nobody was coming down the stairs.

She was still standing in his arms when Angélique returned with the jug of lemonade.

"Let's go through to the sitting room," said Angélique, "and then I'll go and find *Maman* so that you can tell her everything." She added, with a little giggle, "And me, too."

Laughing among themselves, the three of them went into the big room of the house while Angélique found some glasses for their lemonade. Thérèse sat beside Emmett on the chaise longue, her arm tucked comfortably through his.

After a few minutes, Angélique returned with their mother in tow. The matriarch hugged her daughter, then shook hands with Emmett.

"So, Captain Richardson," she said. "Tell me about your conversation with my husband."

Emmett accepted the cool beverage that Angélique handed him, then addressed her mother.

"I requested *Mademoiselle* Thérèse's hand in marriage," he replied shyly. "Her father told me that we may proceed on the conditions that I agree to baptize any children we have in the Catholic religion and that we wait until the war is over for the wedding."

The girls grinned at each other at the mention of children from the marriage, but *Maman* looked seriously at Emmett.

"Well, I'm sure this war will be over soon," she told him. "The German army is losing everywhere, and the Allies will soon be victorious. We'll start with some of the preparations now, at any rate. And you, *ma fille,* " she turned to Thérèse, "must report to Dhala each day and learn how to cook. I'm sure that Captain Richardson will not have servants to do the household chores for you on an officer's salary, so you must learn household tasks." She looked at Emmett again.

"And I'll ask my husband to hire a tutor to teach Thérèse English," she added. "We can't have her not being able to speak her husband's mother tongue."

"But Emmett speaks French, *Maman,*" interjected Thérèse.

"Your husband will probably take you to live in his country, so you must speak the language," Madeleine replied.

Thérèse felt a little annoyance at her mother, as this wasn't a foregone conclusion to her. She was still hoping that she could convince her future husband to agree to remain on the estate and help her father run the plantation. Still, her mother was a practical person, and she supposed that it was only right for her to speak Emmett's language.

She was going to be married! It was actually happening, and she felt sure that the war would soon be over. Wouldn't it be wonderful if she were to be a married woman before the end of the year? Her emotions bubbled over with happiness, and she felt again that she was the luckiest girl in the world.

16

December 1918

The war was over at last. The Allies had finally overcome Kaiser Bill's army after many bloody battles in Europe. Thérèse's family had waited in fear of telegrams arriving at the Big House with news of the death of Rémy or Dominic but, happily, both boys survived the war. However, Rémy had an injured hand which, although it had been operated on by army surgeons, never returned to its previous state and was frequently hidden in the young man's pocket.

Dominic, on the other hand, although his body was whole, didn't seem to be himself after his return from France. His eyes held a haunted look, and he would often start and look frantically over his shoulder, especially if there was a sudden, loud noise in the house. He could often be found staring into space with tears in his eyes and, when someone approached him to ask what was wrong, he would hastily dash the tears from his eyes and retreat to his bedroom. He spent many hours a day in there, and sometimes would have to be called repeatedly to come to luncheon or dinner. Their mother tried to give him warm hugs and to order special dishes from the kitchen to cheer him up, but he didn't respond to either with much pleasure. Thérèse knew that *Maman* was worried about him, although her father was becoming impatient with his younger son's melancholy. There wasn't much doubt in Thérèse's mind that her brother was suffering from the condition that everyone was talking about, and that had been recently recognized by doctors, shell shock. She had heard some of the neighbours talking about it, and felt certain that this applied to Dominic.

On November 11, 1918, the Armistice was signed. The Treaty of Versailles that was drawn up in 1919 punished Germany severely for starting and continuing the war for four years. Its colonies were given away to the Allies, and many harsh economic sanctions were imposed on the country. Germany was to suffer greatly for the next twenty years, and this caused the Germans' feeling of nationalism to once again strengthen, re-energizing their nation. Hunger and many other privations racked the country and made the German people anxious for a new leader who would lead them out of the dark.

Meanwhile, Thérèse and her mother were finally able to prepare for the wedding. They had looked at many beautiful white organza, silk and tulle gowns, and Thérèse was starting to feel overwhelmed. On what seemed like their tenth visit to the dressmaker in Port Louis, they had finally settled on a white lace gown with *broderie anglaise* on the bodice and cut in the new mid-calf length that had recently emerged from the Paris couturier salons. Thérèse had agonized over the new wedding veils, which came down very low over the forehead, and were held in place with a large white bow, before settling on a more becoming white cloche hat that framed her oval face. She knew that she looked striking in white, with her dark hair and eyes, and that her bridegroom would probably be pleased. Her two younger sisters, Angélique and Marie-Anne, and cousin, Solange, would wear light blue gowns cut in the same fashionable mid-calf length as her wedding gown, while her littlest sister, Celeste, would be adorable as the flower girl in a pink, ruffled organza gown.

The wedding, as promised to Emmett, was to be held at the army base, but Madeleine had insisted that her cook, Dhala, and the kitchen staff at the Big House provide the food, as the family didn't think that they or their neighbours could stomach plain, stodgy English food. There would be local delicacies like curried goat and lamb stew, as well as vegetables like okra, sweet corn and yams, with copious amounts of fruit such as papaya, grapes and mangoes for dessert. The wedding cake, which Dhala baked herself, was made from coconut and vanilla, with a delicate whipped white frosting, and figurines of the bride and groom (in uniform) posed on top. As instructed by her mother, Thérèse had been learning to cook, and had spent many hours in the hot, steamy kitchen with Dhala. The cook had been impressed with how conscientious her student was, and how quickly she had learned to make pastry and to serve up delicious meat and vegetable dishes.

"You will make your husband very happy, *Mademoiselle* Thérèse," she commented. "The way to a man's heart is through his stomach." Thérèse smiled secretly to herself. She wasn't so sure that it was *that* part of a man's body that caused him to love a woman. Her mother had spoken to her on a couple of occasions about what would be expected of a wife, both in the kitchen and in the bedroom. Although she already knew what went on in the bedroom, Thérèse listened attentively but asked her mother few questions.

"Just let him lead the way, *chérie,*" Madeleine confided. "The man knows what to do. You must just follow his lead, and never refuse him! A wife's duty is to always be acquiescent to her husband's needs."

"Yes, *Maman,*" she replied, thinking to herself that her mother's submitting to her husband's needs had now got her twelve children, and that her husband still didn't seem to be satisfied. She knew that Emmett adored her and hoped that she would be enough for him. She supposed she would soon find out, but was still excited at the prospect of the wedding.

The wedding day dawned bright and sunny. The temperatures at this time of year were still warm and, as Thérèse made her way out to the garden early that morning, the birds of paradise were in full bloom and looked remarkably like stationery birds in the flower beds. The huge palm trees in the garden were home to hawks and orioles, and some of these were calling to each other in the early morning sun, flitting in and out of the trees. The grass in the garden was looking parched, despite the gardening staff's efforts to keep it watered. At least the rainy season wouldn't arrive until after Christmas, and Thérèse was glad that her mother had insisted that the wedding be held before the festive season started.

She looked down at the small engagement ring that Emmett had bought her several months ago, and a little frisson went through her as she realized that, by the end of today, she would be wearing a gold band with it. People would be calling her "*Madame* Richardson," instead of "*Mademoiselle* Lemieux," and the thought gave her a little thrill. Married to the man she loved most in the world! Who would have thought that this wonderful dream would have come out of the darkness of war? She certainly would never have met him if it hadn't been for the European conflict, and she murmured a small prayer of thanks for the things that had happened over the last couple of years.

She made her way back to her room and lay down again on her bed but couldn't sleep for excitement. This was the day that every young girl dreams of. In the back of her mind was a small dread of leaving the island and her beloved family behind and going to a small, cold island half-way around the world. Emmett had made it very clear that he intended to return to England once the war was done, as his elderly aunt needed his care and attention. Her husband had passed away recently, and as his aunt wasn't getting any younger and had been very good to him as he was growing up, the least he could do was to go back home and offer her food and shelter. He told Thérèse that it was wonderful that she had learned to cook while on the island, but that his aunt would be teaching her how to cook the English way, which was what would be expected on the table every day at noon. Tea would be eaten in the evenings, with sandwiches or salads prepared by herself. The colonial habit of eating a large dinner in the evening was frowned upon in the British Isles. Thérèse pushed the thoughts of life with her young husband and his elderly aunt from her mind and got up, wrapping her dressing gown around her.

She went downstairs and found her mother sitting at the dining room table nursing her youngest child, a baby boy named Albert, born just before the end of the war. Her mother smiled warmly and held out a hand to her. Thérèse took it and sat down beside her.

"Are you excited about today, *ma chérie*?" *Maman* asked her daughter.

"Yes, and nervous," Thérèse replied. "I still can't really believe it's happening."

"Well, in a few hours, you'll be a married woman," her mother smiled.

"I can hardly wait. Emmett's going to be a wonderful husband, and I'll do my best to make him a dutiful and loving wife."

"I have no doubt that you will, *chérie*, as you have always been a dutiful and loving daughter."

Thérèse got up and gave her mother a quick hug, then poured herself some coffee. Dhala came in with some eggs and fruit for the two women, and Thérèse's brothers and sisters started arriving for breakfast in little groups of two and three. Her sisters were especially loving towards her, and little Celeste, who was excited to be a flower girl at the wedding, gave her an excited hug.

Papa eventually came in, leaned over and gave Thérèse a kiss on the top of her head as he passed her to his seat at the head of the table. She smiled to herself and thought that he was probably relieved to have his eldest daughter married off and happy, and therefore unlikely to spill his secret to his wife. Now that she had got what she wanted, she no longer needed to blackmail Paul about his affair with the housemaid, and therefore could keep her lips sealed. She wasn't sure that she really could have gone through with hurting her mother in that way, anyway. It was best forgotten, as much as it could be.

At eleven o'clock that morning, Thérèse was helped into a horse and carriage by Henri, and her father and Angélique climbed in behind her. She knew she looked beautiful in the white lace dress and was very glad of her decision to wear a hat, rather than a veil, in the intense heat. She carried a small bouquet of magnolias and fiddled anxiously with the ribbon around it as they rode.

The ride to the army base seemed interminable but, finally, it was over and they had arrived. There were two rows of English soldiers standing outside in the sweltering heat, and a cheer went up as Thérèse stepped down from the carriage, holding onto Henri's hand to steady herself.

Her father offered her his arm and, as he did so, the young soldiers each raised a ceremonial sword and proceeded to hold them overhead and crossed with one another, forming an arch. Thérèse and her father walked slowly underneath it and up the stairs of the base, followed by the bridesmaids and flower girl who had descended from the other carriage. Once inside, she gasped at how beautifully the main hall had been decorated, with exotic flowers and Union Jacks.

They proceeded down the hall and into the chapel. As they walked in, the enormous congregation of wedding guests all stood up. It seemed just about everybody who was anybody had come to attend her wedding! If Thérèse hadn't felt nervous up to this point, she suddenly felt terrified and was aware that she had broken out in a sweat. She hoped it wouldn't be noticeable to the guests, and especially not to her new husband.

Emmett was standing at the end of the altar with his staff sergeant and best man, Roger, beaming proudly at her. Thérèse thought how handsome he looked in his uniform, and her nervousness suddenly disappeared. She had never felt happier than she did at this moment. She smiled up at him warmly and kissed her father's cheek, as he handed her over to her bridegroom.

Père Lavallière, their local priest, officiated the ceremony and the wedding mass was performed. Emmett spoke clearly during the recital of the vows, but Thérèse's responses could barely be heard. However, she beamed when Emmett placed the plain gold band on her left hand and couldn't help but glance down at it every few minutes.

Finally, the ceremony was over, and they walked back down the aisle of the chapel, to the cheers and thrown kisses of the wedding guests. They had decided to forgo the receiving line outside the chapel, due to the intense heat, and the wedding party now proceeded to another part of the base, where the banquet hall was housed. When they stepped inside it felt much cooler, and Emmett and Thérèse, who had been fanning herself to stay cool, were now able to stand in line to receive the good wishes of the many guests.

Her mother had made good on her promise of a sumptuous wedding feast, and Thérèse drank several glasses of cool white wine, as well as a glass of port with her wedding cake. After the dinner, speeches were heard, and Emmett distinguished himself with a heartfelt and sincere thanks to her parents for allowing him to marry their daughter, and also a toast to the British Empire and the end of the war.

The dance then began, and Thérèse grabbed her husband's hand.

"Oh, no, darling, I don't dance," protested Emmett, pulling away from her.

"What do you mean, you don't dance?" She stared at him incredulously.

"Well, I mean . . . I've never learned . . . my aunt and uncle didn't approve of dancing," he sputtered, looking embarrassed.

"But it's our wedding day!" protested Thérèse.

"Well, why don't you dance with one of your brothers, or Roger?" he suggested hopefully.

"I didn't marry Roger," she announced firmly, pulling him out of his seat by the hand and down the steps of the dais to the dance floor. It occurred to her that, truthfully, she didn't know very much about her new husband, other than that he was handsome, kind and born in England. She had never met a man who didn't know how to dance. It was one of the required disciplines on the island for men and women, and she was very good at it.

"Just follow what I'm doing, and try not to step on my toes," she murmured in his ear as she started leading him around to a romantic waltz number. She exchanged looks with her father, who was playing the violin with the band. His expression conveyed that he knew about her husband's inability to dance, and Thérèse thought she saw contempt on his face. She turned her back on him and whispered in Emmett's ear, as she held on to him firmly and guided him around the dance floor. Most people looking at them would have thought she was whispering sweet nothings to him, but she was in fact giving orders about where to turn and how many steps to take in each direction.

She didn't know it then, but this was to be the first and only time she would dance with her husband.

17

The wedding was over, and Thérèse and Emmett had left the reception hall amid cheers and wishes for their good luck and happiness. After a short carriage ride, they arrived at the married quarters on the base, where they would spend their wedding night.

She was nervous about what was coming next but tried to hide it beneath an air of confidence, holding tightly on to her new husband's hand during the trip. Once they arrived, Emmett got down from the carriage, lifted out his bride and tipped the driver generously. Thérèse gave him a happy kiss on the lips, and they walked into the base together, arm-in-arm.

They were shown to their room, a relatively small space for two people, but with a fairly large double bed dominating it. Thérèse's heart did a little jump as she compared it to the small single bed she had slept in at home on the estate, and tried not to feel more nervous about what was coming.

Emmett turned to her. "Would you like to use the bathroom first?" he asked solicitously.

She nodded and removed her coat, hanging it on the hook beside the door. She put her small suitcase down on the floor, opened it and removed a small bag containing her washcloth, toothbrush and some eau-de-cologne. She then pulled out the beautiful full-length lace nightgown she had chosen for her honeymoon and went into the bathroom.

She emerged several minutes later to find Emmett sitting in the only armchair in the room, smoking a cigarette. He jumped up when he saw her and stubbed his cigarette hastily out.

"You're so beautiful, Thérèse darling!" he exclaimed, pulling her into his arms. She could taste the cigarette on his lips as he began to kiss her but didn't find it unpleasant. As his kisses became more urgent, she moved out of his embrace.

"Go and get washed," she said breathlessly. He nodded and turned quickly away from her, grabbing his overnight bag and disappearing into the bathroom.

She looked around the room, then lifted up the covers on one side of the bed and climbed tentatively in. The sheets felt cold against her arms and legs, but she knew she would soon be warm. She pondered what was about to happen and wondered how she would find it. *Maman*'s description of what happens between a man and a woman kept running through her head, and she hoped it wouldn't be as unromantic as it sounded. A little shiver of fear and anticipation went through her and she lay there staring at the ceiling for a few minutes. Emmett eventually appeared, shutting the bathroom door quietly after him. He climbed into bed on the other side, then leaned over and gazed at her face.

"I love you so much, Thérèse," he whispered, taking one of her hands in his and kissing it.

"I love you too, Emmett," she replied breathlessly, leaning forward and kissing him gently on the lips. His response was to gather her in his arms and start kissing her over and over, on her face, arms and neck. She let out a little sigh and allowed herself to relax and respond to him. Before very long, she experienced the warm feeling she had felt previously and found her breathing speeding up.

They gave themselves to one another with love and tenderness. It was over fairly quickly, and she lay still afterwards, thinking that it wasn't as bad as she had been afraid it would be.

"It will be better next time, I promise," he murmured, as he held her tightly in his arms. "Did I hurt you?"

She shook her head and looked into his eyes.

"Have you had experience of this before?" she asked him, candidly. She knew that soldiers often associated with women of easy virtue when they were far from home and needing comfort.

"A little," he replied hesitantly, then hastened to assure her, "but it didn't mean a thing."

"That's alright," she answered. "I'm glad you knew what to do."

He smiled at her then rolled onto his back, pulling her tightly against his side.

"Go to sleep now, my angel," he murmured against her hair. She snuggled closer to him and closed her eyes. They were both asleep in minutes, worn out after the long and exciting day they had had.

18

They arose early the next morning and washed and dressed in the half-light. She was once again a little nervous to be alone with him and hid herself in the bathroom to change out of her nightgown.

"Shall we go to my parents' house for breakfast, or do you want to stay here and eat at the base?" she asked Emmett.

"Let's go to your parents' house," he replied. "I'm sure that they'll want to make sure that their daughter is still in one piece!"

Thérèse giggled and kissed him on the nose.

"I'm certain they knew you'd take good care of me," she answered. "Come on, then! We'll see if we can get a carriage to take us back, then ask Dhala to make some breakfast for us."

He put his arms around her and looked sincerely at her as he asked his question.

"You've had servants to take care of you all of your life. Do you think you'll be alright having to cook and clean for us when we return to England?"

She gazed at him intently. This was her final opportunity to ask him about the one thing that was marring her happiness - the thought of leaving her island and family.

"Is there any chance at all that you might change your mind about going back to England, Emmett?" she asked him in a quiet voice.

He broke away from her, seeming troubled.

"I've thought about it, "he said. "But my elderly aunt needs me. She hasn't been coping all that well by herself since my uncle died, and I made a promise to her that I'd take care of her when I returned from the war. Also, I have the house over there in London. Here, we'd probably have to live on your father's charity for a while, or perhaps forever, and

I don't know whether I want to do that."

She smiled. "Yes, there is that. *Papa* isn't always the easiest person to get along with, either. And there are the other children who will be underfoot, as well. We'll want to have children of our own, and then it will get really crowded!"

"I'm glad you see things in that light," Emmett answered her. "I was afraid that you wouldn't want to leave the island at all. England is very different, as well as halfway across the world."

"I knew that when I agreed to marry you. I'll be happy, as long as I'm with you."

He smiled and kissed her, then they put on their coats and went downstairs to try to find a carriage.

Emmett and Thérèse arrived at the Big House about half an hour later and went into the house quietly. They were greeted by some of the servants, who congratulated them warmly and told them that they would let Dhala know there would be two more people for breakfast.

They went into the big dining room, where Thérèse's father was already sitting reading the newspaper. He rose when they came in, shaking hands firmly with Emmett and kissing Thérèse on the cheek.

"My wife will be down shortly," he told Emmett, then gestured to the kitchen servant to pour them some coffee.

"Have you decided when you would like to take your bride back to England?" he inquired of Emmett, once they were seated at the big table with their coffee and some papaya juice. Thérèse started at the question and looked intently at her father. She had the feeling that he would be glad to be rid of her and was just waiting for Emmett to take her away. She had kept his secret about the affair with Eugénie, but she suspected that her father lived in fear of her telling her mother. It obviously never occurred to him that Madeleine might find out for herself.

"Yes, I think perhaps in two weeks," Emmett replied, to Thérèse's surprise. She had expected much longer than that. Perhaps two months to pack up her things and say goodbye to all of the friends and neighbours on the island? But two weeks?

"That seems reasonable," said her father. Of course he would say that! Thérèse wondered what her mother would think. She didn't think she'd be prepared to part with her eldest daughter so quickly.

As it happened, Madeleine didn't seem all that surprised that Emmett wanted to leave so quickly. Maybe she had already spoken with him about it, or at least discussed it with her father? She promised to help Thérèse pack all of her clothing and belongings, and to host a small party for her just before she left. She looked sad when she spoke about it, but not overly distressed. Thérèse supposed that a woman who had lost two sons to the war wouldn't have that much trouble letting a daughter leave home with her new husband. That was the way of the world, after all.

All the same, she hoped that her mother and other siblings would miss her once she was gone. Going to England was a big adventure for her, and she was looking forward to settling in a new country, even though she had harboured a small hope that Emmett would agree to stay in Mauritius. However, with the terrible war being over, the world was changing rapidly and she knew it would be good to start a new life in a new country. With Emmett by her side, she felt that she could do anything, although she wasn't looking forward to the long sea voyage to get there.

The two weeks passed quickly in a flurry of preparation. Thérèse and her mother worked tirelessly at sorting through her wardrobe and childhood possessions to decide what she should bring with her to England, and the servants packed everything into trunks under Madeleine's supervision. Madeleine commissioned her dressmaker to make Thérèse a navy blue sailor suit for travelling, in the new shorter style, and they purchased a smart cloche hat to match. She felt very grown up, and much older than her years when she put it on for the first time.

Emmett, meanwhile, finished up his business at the military base and obtained the necessary signatures on his discharge from the British army. He only had one suitcase of clothing and a small travel bag that contained the few possessions he had brought with him from England.

The party that Thérèse's parents hosted for the young couple's farewell was a successful affair. All of their neighbourhood friends attended, as well as the girls she had gone to school with and their parents. The food was excellent, as always, prepared lovingly by Dhala, and the music and dancing went on until well past midnight. Thérèse and Emmett stayed at the Big House for their last night on the island and took breakfast with the family in the morning.

"I can't believe you're really leaving, Thérèse," said Angélique, hugging her sister tightly. "I'm going to miss you so much!"

"I'll miss you too, Angélique," Thérèse replied, tears forming in her eyes. "You're my best friend. You know that, don't you?"

"Yes, and you're mine," her sister replied fervently.

"You played a big part in bringing Emmett and me together, and I'll never forget that. You'll have to come and visit me in England, once you get married yourself."

"Oh, I will!"

The two girls clung to each other for a few minutes, then some of the younger children started to demand their turn to embrace their older sister, particularly the little ones. Thérèse kissed them all and told them how much she'd miss them, promising to come back and visit before too long.

Little did she know it that she would have little ones herself before she could fulfill that promise.

19

On the morning of sailing, Thérèse awoke at her usual five o'clock, rolled over and threw her arms around Emmett for a brief moment, smiling to herself as she remembered the night before. Their lovemaking was becoming more passionate, and she was starting to learn some new ways to please her husband. She had had no idea how satisfying and pleasant marital relations could be, and she was very grateful to Emmett for not rushing her or making her feel inadequate. She knew she was less experienced than he, but she was rapidly catching up.

She untangled herself from her husband and rolled out of bed, quietly putting on shoes and tiptoeing out of the room to go down to the garden for the last time. Nothing stirred in the house as she made her way down the stairs and out onto the verandah. The huge garden was quiet, with only a few jacanas calling to each other in the dawn light. She stooped over the flowers as she had done every day for so many years and reflected on how much she would miss her morning ritual here, and the family she was leaving behind. She was sure she was in for a great adventure in England, but she had never been away from her family before and she knew it was going to be difficult at first. However, she was sure that Emmett's love for her, and her own sense of curiosity and adventure, would make it easier.

She returned to her bedroom after a few minutes of wandering around the garden and saying silent farewells to the flowers and plants, and gently shook Emmett awake.

"We have to go down to breakfast soon, darling," she murmured in his ear. "Breakfast for us is going to be at six."

He stirred, then smiled up at her, stretching and yawning in the half-light.

"Just give me a few minutes to wake up", he replied. "Why don't you get dressed and go down to your parents while I get ready?"

She nodded, put on her Chinese dressing gown, slipped out of the room and went into the bathroom down the hall to start her daily preparations. She brushed her teeth, combed her hair and dressed quickly, then went down the stairs to the dining room.

Maman was sitting at the table, nursing baby Albert. She smiled up at Thérèse and held out her hand to her. Thérèse bent and gave her mother a gentle kiss on the cheek and her mother responded by stroking her hair tenderly.

"I don't know what I'm going to do without you*, ma fille,"* she said softly, her eyes filling with tears. "You've been my rock for the last few years, and I'll miss you so much."

Thérèse hugged her mother tightly, including the chubby baby in her embrace.

"I'll write often*, Maman,*" she murmured. "And I'll try to come back and visit as often as I can."

Her mother nodded and dashed the tears off her cheeks with clenched fingers.

"Yes, I'm counting on that, Thérèse," she replied, quietly. "I don't think

I can handle *Papa* for the rest of my life unless I can have some understanding from another person who knows what he's like."

Thérèse grimaced to herself. She was surprised her mother was admitting to her that life with her father wasn't easy. She supposed that *Maman* saw her now as a fellow wife who was learning how difficult marriage could be. For her though, it had been nothing but blissful so far, and she didn't expect it to change in the near future. She felt sympathy for her mother, as she'd seen the things *Papa* got up to and didn't envy her the life she led and the annual pregnancies, which must be exhausting. She squeezed her mother's hand tightly, then sat down and poured herself a glass of mango juice. Henri, the butler, silently entered the room and bowed to Thérèse, then asked her what she would like for breakfast. She ordered eggs and croissants for herself and asked him to bring the same for Emmett.

After breakfast, at which *Papa* had presided and discussed European politics with Emmett while *Maman* and Thérèse ate silently, they all got ready for the carriage drive to Port Louis. *Papa* had suggested that they all travel together to the port city before the other children were awake and before the heat of the day became too extreme. Thérèse and Emmett's boat, the "*Impératrice de l'Océan*," was sailing at eleven o'clock and they wanted to be installed in their cabin, then seated in the dining room by that time.

The drive to the harbour was long and tedious, and Thérèse could feel the sweat trickling down her back as she sat upright on the hard carriage seat in her new sailor suit and cloche hat. The navy blue suit, though smart, wasn't very practical in the early heat of the day, and she was looking forward to changing into a summer dress once they boarded the boat. She noticed Emmett wiping sweat off the back of his neck as he sat in his dark morning suit and tie. *Maman* and *Papa* looked similarly uncomfortable. They would be glad to get back to the cool interior of the house.

They arrived at the dock at around nine o'clock and were helped down from the carriage by Henri, who pulled all of their baggage to the ground and placed it in a small cart, which had been supplied by a young porter. They proceeded to the gates of the harbour, and then it was time to say farewell.

Thérèse's mother pulled her into her embrace, tears once again springing into her eyes.

"Take care of yourself, *ma chérie,"* she murmured against Thérèse's hair. "Write often and let me know all of your news. I'll think of you every day in your new home."

Thérèse felt the tears coming into her own eyes as she squeezed her mother tightly.

"I will, *Maman,"* she replied. "And take care of yourself, too, and the other children. You'll be in my thoughts every day, too."

They clung to one another for a few minutes, each with her eyes closed and tears now coursing freely down their cheeks. The reality of this moment hadn't really hit Thérèse until now, and it finally dawned on her that she was leaving her family and her childhood home for good, trading it for a new country where she knew nobody but her husband and barely even spoke the language. It suddenly became a daunting proposition, rather than an adventure. It was with these melancholy thoughts that she turned to her father and gave him a quick hug.

"Thank you, *Papa,* for everything you have done for me. I shall miss you," she said dutifully.

He pulled her into a warm embrace and, for a moment, she could almost forgive him for the things he had done and his selfishness. He had been her only example of a husband and father, but she knew that her own husband was going to be very different from him. She wasn't so sure she would miss her father in the way she would miss her mother and brothers and sisters, but she would miss him nonetheless. He hugged her tightly and exhorted her to be a good and dutiful wife to her husband, as well as a credit to him and their family. She nodded and told him that she would do her best.

Her parents embraced Emmett and asked him to look after their daughter in her new home in England. He told them that he would help her with her English and teach her the ways of society in that country halfway across the world, and that he would try to make her happy there. The prospect of what was coming now seemed much more real to Thérèse, and it somewhat took away the excitement of her new adventure.

She took her husband's arm and bade her parents a final goodbye, then turned, and they started walking towards the ramp that would take them on board the boat. Thérèse looked up at the huge ocean-going liner, realizing that this would be her home for the next two weeks, and that when she finally left it, she would be stepping into a completely new place and beginning a very different life. She hoped she would be up to the challenge, and the expectations that would be put on her.

20

Thérèse found life on the ship very exciting. She enjoyed the gentle rocking of the boat and looking out into the endless ocean once they got out of port. There were so many new people to meet, and many of them looked at her husband with admiration when they found out that he had been a soldier in the British army. She felt proud of him and would often take his arm possessively as they strolled along the decks, breathing in the fresh, salty air. At first, birds circled around the ship, but eventually there were very few to be seen. It was a whole new world she had never seen before, and she realized just how sheltered she had been growing up in her island home.

She was introduced to the captain on the first night. He was a tall, imposing man who looked dashing in his naval uniform. His eyes lingered on her face and figure as they were introduced, and she felt that he held on to her hand for a few seconds longer than was necessary as they shook hands.

"You have a beautiful wife, Captain Richardson," he said to Emmett.

"Yes, I'm very aware of that, Captain," replied Emmett. "I ask myself every morning when I wake up how I came to be so lucky!"

Thérèse giggled and laid her head briefly on Emmett's shoulder before responding,

"It's a pleasure to meet you, Capitaine Alexandre."

"The pleasure is all mine, *madame*," he said, looking her squarely in the eyes. "Perhaps *monsieur* and *madame* will join me at the captain's table for dinner tonight?"

"We would be honoured," replied Emmett quickly. He knew that sitting at the captain's table wasn't a favour that was accorded to everyone on the boat, and he thought it was well worth taking advantage of.

As they walked down the deck, Emmett whispered to Thérèse.

"You've made quite a conquest with the captain, *ma chérie.*"

"Do you think so?" she asked, coyly.

"Oh, yes," Emmett answered. "Most people don't get invited to his table on the very first night unless he knows them. I believe the food is generally better at his table, but it's also a feather in one's cap to be asked." He smiled knowingly.

Thérèse was becoming aware of the effect that she had on men, and realizing that it was something that she could possibly take advantage of. Already Emmett was eating out of the palm of her hand and could refuse her nothing. She knew she was always in demand when she was younger and the neighbourhood boys came to dances at her house, but it wasn't something that she'd expected would continue into adulthood. She tucked the information away in the back of her mind, to be used whenever an occasion might present itself.

She dressed herself carefully in a dark blue silk dress for dinner and styled her hair with a diamond clip. Her mother had never allowed her to use lipstick, but now that she was a married woman, she had purchased some at a little boutique on the island before leaving and applied it to her lips now. As Thérèse gazed at her reflection in the mirror, she saw that her eyes were sparkling and how the lipstick added colour to her entire face, not just her lips.

When she and Emmett walked arm-in-arm into the dining room that evening, the captain caught sight of them and waved them over.

"*Monsieur* and *Madame* Richardson!" he called out. "Come and sit by me."

Thérèse hurried Emmett over to the table and seated herself in the chair beside the captain, with Emmett to her left.

"You look charming this evening, *madame,*" he murmured quietly to her. Then he turned to the lady who was seated on his other side. "Please meet my wife, Sophie. This is *Capitaine* and *Madame* Emmett Richardson, *ma chère*. The captain fought in the British army."

Neither Thérèse nor Emmett corrected him about the fact that Emmett hadn't actually fought in the army. He had done his part with the ordering of supplies for the army base, but the captain and his wife didn't need to be any the wiser.

Madame Alexandre bowed her head to Thérèse and Emmett, but Thérèse caught a sour look on the lady's face as she looked her up and down. She was considerably older than Thérèse, and quite a bit plumper. Thérèse got the impression that she was jealous of any attention her husband paid to younger, prettier women. Her father flashed quickly through her mind, and she realized that the captain's wife probably had reason to be jealous. Were all married men guilty of flirting, or worse, with attractive young women? However, she felt she didn't have to worry about Emmett. He was completely devoted to her and didn't have eyes for anyone else.

Thérèse and the captain kept up quite a conversation during dinner, with Emmett adding comments every so often about the war and what he felt was coming in the future. She could feel the captain's eyes upon her from time to time, and also those of his dowdy wife, who seemed very annoyed to be virtually excluded from the conversation. Thérèse knew that she hadn't made a friend there and vowed to try and butter her up the next time they met on the ship. She didn't like the feeling of being disliked just because she was younger and more attractive.

Life continued on the ship at a leisurely pace. Thérèse and Emmett spent the days wandering the decks, sometimes sitting and chatting with other passengers. They met quite a few British couples, and Thérèse tentatively tried out her English with them. Emmett had been coaching her patiently every evening after dinner, to supplement the lessons she had had on the island with a tutor, and she was a quick and eager pupil. He sometimes laughed indulgently at her pronunciation, but mostly commented on how fast she was learning and what a clever wife he had. He had presented her with a slim, leather-bound French-English dictionary on their first night on the ship, and she often amused herself by making up conversations about everyday situations so that she could widen her vocabulary.

They continued to sit at the captain's table every night, and Thérèse made efforts to include *Madame* Alexandre in the conversation, as well. She felt the lady slowly warming to her and not glowering at her anymore when the captain addressed her. Thérèse had always been loved by everybody and didn't want to feel that someone could dislike her because of her appearance.

About a week after they had started their journey, she woke up one morning feeling rather ill. Emmett came out of the bathroom and bent to kiss her as she lay in bed, feeling nauseated.

"Wake up, sleepyhead," he murmured, kissing her tenderly on the cheek. "Ready for breakfast?"

The thought of breakfast turned her stomach and almost made her jump out of bed and run into the bathroom.

"Oh, I couldn't," she replied. "I don't feel well today. You go down by yourself. I don't think I could eat anything."

"Seasick?" he asked her, surprise showing on his face. "Up till now, you've had really good sea-legs."

"Yes, I know," she replied. "There must be some bigger waves today. I really don't feel well at all."

"Well, that's alright, darling. You just stay put and I'll come and see how you're feeling after breakfast."

The word "breakfast" tipped her over the edge, and she ran into the bathroom and threw up violently into the toilet. When she came back, pale and shaking, Emmett was still there waiting for her, concern showing on his face.

"Are you going to be alright by yourself?" he asked. "I can stay with you, if you like."

"No, you go ahead and have your breakfast. I'll just rest in the cabin for a while."

She stayed there for an hour, feeling horrible and trying to sleep so that she didn't have to experience the nausea. Gradually, the feeling lessened, and she was finally able to get herself out of bed and put on some clothes. She rinsed her mouth and brushed her teeth, then went out of the cabin to get some fresh air.

As she walked along the deck, she started to feel better and began to keep an eye out for her husband. She finally found him, deep in conversation with an Englishman, who he introduced as Mr. Armitage, a civil servant from London. The gentleman bowed politely and immediately began speaking to her in precise, but accented French.

"Your husband tells me that he was in the British army, *madame*," he said. "And that he was in charge of the supplies at the base on your island."

"That's correct, sir," she replied. "And I believe he was very efficient at it."

"Yes," Mr. Armitage answered. "I've been telling him that he should look me up when you arrive in London. I believe I may be able to find employment for him."

"Oh, that's wonderful!" said Thérèse, turning to Emmett and squeezing his arm. He was looking very pleased.

"The King and country are always anxious to reward those who give service in time of war," explained Mr. Armitage. "My department is on the lookout for intelligent and experienced ex-soldiers who'll be able to help us in the accounting area. I'm sure your husband will do a good job for us."

"Oh, yes," breathed Thérèse. "He will be a very reliable and trustworthy employee for you, I'm sure of that."

"I believe so, in talking to him," said the civil servant. "You make sure you look me up, Captain Richardson."

Emmett smiled as Mr. Armitage passed him his card, then tipped his hat and bade them good morning. He walked away along the deck and Thérèse and Emmett gazed after him, then smiled at one another.

"What a marvellous opportunity that could be!" said Emmett, excitedly. "Are you feeling better, darling?"

"Oh yes, much, thank you," she replied. "I suppose it was just some stronger waves rocking the boat this morning."

Emmett looked puzzled, as though he hadn't noticed anything unusual, but then turned to the subject at hand.

"I'll definitely look up Mr. Armitage when we arrive in London," he told her. "I was wondering what I was going to do for work when we got back. The civil service is an admirable institution, with good pay and a pension. I could do much worse than work for them."

Thérèse smiled happily and squeezed his arm. She was sure that her life with this man was going to be wonderful and that he would look after her very well. She had sensed that the minute they met, and when he started courting her. He already had a house waiting for them when they arrived, and now he would have a job to support them. She promised herself that she would be the best wife and housekeeper she could be, even though she had never really done that sort of work at home on the island. She was certain she would learn how, and that she would enjoy every minute of it. Little did she know that things don't always turn out as planned, but she was an ingenuous young girl with unrealistic dreams. She did have Emmett's love, though, and that would never change.

England

21

The journey continued, with every day bringing Thérèse that much closer to her new life. The only cloud on the horizon was the seasickness that continued to plague her. It would hit her at odd times, sometimes in the morning, sometimes throughout the day, and not always when the ocean was unsettled. One day, it came over her when the sea was as calm as a millpond, and she thought despairingly that she was a terrible sailor, and that it didn't bode well for any future trips she might take back to Mauritius to visit her family. She supposed that some people just weren't cut out to travel by boat, but that she wasn't going to let that stop her from visiting her beloved island in the future. Emmett had already assured her that he would allow her to return as often as she wanted, even if it meant he stayed at home while she travelled alone. She marvelled at how easygoing he was and how he didn't try to order her around, like some husbands she had observed in the past.

After two weeks on the ocean, she was having a better day with her queasiness, and was up on deck getting some fresh air. She gazed out at the horizon, enjoying the warmth of the sun on her back in spite of the ocean wind that ruffled her hair. The ubiquitous gulls flew high up in the air, often encircling the main mast of the ocean-going liner. As she looked out to sea, she thought she saw a small dot on the horizon.

She ran down the deck to Emmett, who was sitting in a deck chair reading an outdated newspaper.

"Emmett!" she cried, excitedly, leaning over him. "I saw something on the horizon. What do you think it is?"

He frowned, then folded up his paper and followed her down the deck to where she had been standing. She pointed in the direction of the dot, which seemed to have got somewhat bigger in the time it had taken her to run to Emmett.

"I think it could be Land's End," he told her.

She shivered with excitement and threw her arms around him.

"Are we getting close to England?" she asked, with mounting anticipation. Could it be possible that this journey would soon be over, and she would finally be able to set foot in her new home?

He smiled at her childish enthusiasm and returned her hug.

"Yes, yes, I think so," he replied. "Land's End is the southern-most tip of England. The Ancient Britons believed that it was where the world ended."

Visions of arriving in London and finally seeing the house where she and Emmett would live together and be happy forever after danced through her head.

"Oh, that's so exciting!" she said. Then, all of a sudden, she was seized with a wave of nausea and moved cautiously out of her husband's arms.

"Sorry, Emmett, I have to go," she murmured, running towards the galley stairs that led to their cabin. The smell of lunch being prepared made her stomach convulse again, and she barely made it through the cabin door and into the toilet.

She would be very glad to have this voyage over with and be done with seasickness.

Two days later, they were pulling into the harbour at Southampton. Thérèse spent as much time as she could on deck, watching the landscape, enthralled by the green and gently rolling land. The white cliffs of the Isle of Wight mesmerized her and reminded her a little of the mountain at home, *Montagne des Signeaux*. She knew this would be a very different land, though, and a climate very unlike where she had grown up, although rain would be something both places had in common. She prayed she would get used to the cold winter rain that Emmett had told her about.

As the huge boat pulled up alongside the quay, she felt butterflies in her stomach, but this time it had nothing to do with the ocean. She was filled with anticipation at being a wife and, maybe some day, a mother, in this new country. She could hardly wait to impress Emmett with her culinary and housekeeping skills. She had learned how to cook quite nicely from Dhala, but really had no idea how to keep house. She supposed that she would learn as she went along, just like any other new wife.

They docked shortly afterwards, and Emmett supervised the unloading of their bags. Thérèse stood on the quay, watching the procedure and trying to attune her ear to the English language being spoken rapidly by the locals and the ship's crew. She had taken her English lessons with Emmett very seriously and hoped she'd soon become fluent in her new language.

The wind was cool as she stood there, and she pulled her jacket closer around her. Grey clouds scudded across the sky, obscuring the rather watery sun, and she shivered. It certainly wasn't warm here, unlike her island. It was autumn, and she had thought it would be a lot more pleasant, though she wouldn't complain. At least she wouldn't have to deal with sweat trickling down the back of her neck from the hot sun here, like she did at home.

Emmett interrupted her reverie, taking her by the arm.

"Come along, darling," he said, with a smile. "The porter will bring our bags to the station, and we'll catch the train to London from there."

A train! She'd never been on a train before and looked forward to the experience. She knew that they travelled fairly fast and that it would be interesting to watch the countryside rushing by. They hurried towards the station, and she was thankful that her nausea had stopped now that they were on dry land.

Emmett steered her towards the station ticket office, the porter following them dutifully with their enormous pile of bags. They purchased their tickets, then went towards the platform where the long train was standing waiting. Emmett led them to the first-class compartments and stood back while the porter opened the door and began loading their bags in.

"First class, Emmett," Thérèse commented, impressed.

"Nothing's too good for my wife," he replied, kissing her cheek as he handed her into the compartment. He thanked and tipped the porter, and they sat down on the comfortable seats in their luxury surroundings.

Thérèse emitted a contented sigh, happy that she was now finally in England. As the train pulled out of the station, she watched the sights of the beautiful port city of Southampton. Once they were out in the countryside, she admired the gentle, rolling hills and small green pastures where sheep and cattle grazed.

Her nausea struck her twice as they travelled towards London, and Thérèse supposed it was due to the motion of the train. She suspected she must be one of those people who just couldn't travel without feeling sick, but it wasn't going to stop her determination to see as much of her new country and the continent as she could. Her mother had told her that she should try to get to France, as her family had many relatives there who would be eager to meet their new cousin from the tropics.

She dozed off at one point, lulled by the gentle rocking motion of the train, and woke up to the screeching of the brakes. They were surrounded by tall, grey buildings and rows of tidy, well-kept houses that all looked the same. Every so often, she would glimpse a narrow street with bright, colourful shops on either side. She watched people scurrying about their business and saw horses and buggies travelling along the streets, as well as the occasional open-air vehicle without a horse, which she had learned was called an "automobile." She had seen pictures of them, but never encountered one on her part of the island.

"We're pulling into London," Emmett said. "It won't be long now."

She leaned forward excitedly and continued to watch the city fly by through the train window. Her sense of adventure was really heightened now, and she knew she would never tire of new experiences and new places. Her life was going to be very interesting from now on, she thought.

They arrived at the busy Victoria Station in London not long after that. Thérèse could hardly contain her anticipation as they descended from the train and found a porter to take their bags for them. The station had a high glass roof, and she could see the grey sky and clouds through it. People went to and fro, jostling each other in their hurry to go about their business. Porters blew whistles, and Thérèse was conscious of the stream of English being spoken around her, most of it incomprehensible to her. She couldn't help but notice the dirt on the station platform, however, and the thick black smoke pouring out of the various trains' engines. She stuck close to Emmett as they made their way out of the station in search of a cab.

"Would you like to take one of the new automobile cabs, darling?" he asked her.

"Oh, yes!" she breathed excitedly, although she quietly hoped that it wouldn't trigger her sickness again. They walked out onto the concourse outside the station where horse-drawn carriages were waiting for passengers to ferry around the city. Emmett spoke to a gentleman in a navy blue uniform and cap and, shortly thereafter, an automobile pulled up beside them.

It was a comfortable Ford with a black interior. Thérèse sank back onto the leather-upholstered seat and gazed contentedly out the window, smiling at Emmett. However, when the cab suddenly lurched forward, she grabbed Emmett's arm and held on for dear life until the driver had shifted gear several times and the motor car finally settled down to a smooth pace. Relinquishing Emmett's arm, she relaxed somewhat into the comfortable seat. She looked out of the window at the scenery as they drove through the city streets, dodging other cars, horse-drawn vehicles and pedestrians. There didn't seem to be any rhyme or reason as to when people could cross the streets, and very often the cab-driver would curse and brake suddenly as someone stepped out in front of him.

Thérèse saw shops, markets, row houses and tall, elegant churches as they made their way to Emmett's house in North London. Many areas were crowded and dirty, but then they would drive by beautiful monuments and houses, and Thérèse would once again be impressed with the city's grandeur. After a forty-five-minute ride, they pulled into a quiet, elegant-looking neighbourhood with more row houses and tidy gardens and gates at the front. Flowers flourished in the gardens, and the houses all looked immaculate.

The cab finally stopped in front of Number 38, a tall, thin but freshly painted house with a twin on the other side. A wooden fence divided the two gardens, and a newly cut lawn adorned the front yard. Rose bushes bloomed behind the low stone wall in the front of the house and Thérèse smiled to herself at the thought of having fresh-cut flowers to display in the house. The cab-driver opened the door for her and helped her to step off the running-board, then went around the vehicle to take the suitcases out of the boot.

"Well, my angel, what do you think?" asked Emmett, putting his arm around her waist as they walked up the stone pathway to the house.

"Lovely," she replied, thinking nonetheless how small and unimposing this house looked, compared to the Big House on her parents' estate. However, she knew that Emmett wasn't a wealthy man, and the fact that he owned a house at all was something to be respected in post-war England.

Emmett unlocked the door and motioned her into the dark hallway. A set of stairs led to the second floor on the left and a long corridor ran the length of the house, with two doors on the right and one at the very end. The doors on the side opened onto the living room and dining room and the one at the end to the kitchen, with an adjoining scullery.

He took her coat and hung it up in the big wardrobe in the hallway, before they made their way down to the kitchen. He opened the door and ushered her in.

"Would you like a cup of tea?" he asked.

"Oh yes, please," she replied. "Or coffee, if you have it."

Emmett frowned.

"The English drink tea," he replied. "Better get used to it, darling, we drink lots of it. I'll teach you how to make it tomorrow morning."

She smiled, remembering that she was now a housewife and would have to learn how to do many new things that she'd never done in Mauritius.

They sat and drank their tea cosily together in the kitchen, then began the onerous task of dragging their luggage up the stairs and unpacking. Thérèse was pleased with the large, spacious bedroom and bathroom on the second floor of the house, and the smaller rooms in the attic, which she secretly hoped would one day house small children.

When they went to bed that night, the bedroom was cold but they hugged each other tightly before saying goodnight. She murmured a prayer before falling asleep, asking God to bless her marriage and her new life in England and to teach her how to be patient with everything she had to learn. She hoped above all to make her husband happy and to be a good wife, as her mother had taught her.

22

The next morning, after rising, washing her face and descending to the main-floor kitchen, Thérèse prepared a simple breakfast of coffee and rolls for the two of them. It was too cold to go outside and dip her face in the morning dew as she had always done at home, but she vowed to herself to continue the practice once the warmer weather came around.

Emmett soon joined her at the kitchen table and requested tea instead of coffee. She reminded him that he would have to show her how to make it, and he obliged her. Not long afterwards, he went to the front door of the house to pick up the early morning post and returned with two letters.

He opened the first one, then set it aside and opened the second. It was a lengthy handwritten missive, and he started to frown in a concerned way as he turned the pages. He finally laid it down on the breakfast table, then took a deep breath and turned to Thérèse.

"Sweetheart," he said. "That letter was from my Aunt Agatha's neighbour. She said that my aunt is becoming increasingly feeble and needs to be taken care of. She's asking me to bring her here to live with us."

Thérèse gaped at him.

"But we just got married!" she exclaimed. "We haven't had much time together, and now you want to bring your aunt to live with us?"

"I have a duty to her, Thérèse," he replied, calmly. "She and my uncle raised me. I wouldn't be here today if they hadn't."

Upon reflection, Thérèse recognized her husband's commitment to his aunt, and asked herself how she would react if her mother suddenly needed to come and stay with her and her new husband. She knew she wouldn't hesitate, but she had hoped that Emmett would take care of his aunt from afar, not have her come to live with them so soon. She looked him squarely in the face.

"Alright, darling," she said. "Write back and tell them that your aunt can come and stay here." She suddenly thought of a practicality. "But where will she sleep?"

"In one of the attic bedrooms," he replied. "It will need to be aired out, and clean linens put on the bed."

Thérèse felt a quiver of anticipation. She'd never done any household chores except for cooking, and this would be her chance to show her young husband what she could do. However, all of a sudden, her anticipation was replaced by a queasy feeling in her stomach, and she put her hand over her mouth.

"That's fine," she managed to choke out, before running from the room and into the toilet, where she promptly threw up. She returned after wiping her mouth and taking a long, cool drink of water from the tap in the bathroom.

"Are you feeling alright, darling?" asked Emmett, looking at her with concern.

"Yes," she affirmed, sitting back at the table with him. "My breakfast just didn't sit very well with me. I think maybe what I thought was seasickness on the boat was actually a tummy bug of some sort."

"You must see a doctor," he replied.

"Let's give it a few days to settle," she said. "I don't want to run to a doctor for everything little thing."

"Very well, but don't leave it too long if you're not feeling better."

The next few days became a whirl of preparation for Emmett's Aunt Agatha to come and stay with them, and Thérèse felt proud of how efficiently she was able to manage things. The attic bedroom shone, and freshly washed linens had been placed on the bed. She made a mental note to sit down and write a letter to her family to tell them how well things were going, once everything was done in preparation for Aunt Agatha. Meanwhile, Emmett had written to his aunt's neighbour to tell her that he would indeed step up to the job of looking after his elderly relative and make arrangements to go up to Yorkshire and bring her back.

Two days later, he renewed his pledge to write to Mr. Armitage from the Civil Service about employment. Mr. Armitage replied by return post, advising Emmett that he would be delighted to conduct an interview with him at his earliest convenience. Emmett obliged him by going to

London the very next day to see him, returning with an offer of employment to start the following week as a junior clerk in the accounting department.

When the day dawned for him to take the trip north and bring home Aunt Agatha, Thérèse stood with him at the front door of the house as he prepared to leave. She had had another bout of nausea that morning, and Emmett had told her to go around to the doctor's surgery and see him. She had agreed, although she had hoped that the feeling would gradually pass as the day wore on and she wouldn't have to go. She had tried brewing peppermint leaves in hot water, as her mother had taught her to do back home, but it hadn't really helped.

She saw her husband into his taxi with a kiss and a hug. He told her it would take a couple of days to pack up his aunt's house, and to expect them to arrive any day. He also promised that, when he returned and had to take up his new job at the Civil Service, he would install one of those new-fangled communication machines in their home. These "telephones" were becoming very popular among the rich, and now the middle classes too, as a way of speaking to one's friends and relatives and of relaying news. Thérèse had seen them at the military base, but her parents hadn't felt the need to own one, as everything on the island could be communicated by letter and delivered the same day by wagon. Still, if they were to install one in their home as well, she could then speak to her family personally, instead of writing. The knowledge of that made her feel very comfortable, and being able to speak to her mother about everything would be very reassuring.

After Emmett had left, she put on her hat and coat and walked to the doctor's surgery. Her husband had given her directions as to how to find it, and she had dutifully written them down. The weather was cold and damp outside, and she hugged her coat closely to her. She hoped that she could make herself understood with her halting English. Oh, well, she would soon have to speak English with Emmett's aunt, so she'd better get practising!

She rang the bell of the surgery and was greeted by a young woman in a nurse's uniform who ushered her in to a waiting room equipped with wooden chairs and about a dozen people sitting patiently waiting.

"Please . . . visit *le docteur*?" Thérèse asked hesitatingly.

The nurse replied in a volley of English, none of which Thérèse understood, and she politely asked her to repeat herself, using phrases she had learned from her book. The young woman frowned, then indicated that she should take a seat in the waiting room and mumbled something about "an hour."

Thérèse sat quietly looking around the room at the other patients until the nurse gestured for her to get up and follow her. She was shown into a small office containing many shelves of leather-bound books and some rather terrifying-looking jars of what looked like animal mummies and parts. The desk was littered with papers and books and didn't exactly inspire Thérèse with confidence.

The tall, bespectacled doctor entered from another door, smiled briefly at Thérèse, then sat down at the desk and started writing. After he laid down his pen, he turned to her and inquired,

"How may I help you, madam?"

"I . . . er. . . not myself feel good . . . *estomac . . . .nausée . . . ,"* she began in a hesitant tone.

"Vous parlez français, madame?" The doctor asked, in slow but careful French.

"Yes," she replied, relieved to be able to speak in her native tongue. Thank goodness young Englishmen and women learned French in their schools!

"I don't feel well, often nauseous and vomiting," she explained.

The doctor looked at her left hand and glanced down at the notes he had brought in with him. He indicated the examination table in the room, and Thérèse climbed nervously on it. The doctor palpated her stomach gently with both hands but, appearing to find nothing, looked up at her with a questioning frown.

"You are married, madam?" he questioned her.

She told him that she was, but only for about a few weeks. He then asked her if she might be *"enceinte."*

Pregnant! She stared at him for a moment, taken aback. She hadn't even thought of that. So soon? She supposed it could happen and, come to think of it, she couldn't remember when her last monthly visitor had come and realized it was some time before the wedding. She was suddenly filled with excitement. What wonderful news to share with Emmett!

""How will I know?"" she asked the doctor.

"You'll notice several changes in your body," he replied matter-of-factly, "and you will not see your monthly courses anymore. You will also gain weight around the middle."

The doctor seemed surprised to have to explain these facts to his patient, but he put it down to her extreme youth. He thought she barely looked old enough to have finished school. He instructed her to return to his office in a month and, if his diagnosis proved to be correct, he would then put her in touch with a local midwife who would assist with the birth and be available to help her with the new arrival. If, however, her monthly event returned, she need not bother to come back to his office.

She thanked the doctor and did up her coat, leaving the office in a flurry of anticipation. She could hardly wait for Emmett's return to tell her young husband about this new turn of events. The small cloud of Aunt Agatha's arrival lingered on the horizon, but she was sure the old lady would be delighted and would want to assist in the child care.

Little did she know how naïve her expectations were.

23

Four days later, Thérèse was washing up the breakfast dishes when she heard a commotion at the front door.

"Emmett?" she called out. His return was the only event she had been anticipating, unless the meat she had ordered from the butcher the day before was being delivered.

She wiped her hands on the towel beside the sink and walked eagerly down the hall that led to the front door. A key was being inserted into the lock, and she could see the shadowy outline of two figures standing on the step through the frosted panes in the door.

She quickly turned the handle on the door and opened it, to be greeted by the sight of her husband and an elderly lady dressed entirely in black, apart from a white feather in her bonnet. Emmett smiled eagerly at her, then surrounded her with a quick hug, before taking his aunt's arm and propelling her through the doorway.

"Thérèse," he said in French, still smiling. "This is my Aunt Agatha." He turned to his aunt and then pronounced carefully in English, "Aunt Agatha, this is my lovely bride, Thérèse."

Thérèse smiled uncertainly at the old lady, holding out a hand to shake and suddenly dropping a little curtsey. Why did I do that? She thought, puzzled. She's not the queen!

The elderly matron looked Thérèse up and down in a silent and disapproving way. She scowled and then looked at Emmett, muttering something of which Thérèse could only catch the words, "too thin" and "so young."

Emmett's pleasure at introducing his new wife to the aunt who had been a mother to him for so many years quickly dissipated, and he looked rather distressed. He again took his aunt by the arm and started hurrying her towards the stairs to the top of the house, saying over his shoulder to Thérèse,

"Would you make some tea, darling? There should be some chocolate biscuits in the kitchen cupboard."

Thérèse felt her heart jump, and her hands were trembling slightly as she went back to the kitchen. Her first impression was that Aunt Agatha seemed to be a grim old lady, and she sincerely hoped that this would not be the start of a strained relationship. She hadn't bargained on having the elderly woman coming to live with them so soon in a country that was still strange to her, especially when she barely spoke the language and wouldn't be able to communicate with her very well. She identified the feeling in the pit of her stomach as foreboding, and not the nausea she was feeling each day. It was similar to the feelings she'd had at home when she had anticipated something bad about to happen.

She brewed the tea and put a plate of biscuits from the box in the cupboard onto a tray, with three cups and saucers. Teaspoons, milk, and sugar with tongs completed the picture, and she carried the tray into the living room, where her husband's aunt was now ensconced in the wing chair by the window. The old lady threw a sour glance at Thérèse, then turned to Emmett and addressed him in English.

Thérèse felt like she was a servant back home as she served the tea and biscuits to her husband and his elderly relative. The only time the aunt made an effort to address her was to remind her that she hadn't brought any napkins. She looked Thérèse squarely in the face as she issued her reminder, then turned back to her nephew and continued to address him, carrying on a conversation of which Thérèse understood only a small amount. The aunt seemed to have an odd accent when she spoke English, an accent Thérèse couldn't really follow and had never heard her husband use. She later learned that it was the accent of the north of England.

Thérèse looked through the sideboard until she found some white linen napkins and gave one each to Aunt Agatha and Emmett. However, she didn't put one out for herself and eventually picked up her cup of tea and left the room, taking it into the kitchen so that she could start preparing the hot luncheon that was expected at noon here in England. She felt very intimidated by her husband's old aunt, who had basically ignored her since their introduction and her first disapproving comments to Emmett. How was she going to help take care of an elderly lady who wouldn't even look at her, let alone make an effort to get to know her? What were she and Aunt Agatha going to say to each other once Emmett took up his job at the Civil Service? Perhaps the old lady would try harder to speak to her slowly in English?

She was making a lamb stew for lunch, in the way that Dhala had shown her, adding some curry powder to the seasonings to give it a little more flavour. She had made the same dish for Emmett when he had come to visit her during their engagement back in Mauritius, and she wanted to show off her newly learned culinary skills. He had praised the flavour and tenderness of the meat, as well as the rich and spicy aroma of the gravy.

Two hours later, she went into the living room, where Emmett was reading a book while his aunt unpacked the trunk that he had carried up to the attic bedroom for her.

"Lunch is ready," Thérèse announced brightly.

"Are you serving it in here?" Emmett asked her.

"No, in the kitchen, as we've been doing since we arrived here," she replied.

Emmett jumped up.

"Oh, no!" He exclaimed. "Aunt Agatha is used to lunch being served in the dining room. We should set up the table in here. She'll never accept eating in the kitchen. She's not a servant."

"I know," said Thérèse, feeling as though she was under attack. "But we've been eating in the kitchen every day. What's wrong with that? We only ate in the dining room at our house in Mauritius because the servants brought the food out to us."

"Well, you're bringing it out to Aunt Agatha," Emmett answered, looking at her awkwardly.

"But I'm not a servant," she said hotly.

"I know you're not, *chérie*, but please don't make things difficult on my aunt's first day here," he beseeched. "We can always make a change in the arrangements in a few days' time, when she's used to being here."

Thérèse stared at him for a minute, then turned and began to pull the big oak table away from the window in order to set it up in the middle of the living room. She took a large white tablecloth out of the sideboard and began to spread it over the table, as Emmett tried to help her. She waved him away and set the table quickly, as she had learned to do at home for a formal dinner, then returned to the kitchen while Emmett went upstairs to tell his aunt that luncheon was served.

The old lady descended the stairs and walked into the living room, grunting slightly as she entered the room and spied the table set for the meal. She threw another sour glance Thérèse's way, then seated herself at the head of the table, which Thérèse had set for Emmett.

Thérèse brought in the savoury-smelling stew, as well as some rice and vegetables to eat with it. She then left the room and returned with a loaf of freshly baked bread and some butter.

Emmett said grace, while Thérèse and the old lady bowed their heads at the table. When Thérèse made the sign of the cross, as she always did after a benediction, Aunt Agatha frowned at her again, then took a mouthful of the hot food. She suddenly threw her fork down on her plate, exclaiming loudly.

Emmett looked aghast at his wife.

"Aunt Agatha says that the stew is spicy!" he pronounced, looking very uncomfortable.

"Of course," replied Thérèse. "Lamb is a very bland meat. It needs something to give it flavour."

"But my aunt's from the north of England, Thérèse," Emmett countered. "They don't like spicy food there, especially not at lunch."

Thérèse felt the colour rising to her cheeks, then spreading down to her neck.

"Well, you never told me that," she admonished her husband.

"I'm sorry, darling," he answered. "I didn't expect you to make a curried dish. My aunt likes only English cooking. It's what she's eaten all her life."

Thérèse looked aghast at him.

"Don't worry," he hastened to reassure her. "Aunt Agatha will teach you how to cook the English way."

Thérèse glowered at him but carried on eating her lunch. Aunt Agatha joined in the conversation, but Thérèse only caught a few words that she could understand. "I'm not eating that!" were the only words she could make out clearly. After her pronouncement, the meal continued in stony silence as the old lady picked out the vegetables and ate several pieces of bread and butter. Thérèse felt cowed by the rudeness of the elderly woman, but knew that she had to show her respect, just as she had back at home to her father, who could be unpleasant.

When the meal was over, and the dessert of fresh fruit had been eaten without any rude comments, Thérèse hastily cleared away the dishes. Aunt Agatha announced her intentions of taking a nap and promptly went up the stairs to her room.

Thérèse washed the dishes in the kitchen and put away the remaining food in the pantry, then returned to the living room, where Emmett was reading the newspaper. He glanced nervously at his wife as she sat down in the armchair opposite him.

"Well," she said, addressing him glumly. "That didn't go very well. I think your aunt hates me."

"Give her time, *ma chérie*," he answered soothingly. "She has to get used to living in a new city and sharing her favourite nephew with another woman whom he loves."

"Well, I'm living in a new *country* and I'm your *wife*," she reminded him indignantly.

"I know, I know," he said. "But you're much younger and more flexible. She's in her dotage and is used to having things her way."

"I heard her say that I'm too thin and too young," she reminded him with annoyance.

"Don't pay any attention to that. It's just her manner."

"Well, why has she come to live with us, then, if she wants everything her way?" she replied hotly.

Emmett came over to her, lifted her out of the chair and enfolded her in his arms.

"She's an old lady, darling," he said gently. "She's losing her memory and can't do things for herself anymore. She needs our help. I promised my uncle before he died that I'd look after her once the war was over."

Thérèse felt tears pricking her eyes. A wave of homesickness suddenly hit her, and she leaned her head on Emmett's shoulder. Her new life wasn't turning out at all the way that she had thought it would. She had never counted on looking after a hostile elderly lady so soon after moving to her new home. She decided to keep her possible happy news to herself for now, until she was sure of what the doctor had told her the other morning. There was no point in sharing the news with Emmett, in case it turned out to be wrong and she'd have to share her disappointment with him. For now, she had to concentrate on getting through each day under the unpleasant circumstances she had suddenly been handed. She felt a huge wave of nostalgia for her mother and her beautiful island and decided that she would write to her mother as soon as possible.

24

January 1919

A month had gone by, and Thérèse was slowly getting used to the turn her new life had taken. She and the elderly aunt mostly ignored one another, and she tried to stay out of the older woman's way. When the three of them shared meals together, she ate quietly at her place at the table, then cleared away the dishes and escaped into the kitchen to wash them and spend some time by herself. On the days that Emmett was at work, she served Aunt Agatha, then did her best to avoid her eyes during their silent meal.

Her relationship with Emmett was somewhat strained by the arrival of his aunt and his loyalty to her. She wished her husband would try harder to convince his elderly relative to be kinder to her niece by marriage. Thérèse was able to understand most of their conversations, but she didn't attempt to join in for fear of a disapproving look from the elderly matron. However, when she was alone with her husband, she tried not to bring up the subject of his aunt, and their relationship resumed its loving and passionate nature. At those times, she felt that she loved him more than ever.

She had written to her mother about her difficulties and had received a sympathetic letter in response. Her mother had also had to deal with elderly relatives when she was a young girl living at home with her family and had done her best to show respect and patience with the old people. Madeleine counselled the same to her daughter. Thérèse had imparted her other news to her, and her mother had been delighted at the possibility of a grandchild. *Maman* had always loved children and was thrilled by any new arrival, whether her own, or that of one of the servants on the estate.

Time had gone by and still Thérèse saw no sign of her monthly visitor. The nausea continued every day, but it wasn't quite as severe as it had been. She decided it was time for a second visit to the local doctor.

It was a grey day as she walked to the surgery again, but occasionally the sun peeked through the clouds, warming the air for a few minutes. She walked briskly along the tree-lined road, smiling secretly to herself at the thought of what the doctor might tell her when she saw him.

Upon her arrival at the surgery, the nurse indicated once again that she should sit in one of the chairs with the other patients. Thérèse looked around and carefully avoided sitting beside the middle-aged woman and small boy who were both coughing without covering their mouths. There was talk of a new influenza bug going around, called the Spanish Flu, that was said to be striking hundreds of people and killing many. It was also said that the soldiers in Europe had brought it back with them from the front, and that it was highly infectious. Thérèse made a silent vow to herself not to go out and about much if it turned out that she was pregnant, and to tell her husband to come straight home after work and not linger at the office.

When the nurse called her name, she jumped up quickly and followed her into the doctor's consulting room. He was already seated at his desk this time, and he smiled warmly at her.

"*Madame* Richardson?" he asked her politely in French.

"My English is getting better," she replied, hesitantly. "You can speak to me in English."

"Well, let's try a little bit of both," he suggested kindly.

Thérèse explained to him that her courses hadn't appeared and that she still felt sick on most days. He asked her if she would be comfortable being examined, and she indicated her acceptance.

After the doctor had finished his examination, he smiled at her in an avuncular way.

"You are definitely pregnant, *madame,*" he announced. "I think you can expect to give birth this summer."

Thérèse's heart leaped. How wonderful! She could hardly wait to tell Emmett the good news. She shook hands with the doctor, and he gave her a card with the name of a midwife whom she was to see as soon as possible.

She scarcely remembered leaving the doctor's surgery and walking back home. Lunch with Aunt Agatha was the usual uncomfortable experience, but her news kept her spirits buoyed and she wouldn't let herself feel intimidated by the old lady.

She decided to take a nap when Aunt Agatha went for hers, partly because the walk to the doctor's surgery had tired her out and partly because she wanted to make the time go faster until she was able to be alone with Emmett and share her secret.

It wasn't until they retired to bed that she was able to talk to him alone. Aunt Agatha conversed with Emmett all through dinner, then decided that they should play cards afterwards.

Thérèse quietly excused herself and went to the kitchen. She enjoyed playing cards, but not with a stern old lady who wouldn't even look at her most of the time. What if Thérèse beat her at her favourite game? She didn't think she could deal with the unpleasantness that might follow.

Thérèse decided to write to her family at home to let them know the wonderful new development in her life. They would be surprised at how quickly this had happened. She thought she had probably conceived on her wedding night, or shortly afterwards. The thought of having an infant of her own to cradle and love filled her with warmth, and she could hardly wait to tell Emmett.

When they finally went to bed, she turned and put her arms around him.

"Emmett*, mon amour,*" she whispered into his ear. "I have news for you."

"What is it?" he murmured, already sounding as though he was falling asleep.

"I'm going to have a baby," she replied.

Emmett was shaken out of his near-sleep and sat up quickly, a look of concern on his face.

"What?" he asked, gaping at her. She couldn't tell if it was in horror or surprise.

"You're going to be a father," she answered.

"Already?" he demanded, a worried look on his face.

"Yes, isn't it wonderful?" she said, with a happy smile.

He immediately started to soften, taking her by the shoulders and kissing her cheek.

"Of course it is," he replied, hesitantly. "Just rather soon. I mean, I thought we'd be married a little longer before this happened."

She became annoyed and turned away from him.

"What did you expect?" she demanded. "My mother has twelve children!"

He hastened to take her in his arms again and kissed the top of her head.

"Yes, yes, I know," he assured her. "And I am happy, I just wasn't expecting this so early."

Then he thought better of his lack of enthusiasm and added, "We'll make the best of it, and I'm sure Aunt Agatha will be thrilled to have an infant in the family. She'll help you take care of him or her."

Thérèse turned her face away from Emmett. She wasn't sure Aunt Agatha would be pleased, and she certainly didn't want her help. She also wondered what Emmett meant by "making the best of it"? Wasn't he happy to be bringing an heir into the world, someone to follow in his footsteps and take care of him in his old age?

Her intuition had been telling her since her visit to the doctor that she was going have a son. In that moment, she knew she was carrying a boy and that Emmett would be extremely proud when she gave birth. Time would tell as to whether her feeling was right, but she suspected that it would be, just like the ones she had experienced in Mauritius.

She turned back to her husband, kissed him on the cheek, then rolled away from him. He put his arms around her from behind and she soon fell asleep, cradled in his arms.

25

Emmett told Aunt Agatha the news the next morning at breakfast. For the first time since their meeting, she actually looked Thérèse squarely in the face. Although she didn't smile, there was a softening of her usual grim expression.

"Well, that's a good thing. I'm glad you're doing your duty, Thérèse," was all she could offer.

Aunt Agatha had had no children of her own and had only taken in her brother's child when he and his wife were unable to take care of him. Emmett was very fond of her, so Thérèse supposed that she had been a good mother-figure to him, but she wondered how much warmth the old lady would have shown to a young child.

"I'll begin knitting a layette immediately," she told the young couple. "The new arrival will need clothes."

Thérèse was quite surprised by the elderly lady's response.

"Thank you, aunt," she said softly.

The old lady nodded, and Thérèse felt that perhaps this would be the start of a more comfortable relationship between her and the other woman in the house.

"Oh, that's wonderful, Aunt Agatha," exclaimed Emmett. "I'm sure Thérèse will be most appreciative."

Thérèse nodded her agreement and thought that she caught a glimmer of a smile on Aunt Agatha's face. She started to think that maybe things weren't going to be so bad here after all.

After breakfast, she decided she would go and visit the midwife whose name had been given to her by the doctor. She put on a warm wool coat and tied a scarf around her head. The damp English winter weather went through her bones, and she always found herself chilled when she went outside for any length of time. On many occasions, she missed the warmth and sunshine of Mauritius, but she reminded herself of how happy she was here with Emmett, and soon a new baby, and she wouldn't trade that for anything, even to get rid of the cold damp of England and a frosty old aunt. She walked down the street, looking forward to her first encounter with the midwife.

Her walk took about twenty minutes, and she finally reached a small but cozy-looking bungalow set amid ageing trees at the end of a long avenue. There was nobody in sight, but a plaque beside the front door read, "Maureen Dalrymple, Midwife and Private Nurse." She walked up to the door and rang the bell. After a few moments, she heard the sound of a lock being drawn back and then the door opened to reveal a portly, middle-aged woman with a warm smile.

"Yes?" the midwife enquired.

"Excuse me, *madame,* but I have been given your name by le *Docteur* Briggs," Thérèse announced.

"Yes?" the lady repeated.

"I will have a baby," Thérèse stammered.

The lady's smile broadened even more and she immediately gestured Thérèse to step into the house and follow her. They sat down in a small but comfortable living room containing a large sofa and matching wing-chair. The midwife indicated the sofa to Thérèse, who sat down politely on the edge.

"When is this baby due?" Mrs. Dalrymple asked Thérèse, with a kindly smile.

"In the autumn," she replied.

"Well, well, that's wonderful! And you are young, so that should make for an easy time. Is this your first?"

Thérèse nodded assent, then proceeded to explain to Mrs. Dalrymple in her halting English that she had arrived in England only a little while ago and had no family here but her husband and an elderly aunt, so didn't know very much about childbirth. The extent that she knew she had learned from her mother and by observing the servants on the estate.

Mrs. Dalrymple assured her that it was a perfectly natural process and that she would be available to assist at every stage. She outlined a set of monthly appointments that would then become weekly as the pregnancy advanced, and asked permission to examine Thérèse. It was given immediately. Then she ushered her into a small room at the back of the house and gave her privacy to get ready for the examination. Afterwards, she asked for Thérèse's address so that she could come and see her at her house for the next visit.

The two women shook hands as Thérèse prepared to take her leave, now feeling much more comfortable and less anxious about the thought of putting herself in this woman's hands in the months to come. She knew that her mother became quite tired and emotional during the second half of her pregnancies, but Mrs. Dalrymple had explained that this was quite normal and expected to happen in any healthy pregnancy. Thérèse felt herself quite buoyant with happiness during the return walk home and let herself in through the front door of the house. She told herself that she should be getting a letter from home very soon and, sure enough, there was one sitting on the table in the hallway as she walked in. How perfect! She had just been thinking of writing a letter to her family, and now she would have plenty to tell them.

Aunt Agatha was sitting in the living room and gave Thérèse a slight nod of the head as she greeted her.

"There's a letter for you on the table, niece," she informed her.

"Yes, I know. It's from my family in Mauritius," she replied.

Aunt Agatha cleared her throat.

"Well, what are you waiting for? Go and put your feet up and read it," she told Thérèse.

Thérèse smiled to herself. Although gruff, the elderly aunt's disposition seemed to be warming somewhat and she felt some hope that perhaps they would eventually become allies, if not friends.

Emmett arrived home that evening with a large box in his hands.

"Whatever is that, Emmett?" she asked, as he bent to kiss her cheek.

"One of those gadgets I've been telling you about, a telephone," he replied, a boyish grin on his face.

He immediately started to open the box and soon revealed a long, thin tube with a sort of clock on the front which had letters and numbers on it, and then a round disc on top with an attachment in the middle of it. It was linked to another cylindrical tube, which he held up to his ear. It was nothing like the one that Thérèse had seen at the army base, which was basically a large wooden box with a speaking tube coming out of it, and Thérèse stared at it with confusion.

"You see, you listen in here," he explained, "And then you talk into this part." He indicated the disc on the top of the tube.

"Everyone who has one has a special number," he went on, "and, if someone wants to talk to them, they have to telephone the operator by means of the dial on the bottom, here." He started rotating the numbers on the dial as Thérèse watched with amazement. "She'll then connect them to that person." Emmett continued his explanation.

"A gentleman is coming over tomorrow morning to install it for us," he said. "You'll be able to telephone me at work if you or Aunt Agatha needs something. And," he went on, with a twinkle in his eye, "you'll be able to telephone your family in Mauritius, if they have one of these gadgets too. But don't do it too often, it's very expensive."

Thérèse threw her arms around her husband.

"Oh, Emmett, you're so good to me," she murmured against his ear.

"Nothing's too good for my wife," he replied. Then he put his arm around her waist and gave it a little squeeze. "And our coming little one."

She smiled and started to kiss him on the mouth but, looking over his shoulder, she caught Aunt Agatha standing in the doorway of the living room, staring at them disapprovingly. Thérèse stepped back.

"Look what Emmett has brought us, aunt," she exclaimed. "We can telephone him at work if we need to."

Aunt Agatha gave the telephone a passing glance, mumbled something about "new-fangled gadgets" and went up the stairs to her room.

Emmett and Thérèse looked at each other and giggled.

"I don't think Aunt Agatha will be using it any time soon," he said quietly, in French.

26

August 1919

The months flew by quickly, and summer was here. The gloomy damp of the English winter slowly metamorphosed into spring, with warmer temperatures and new buds on the trees, and then the birds began to sing again. Once summer appeared, Thérèse felt better in general than she had been feeling all year. The constant grey clouds and dark, oppressive winter weather had weighed on her, and she was happy to feel the sun on her back when she walked down to the greengrocer's, or to visit Mrs. Dalrymple. For the rest of her life, she would feel hemmed in by the English winter and could never quite put her finger on why this was. It was only later that the syndrome was given a name, but this was completely unknown in the post-war years of the early twentieth century.

Emmett did his best to cheer her up. Her figure had bloomed nicely with her pregnancy, and she had a rosy glow on her cheeks. One day, he called her his "English rose," but she hastened to remind him that she had grown up in the tropics.

"My tropical rose, then," he replied, chucking her under the chin.

She had smiled at him.

"I'm not feeling very rosy," she said.

"Are you feeling sick again?" he enquired, looking alarmed.

"No, no, that's gone away. I just feel . . . sad," she answered.

He put his arms around her.

"Is Aunt Agatha getting on your nerves?" he asked solicitously.

"No, she's alright. She seems to be making a bit of an effort to make me feel comfortable, what with the baby coming."

"She hasn't really been around babies much," he said. "I was already three years old when she adopted me. Of course, there was her younger sister, Aunt Theodora, but they were quite close in age, so she probably doesn't remember her as a baby."

"Well, I hope she's prepared for the crying at night and the endless nappy changes!" warned Thérèse.

"I'm sure you'll cope marvellously with all of that, darling," he said. "What with your mother having twelve children."

"Number thirteen's coming this winter," Thérèse reminded him. "Fancy my mother having a baby that will be younger than my child. It's strange to think that I'll have a brother or sister who's younger than my own son."

Her mother had written to her with the news in the spring, when Thérèse was already three months pregnant herself. It wasn't unusual for large colonial families to continue adding to their numbers after their own children had married and produced their own offspring, but the thought of her mother and herself being pregnant at the same time seemed rather odd to Thérèse. However, she knew that she herself was a young bride at twenty, and that her mother was still in her child-bearing years. Besides, Madeleine was a great comfort to her daughter, reassuring her when she became alarmed at the first kicks from the baby, and then by the painless contractions that she had been experiencing lately. Thérèse had been happy to telephone her mother with her questions, at Emmett's urging, although he warned her again of the high cost of talking too long on a telephone call. Still, speaking to her mother rather than awaiting a reply to a slow-to-arrive letter was very comforting. Thérèse was grateful that her husband had seen fit to invest in a gadget that would bring such solace to his bride.

"You're still sure that we're having a son?" Emmett asked her, smiling.

"Oh, yes," Thérèse answered him. "My intuition is telling me the baby will be a boy, and I'm starting to trust it. I always seem to know when I'm getting a letter from home, and I haven't been wrong yet."

Emmett looked at her admiringly.

"Yes, that's true," he replied. "My wife is also a little bit of a witch, I think."

"Not a witch, just a person who knows things," she remonstrated. She suddenly turned sombre. "I told you that I knew what was going to happen with my brothers before it happened."

"Yes, I know."

"Well, don't you think that's rather telling?"

He ducked his head and didn't look at her, then said sheepishly, "I suppose it is."

Annoyed, she told him, "Just wait until the baby's born. You'll see."

He smiled fondly at her, then kissed her cheek.

Only a few days later, Thérèse was preparing luncheon in the kitchen, a tasty pork dish that she had learned from the recipe book Aunt Agatha had given her. The elderly lady had insisted that Thérèse had to learn to cook the English way, but had declined to teach her herself, preferring to give her a cookery book. Thérèse had dutifully taken the book from her, feeling rather resentful that the old lady didn't like her Mauritian cooking. However, once she had glanced through it and found some recipes that seemed quite interesting, she had discovered that she could make a meal that tasted good and was also easy to prepare.

The first day that she served up a lunch from the recipe book, she had waited with bated breath while Aunt Agatha took her first mouthful. The sour look on the old lady's face didn't change, but she did nod her approval and proceeded to eat the meal with gusto. Thérèse was relieved, and decided to cook her way through the book, trying out all of the recipes. She was mostly successful, and the only thing that baffled her was pastry for the steak and kidney pie. However, after several attempts to get it right, the dough finally behaved itself beneath her hands and she was quite pleased with the results.

She stood in the kitchen peeling potatoes to go with the pork. As she leaned over the sink, she suddenly felt a sharp pain in her abdomen. She let out a little yelp, then straightened up and continued to peel potatoes. However, a few minutes later, the pain came again and she winced, then waited for it to subside. This continued all throughout the preparation of the meal and, finally, when it was ready to be served, she went and found Aunt Agatha in the dining room. As she opened the door to announce that luncheon was ready, the pain came again, only it seemed stronger this time. She put her hands over her stomach and doubled over.

"Whatever is the matter, niece?" demanded Aunt Agatha, looking concerned in spite of herself. Her nephew's young wife was certainly not behaving with much decorum.

Gasping, Thérèse straightened up and faced the old lady.

"I have pains in my *estomac*," she replied, reverting to French in her discomfort.

"Hmmm, well, you'd better serve luncheon, then go and lie down," was Aunt Agatha's answer. She certainly wasn't showing much compassion, but then Victorian ladies never allowed themselves to show pain and expected the same of others.

Thérèse brought the dishes of carved pork, potatoes and freshly cut green beans into the living room while the old lady waited at the table, fiddling with her napkin. Thérèse had noticed that, although Aunt Agatha's memory didn't seem to be slipping too much, she had developed some odd habits in the last few months. She supposed they were due to the senility that Emmett had told her his aunt suffered from.

Luncheon proceeded in silence, as usual, with the aunt nodding at the flavourful pork, but not passing any comments on the food as she usually did. Thérèse suddenly felt the sharp pain in her abdomen again, and stopped eating while it continued for a few moments, then passed.

She looked up and Aunt Agatha was staring at her.

"Whatever's the matter now, Thérèse?" she asked again, looking annoyed at having luncheon interrupted with such a display.

"I have another pain," Thérèse replied. "I think . . . maybe the baby . . ."

"But it's not due for another month, is it?" sputtered the old lady.

"They come when they are ready," Thérèse replied, remembering her mother in the past suddenly going into labour with one of her younger siblings and having to retire to her room.

She stood up.

"Finish your lunch, Aunt *Agathe,*" she said, pointedly calling the old lady by the French version of her name. "I'm going to telephone Emmett, then go and lie down."

"But you can't interrupt him while he's at work!" Aunt Agatha was most indignant. "That's only for emergencies."

"I'm sure that Emmett will consider his wife giving birth to their child an important enough reason to leave work," she replied. "Besides, he'll have to go around and fetch the midwife. I don't think I can walk that far with these pains."

Aunt Agatha shrugged, then returned to her lunch.

"Very well, do what you think is best," she said, grudgingly.

Thérèse went out into the hall and took the telephone earpiece off its stand. She dialled the number of the operator, then responded to her query with the number for Somerset House, where Emmett worked. This was the office of the British Civil Service, and Thérèse had been very proud of her husband when he had started working there. He had quickly been promoted to the lower management level from the clerical ranks because of his agility with numbers and his record of four years of military service during the Great War.

She quickly informed Emmett's personal secretary of the situation and asked that she tell him he would need to stop at the midwife's house on his way home from the office. The secretary, Louise, replied that she would call a taxi for him immediately.

Thérèse went up to her room and lay down on the bed. The pains were getting worse, and seemed to be getting closer together, but she tried to be stoic and not let Aunt Agatha hear her groaning. The minutes ticked by slowly, and she closed her eyes and tried gritting her teeth with each pang. She couldn't help but feel excitement at the anticipation of finally holding her baby in her arms, but she knew that there were going to be many painful hours before that could happen. She had sat with her father on the occasion of more than one of her mother's births, and she remembered hearing the stifled screams coming from upstairs. She had never actually witnessed a birth on the island, but she knew that it was a long and difficult business.

She eventually heard footsteps on the stairs and, after a brief knock on the door, Emmett burst into the room in a high state of anxiety. He was followed by Mrs. Dalrymple, who carried a large black bag in her hand. She glanced briefly at Thérèse, then smiled professionally.

"Darling, are you alright?" Emmett asked in a worried voice, taking her hand in his and kissing it fervently.

"Yes," she replied weakly, smiling at the concern on his face. "Everything's alright, it's just . . . rather painful."

"This wasn't supposed to happen yet!" he answered.

Mrs. Dalrymple intervened. "Baby decides when to come along," she said in an efficient tone, removing her coat and putting it on one of the armchairs in the bedroom. "He or she won't wait for anyone."

Emmett frowned, then Thérèse started to feel another pain coming on.

"Mr. Richardson, you go downstairs for now," said Mrs. Dalrymple, busying herself with emptying her bag, then washing her hands at the sink in the bedroom. "I'll let you know periodically when things are happening, but this room is no place for a man."

Emmett nodded, then bent over and pressed a kiss on Thérèse's forehead.

"I'll leave you in the midwife's capable hands, darling," he said. "I'll be thinking of you all the time downstairs."

Thérèse nodded, then clenched her teeth as the pain became stronger.

Mrs. Dalrymple patted her arm and said kindly, "Don't worry, Mrs. Richardson. Everything's going to be fine. It's all happening as it should."

The hours went by as night fell, and the pain became worse and worse. Thérèse didn't think she could bear it, but she didn't want Mrs. Dalrymple to think her a coward, so she tried to just clench her teeth and get through each contraction. Sometimes she would whimper softly, but she didn't scream, no matter how much she wanted to. The midwife wiped her forehead and cheeks with a cool cloth after each agonizing episode and, at one point, offered her hand for Thérèse to hold onto.

After a particularly long and painful contraction, Thérèse looked at Mrs. Dalrymple and said,

"How can women go through this?"

Mrs. Dalrymple smiled at her and replied, "We've been doing this since Eve, my dear. It's part of our ordeal as women. God punished her for her transgressions by making everything to do with childbirth painful. Why, your own mother went through this."

"Yes, she's had twelve children and is expecting the thirteenth," Thérèse said.

"Well, there you are, then," Mrs. Dalrymple rejoined.

Suddenly, the thought of her mother filled her with pangs of homesickness. Tears filled her eyes and she put a hand up to dash them away.

"I wish she could be with me now," she couldn't help blurting out.

"Don't worry, my dear, you're a brave, strong girl," Mrs. Dalrymple patted her shoulder. "She'd be very proud of you."

Thérèse smiled at her through her tears.

"Thank you, *Madame* Dalrymple. You're very kind."

She immediately felt another contraction coming on.

"Oh, *mon Dieu*, so soon?"

"It's a sign that Baby's getting ready to greet the world," answered Mrs. Dalrymple. "Let me examine you once more, my dear, and we'll see what's happening."

Sure enough, the baby was trying very hard to make his appearance. Thérèse soon felt a different pain coming on, a burning, searing urgency. Mrs. Dalrymple smiled with satisfaction.

"Baby is on his or her way," she informed Thérèse.

"His," said Thérèse, emphatically, even more sure in the midst of her agony that this baby would be a boy.

Mrs. Dalrymple positioned herself at the side of the bed and got ready to deliver the baby, telling Thérèse to start pushing the minute she felt her muscles starting to tighten again.

It was all over very quickly, and suddenly Thérèse heard a loud bellow.

"It's a healthy boy," announced Mrs. Dalrymple. "And it's a good job he came a bit early, otherwise he would have been a giant, and this would have been a whole lot worse."

Thérèse couldn't help letting out a little laugh, so relieved was she to have the terrible pain stop. Her insides felt bruised, but she was happy to have survived the ordeal and to have a healthy little son to present to Emmett. Mrs. Dalrymple busied herself with cutting the cord, then taking the infant over to the sink in the corner of the bedroom to wash him. He objected loudly, and Thérèse tried to get a glimpse of his face as the nurse performed her task. All that she could see was a thatch of dark hair, and the thought struck her that her son had inherited his dark colouring from her French family.

The midwife finally wrapped him up in a white blanket and brought him over to her. She held out her arms eagerly to take him and was finally able to look at his little face as she held him tightly against her. She looked at the angelic features and immediately felt the strongest rush of love that she had ever felt in her life. She loved her husband and her siblings and parents, but this was something far stronger than even that.

"Oh, he's beautiful," she breathed, kissing the tiny forehead and searching his face. He hadn't cried since that first yell after coming into the world and was now making little mewling sounds, turning his head in both directions. The little one bore a strong resemblance to her mother and one of her brothers, and she felt that sudden homesickness hit once again. Tears filled her eyes, and she smiled gratefully at Mrs. Dalrymple for everything she had done.

"I'll go and fetch your husband, my dear," the midwife replied, softly patting Thérèse's hand.

"I'm sure he's eager to see his son and heir."

Shortly after Mrs. Dalrymple left the room, Thérèse heard Emmett come bounding up the stairs and then the bedroom door burst open. He dashed to her side, enveloping her in a warm embrace.

"Thank you, my darling," he whispered, kissing her on both cheeks and then her mouth. "Thank you for my son."

She smiled up at him, then returned to gazing at the little boy cradled in her arms. "What shall we call him?" she asked.

"I've been thinking about that," he replied. "What about David?"

"David," she repeated. "It's not a name that I know. It isn't a French name."

"It's Welsh, but it's becoming very popular in England at the moment," he replied, adding, "It's the prime minister's name."

Thérèse didn't pay any attention to politics, but she liked the sound of the name.

"Yes," she said. "I think that would be a fine name. We must talk to the priest at the local Catholic church to see about getting him baptized."

Emmett nodded. He remembered well that he had signed an agreement with Thérèse's father that their children would be raised Catholic before he would allow them to be married. They hadn't gone to church since they had arrived in England, but Thérèse made the silent promise to herself that they would start to go as soon as she had arisen from her childbed.

27

Thérèse had thought she would be up and about in two or three days, as her mother had been after each of her births, but Mrs. Dalrymple had other plans. She informed Thérèse that she must stay in bed for two full weeks after the birth, to allow her insides to heal, and said that she would come every day to see her, to feed her meals and to help with the baby.

"But I'm not ill!" Thérèse replied hotly, when Mrs. Dalrymple had made her announcement. "I want to take the baby for walks in the park with Emmett in the new perambulator that he bought."

"Oh, no, my dear," replied Mrs. Dalrymple firmly. "Fresh air is bad for Baby when he's little, and you'll do yourself an injury if you go out this early."

Thérèse thought this was wrong, but found herself unable to argue with Mrs. Dalrymple's firm pronouncements. After all, Mrs. Dalrymple was the midwife, and had been very kind to Thérèse. She chafed at having to stay in bed for so long, and complained bitterly to Emmett, but she did stick to the rules as she had been told.

After two weeks, she was finally able to get out of her bed and bring her little son downstairs to meet Aunt Agatha. The elderly lady had a horror of "sickrooms" and wouldn't mount the stairs to take a look at her great-nephew until the prescribed two weeks had passed. By now, Emmett had returned to his job at Somerset House and the two women were alone in the house with the new addition.

Thérèse placed the tiny boy in Aunt Agatha's arms, and he squirmed a little at being held by a stranger, but then settled down and looked seriously up into the old lady's face.

"Well, he's a handsome little fellow, isn't he?" she said to Thérèse, almost smiling.

"We think so. He looks like my mother."

"Oh, no," replied the elderly matron. "Definitely his father."

Thérèse pursed her mouth at being contradicted, but then thought better of disagreeing and smiled at the old lady. At least Aunt Agatha wasn't disapproving for once and seemed to take quite quickly to the baby. As he grew older, he was to become his great-aunt's favourite of Thérèse's children, perhaps because he reminded her of Emmett when he was a young boy.

Later that evening, once Thérèse, Emmett and Aunt Agatha had finished their supper and were sitting at the table drinking tea while the baby slept soundly in his cradle, Thérèse announced to Emmett that she would like to go around and see the local Catholic priest about baptizing the baby.

Aunt Agatha turned to Emmett, looking aghast.

"You'll be baptizing him in the Methodist church, correct, nephew?" she queried.

Emmett faltered for a moment then, looking down at the table, replied to her,

"No, aunt, the baptism will be in the Catholic church."

A look of disgust, mixed with anger, came across the elderly matron's face.

"You were raised in the Methodist church!" she spluttered.

"Yes, but I promised Thérèse's father that our children would be raised Catholic" he explained calmly.

"Well, that promise doesn't have to be binding.".

"It does when I signed a legal document saying that would be the case."

The aunt's mouth opened briefly, then shut again. She stared at Emmett for a moment, then shot an icy gaze at Thérèse before looking back again at Emmett.

"I cannot believe that you would consent to raising your children in that antiquated, barbaric church!" she expounded before standing up and sweeping out of the room.

Emmett and Thérèse stared at each other.

"Well, what are we going to do now?" Thérèse asked her husband. "Imagine her referring to my church in such a way."

He took one of her hands in his and raised it to his lips.

"Don't worry about it, darling," he said quietly. "I promised your father our children would be raised in the Catholic church, and I don't intend to go back on that promise. But I knew that Aunt Agatha would object, as she's an ardent supporter of the Methodist church. It's one of the reasons why I haven't advocated for us to go to church at all since we got back from Mauritius. I knew it would cause an argument."

"Well, Emmett, you're the master of this house," Thérèse replied, looking him squarely in the eyes. "You don't have to let your aunt get the better of you in a disagreement."

"I know," he said, but he looked uncomfortable. "It's just that she raised me and . . . "

" . . . and she was good to you," Thérèse finished his sentence for him. "But you're not a child anymore. You're a man, a married man, and a father as well, and you make the decisions in this house."

She knew this to be true, but she was also well aware that he would do anything to make her happy. Thérèse had known that she could easily convince him to see things her way from the moment they'd met, and she wasn't going to let an elderly relative get in the way of that. She knew he loved her too much to let that happen.

"I've no objections to going to the Methodist church once in a while," she threw in as a compromise, because he was looking increasingly uncomfortable. "But I draw the line at baptism. My son must be baptized Catholic."

"I know, I know, my dear," he replied, avoiding her eye.

"I'll go and introduce myself to the priest and find out when would be an agreeable time for the baptism, but you must tell your aunt that there's no question of David being baptized a Methodist."

Thérèse knew that her parents would disapprove of their grandchild being anything but a Catholic, and her father especially would be incensed. That, however, didn't bother her as much as the thought of letting her mother down. She resolved to go around to the local priest as soon as possible, maybe the very next day.

"Do you know who the priest is in this neighbourhood?" she asked Emmett.

"I'm not sure of his name. I think it's Father Hugh something . . ." his voice trailed off.

"Never mind," she replied quickly. "I'll stop in at the church and talk to the curate."

Emmett nodded, then Thérèse turned her attention to clearing the supper dishes. As she went into the kitchen, she thought to herself that Aunt Agatha would probably raise objections tomorrow morning at breakfast, so she had better go around to the church as soon as possible before she lost her resolve.

In fact, Aunt Agatha didn't voice any objections at breakfast. She maintained a stony silence, reading her newspaper with seeming great interest and avoiding Thérèse's eyes. When Thérèse had finished her breakfast, she picked up the baby from his cradle and turned to address the old lady.

"I'm going to the church this morning, Aunt Agatha," she announced, "to speak to the curate about a meeting with the priest to discuss the baptism."

Aunt Agatha sniffed loudly and continued to pore over the pages of her newspaper, saying nothing. Thérèse concluded that the war between her and the elderly aunt, which had reached a truce from the announcement of her pregnancy, had resumed and might not end for some time.

After she had dressed baby David in a little coat, hat and bootees, she took him down the stairs and out the front door to the enormous perambulator that Emmett had purchased not long before he was born. She tucked him in safely under his blanket, then started the short walk to the neighbouring parish church. The September weather was beautiful, the sun shining warmly and a light wind blowing through the leafy trees. What a wonderful feeling! Thérèse admired the flowers in the gardens of the tidy houses, making a mental note that she would like to plant some exotic flowers in the front garden of her house next year. She wondered whether magnolias and bougainvilleas would survive in the cooler English climate and thought she should probably get some advice from one of the local gardeners. If not, roses and chrysanthemums would do. Perhaps she would plant some rhododendron and hydrangea bushes, as well.

Arriving at the church, she walked up the path through the churchyard and up to the big front doors, where she pulled the rope for the bell. It was a large, old church, built probably in the beginning of the seventeenth century, and was set amongst some very old and majestic-looking trees.

After several minutes, she heard somebody pulling on the door from the inside and, a few seconds later, a young curate appeared.

"Good day, may I help you?" he inquired politely.

"Is the priest here?" Thérèse asked him. "I would like to arrange a . . . er . . . *baptême* for my son."

She had temporarily forgotten the word for baptism, but the curate seemed to understand what she meant.

"A christening, madam?" he prompted.

"Yes, that's right," she answered.

"Are you a parishioner of this church?"

She frowned at the unfamiliar word and stared at him.

"Do you attend this church?"

"No, but I am *Catholique.* I wish for my son to be baptized."

The curate nodded. "Follow me," he indicated, opening the church door and ushering her in to the lobby with the pram.

The church was dark inside, and she caught a glimpse of wooden pews and the magnificent altar with an ivory Jesus on the cross, His head crowned with silver thorns and tears on His face. The sanctuary was much bigger than the chapel she and her family had attended back in Mauritius, and she was surprised at this, since England was mostly Anglican. There must be a fairly large Catholic population in North London, she thought.

"Wait here a moment," indicated the curate. "I'll find Father Dougherty."

"Oh, he is here?" she asked, surprised that the priest would be present on a weekday. At home, only the curate would be present during the week, with the priest appearing for Mass at the appointed times.

He nodded, then disappeared down the nave, reappearing a few minutes later with a portly priest, with a mostly bald head and a cherubic round face behind him.

"You would like to arrange a baptism, madam?" asked the priest, dismissing the curate with one hand. He had an odd accent when he spoke, and Thérèse had to really concentrate to understand what he was saying.

"Yes," she replied, indicating her sleeping baby in the pram.

"You're not from these parts?" he asked.

"No, I'm from the island of Mauritius," she answered.

"Ah, a foreigner," he said.

Thérèse must have looked somewhat annoyed, but then his face softened and he smiled at her.

"I'm a foreigner meself," he said, "from Ireland."

So that explained the unfamiliar accent! She didn't expect that he would speak French, so she carefully explained her situation and requested a date when the baptism could take place.

Father Dougherty explained that Thérèse and her husband would have to come to Mass one morning during the week, then they would have the baptismal service on the following Sunday. She told him that Emmett worked during the week, so it was agreed that they would attend this coming Saturday morning at 9 o'clock. The priest told her it would be necessary to have godparents attend the service. She told him that Emmett had no family, other than an elderly Methodist aunt who wouldn't set foot inside a Catholic church, and that her family all lived in Mauritius. He replied that the curate could step in as a proxy godfather if she would name one of her relatives as the actual godparent. One of the female parishioners could do the same for the godmother.

Thérèse pondered whom she could possibly invite to be the godparents of her son, when her family all lived so far away, but thought that Emmett might have some ideas on the subject.

She bade the priest farewell and began the walk back to the house, once again basking in the warm sun on her back as she walked. She had reached her road and was walking by an older-looking row house, when a head suddenly popped up above the garden wall. A slender young woman wearing a flowered silk scarf on her head and holding a garden trowel in her hand was busily weeding her flowerbeds and smiled at Thérèse as she strolled by.

"Good morning," she said brightly, "Oh, you have a baby. May I look?"

Thérèse smiled back at her, proud to show off her little boy. He was looking around in his pram and gazed at the young lady who came through the garden gate to bend down and inspect him.

"Oh, he's beautiful!" she exclaimed. "How old?"

"About two weeks," replied Thérèse.

"He's a big boy for two weeks," said the lady.

"Yes, I suppose."

"Have you just moved in around here? I don't think I've seen you before on the street."

Thérèse told her that she had lived here since last winter but had been pregnant, so hadn't gone very far in the neighbourhood. Besides, she was still trying to avoid the Spanish flu.

"You have an accent," replied the lady. "Where are you from?"

"The island of Mauritius."

"How exotic! Well, I'm pleased to meet you. I'm Adelaide Baumgarten. I originate from Germany."

Thérèse frowned somewhat at the thought of meeting someone who came from the country with which Europe had been at war, but she was quite taken with the easygoing charm and pleasant manner of this young woman. They shook hands and Adelaide said warmly,

"Well, I'm at home all the time and I have three children of my own. If you ever need something, or feel like a cup of tea, just come around."

"That's very kind of you," said Thérèse. "We have a telephone. I could always telephone to you, if you give me your number."

"Oh, we haven't got one of those," said Adelaide. "I can't be bothered with all these modern contraptions."

"Do you mind if I just come around without letting you know first?" Thérèse asked.

"Of course not. You make sure you do!" came the answer.

Thérèse bade her goodbye and walked back to her own house, smiling to herself. She had made a friend in the neighbourhood! This would be a very welcome change from spending the day with Aunt Agatha in uncomfortable silence, the old lady making clear her disapproval of her niece by marriage and her great-nephew's Catholic baptism.

Sunday morning dawned bright and sunny, and Thérèse awoke and fed her baby before preparing breakfast. She returned him to his cradle to sleep a little longer, then dressed carefully for the baptism ceremony, choosing a lavender silk suit and a white blouse with a large bow. She wanted to look demure and respectful for the mass, and also to impress on the congregation of the church that her husband was a hard-working man who could afford to dress his wife in an elegant fashion.

Emmett came downstairs for breakfast and kissed her on the cheek as she made the tea for the two of them.

"You look lovely, darling," he said, as he sat at the table and helped himself to two pieces of toast.

She smiled at him, then sat opposite him at the table

"Do you think Aunt Agatha will join us?" she asked, tentatively.

"Oh, no," he replied, uncomfortably, "You don't need to worry about that. She'd rather walk on hot coals than set foot in a Catholic church."

"Why does she feel that way? You've told her that you promised to raise our children Catholic."

"Yes, but she was brought up in the Methodist Church of England and the English still remember the reign of Bloody Mary, even though it was four hundred years ago."

Thérèse vaguely remembered a sixteenth-century English queen from her history books who had burned many English bishops at the stake. Fancy a grudge carrying on for all of those centuries! Of course, she was forgetting the animosity that her father felt for the English, which had been going on between the French and English since the days of William the Conqueror, and which had been made worse by an English king who broke away from the Catholic church and started his own.

She shrugged her shoulders and the meal continued in silence. Afterwards, she went upstairs to wake up the baby and dress him in his christening gown, a beautiful French lace gown that her mother had sent her while she was pregnant. She finally wrapped him in a white blanket and took him downstairs with her.

She and Emmett bundled the baby into his perambulator and began the walk to the Catholic church.

She enjoyed the beautiful autumn day and once again the feel of the sun on her back. Thank goodness Aunt Agatha hadn't appeared at breakfast and spoiled her pleasure at the upcoming ceremony. Emmett raised his hat to some of the neighbours who were already outside in their gardens, weeding and hoeing the flowerbeds.

When they reached the church, they were met by the young curate, who directed them to the front pew and indicated that they should sit there. The church slowly began to fill up with parishioners, and Thérèse smiled at anyone who happened to catch her eye. Father Hugh Dougherty finally emerged from the vestry and took his place at the altar.

Thérèse followed along with the responses to the priest's words and indicated to Emmett when he should kneel or sit down. Finally, Father Hugh introduced Thérèse and her husband to the congregation, then indicated that he would be performing a baptism. The curate and a matron from the church stood up and took their places beside him as Thérèse, followed by Emmett, walked up to the altar and gave her baby to the priest.

The baptism was over quickly and little David was as good as gold. He didn't even flinch when Father Hugh held him over the font and made the sign of the cross on his forehead with the holy water.

When it was all done, the priest recited a final prayer, and everyone exited the church to the sounds of the organ playing softly.

Thérèse introduced her husband to the priest and they started chatting about their military service during the war. As Thérèse looked around at the parishioners coming out of the church, she spotted the young woman whom she'd met the other day when returning from the church.

Adelaide walked up to her and grabbed her hand.

"So nice to see you again," she said with her friendly smile. She then indicated her husband. "This is Victor."

Thérèse bowed her head and the young man smiled at her. She turned to find Emmett, who had paused in his conversation with Father Dougherty.

"This lady is our neighbour," she explained. "I met her when I was walking to the church the other day. She wants me to come over for tea."

Emmett shook hands with both of them.

"Yes, I've seen you on our street once or twice," said Emmett politely. "It's a pleasure to meet you. And," he smiled warmly at Adelaide, "thank you for inviting my wife over. She's fairly new to this country and doesn't know very many people."

Adelaide smiled graciously.

"Why don't the two of you walk back with us to our road?" she asked. "Perhaps you'd like to come in for a pre-lunch drink?"

Thérèse was going to accept her invitation, but Emmett spoke first.

"Thank you, but no. We have my elderly aunt living with us, and she will be waiting for us back at the house to have lunch."

Thérèse felt deep disappointment in the pit of her stomach. Finally, a chance to talk to someone other than Aunt Agatha, and Emmett had rejected the invitation before she'd even had a chance to speak. She supposed that Aunt Agatha would wonder where they were if they didn't go home directly after church, and would be expecting her to start cooking lunch, but she would have loved the opportunity to spend time with some new people.

"I'll come around during the week," she assured Adelaide, who smiled at her once again with that warm, friendly smile. "But thank you."

"You do that, my dear," replied Adelaide, then turned away to go and find her children, who were running around in the churchyard.

It was two days later that Thérèse finally decided she would go and visit Adelaide, not wanting to seem too eager by going the next day. The nice weather from the weekend had disappeared, and the day was grey and cloudy. She walked up the road, pushing the perambulator with an alert David in it, then let herself in the garden gate of the tall house where her new acquaintance lived.

She rang the doorbell and, when nobody came to answer it, knocked nervously and waited. She heard noises on the other side of the door, then finally it opened. Adelaide, once again wearing a scarf on her head, peered at her, looking puzzled at first but then, suddenly remembering, ushered her in.

"Oh, do come in, Thérèse," she said. She was holding a child who looked to be about three on her left hip. He hid his face in his mother's shoulder when Thérèse tried to say hello to him.

Thérèse lifted David out of the pram and entered the house, noting that it was rather dismal and dark inside, that the carpet was thin and the paint peeling in places. Adelaide ushered her down the hall and into the kitchen, apologizing for the toys on the floor. She indicated the child in her arms.

"This is Georgie," she said. "And what's your little boy's name?"

"David," replied Thérèse.

"Well, we've got two patron saints there," said Adelaide. When Thérèse looked puzzled, she explained that George and David were the patron saints of England and Wales.

Adelaide went to the back door.

"Sarah! Alastair! Come inside!" she called.

Two rather unkempt children appeared a few moments later. Their clothes were dirty and their hair looked unbrushed. Thérèse had a quick flashback of her own younger brothers and sisters, and how her mother always made sure that they were clean and tidy. She would be shocked at this young mother and her small tribe of children.

"Sit down, my dear," said Adelaide, moving some dishes and newspapers off the table to make room for Thérèse.

Thérèse obliged, removing David's little jacket as she did so.

"There's some tea already made," announced Adelaide. Then she smiled conspiratorially, "Or would you like a little drinkie?"

"Yes, tea would be nice," replied Thérèse, confused.

"No, I mean a drink," said Adelaide. When Thérèse looked puzzled, she added, "Alcohol. Wine? Beer?"

"Oh, no," answered Thérèse. It was altogether too early in the day to start imbibing alcohol. She suddenly remembered Adelaide's offer of a drink after church and wondered if that was something that her new friend did on a regular basis.

"No, thank you."

Adelaide smiled and poured a cup of tea for Thérèse. She passed it to her, then went to a cupboard and brought out a half-full bottle of something and a shot glass. She filled it up generously, then smiled at Thérèse.

"Bottoms up!" she said, as she sipped at it.

Thérèse smiled hesitantly. Emmett barely drank at all, and Aunt Agatha didn't touch liquor. She wondered if this girl was an example of young British womanhood, although she remembered that Adelaide was of European descent, or whether she perhaps had a problem. Regardless, Thérèse felt that drinking liquor in front of children wasn't proper. She finally decided that it wasn't up to her to pass judgment, especially when Adelaide had rescued her from a morning with Aunt Agatha.

"Tell me about yourself, Thérèse," Adelaide said as she sat down, pulling her youngest child onto her lap. The child seemed to be a permanent fixture in his mother's arms and rarely spoke, mostly uttering sounds and pointing to anything he wanted. The older two, figuring that their introductions to the visitor were over, went back outside to play in the garden once again.

Thérèse proceeded to tell her new friend about her youth in Mauritius and about meeting Emmett outside the army base that morning. She also told her about her parents and twelve siblings, and Adelaide was quite surprised.

"How does your mother manage twelve children?" she asked. "I find three enough of a handful!"

"My mother has help," replied Thérèse. "She has nannies and maids."

Adelaide looked at Thérèse with new respect.

"So, you left all of that behind to come to this cold little island and run your own household, complete with a crotchety old aunt?" Adelaide asked. Thérèse had told her about her difficulties with Aunt Agatha and the dowager's objections to David's being baptized in the Catholic church. As Adelaide was Catholic herself, she understood Thérèse's awkward position.

"What a strong woman you are, Thérèse," said Adelaide, admiration in her eyes.

Thérèse had never thought of herself as being strong. She had always thought that she had done what she did out of love for Emmett, and that Aunt Agatha was simply her cross to bear. She had had to endure the rejection and disapproval of Emmett's elderly relative as part of her duty to her husband, and she was content to do so, to some extent.

"I wouldn't put up with it," rejoined Adelaide, when she told her how she felt. "I love my husband, but he's not bringing any old ladies to live with us. I've got enough to do with these three."

She ended her pronouncement with another swig from her glass, and Thérèse wondered if this was how she coped with her daily struggles. Adelaide's husband seemed like a nice man from what she had seen of him, and she doubted whether he contributed to his wife's problems.

The morning went by quickly as the women chatted, and eventually little David started fussing. Thérèse told her new friend that she should go home and feed the infant, and that lunch also had to be prepared for herself and Aunt Agatha.

She noted that Adelaide had only consumed one glass of alcohol during her visit, so she dismissed this as a medicinal tonic to help her friend to get through a day with small children. At the time she didn't think it all that important but, as she was to later find out, it would have tragic consequences for Adelaide's life.

She walked briskly back to her own house, comforting little David as he became more and more agitated. She let herself in with her key and encountered Aunt Agatha, fuming at the door.

"Where on earth have you been?' she demanded.

"I went to visit our neighbour, Mrs. Baumgarten," replied Thérèse.

"You went to visit the German woman?" Aunt Agatha's eyebrows shot up, her mouth pursing as it always did when she disapproved.

Thérèse felt her face growing hot. This old lady certainly had a habit of making her feel guilty.

"Yes, I did," she replied. "She is our neighbour, and she has been kind to me."

Aunt Agatha sniffed and turned away. Thérèse thought she heard her mutter something under her breath about "fraternizing with the Huns."

It was true that the British had been at war with the Germans, thought Thérèse, but the war was over and a very stringent treaty had been drawn up in Versailles to keep the Germans from ever declaring war on the rest of Europe and the world again. She had heard Emmett speak of the dire poverty in Germany and the way the nation was struggling to get back on its feet. But Adelaide hadn't even been living in Germany throughout the world war and was a potential friend. Thérèse felt that, other than Emmett, she had been starved of people her own age since she had come to England and, since Adelaide also had children, she could be a good mentor for her.

She sighed and removed her coat, then picked up little David from his pram and took him into the kitchen. She fed him, then laid him down for a nap in his cradle while she prepared the lunch. She took some cold beef from the icebox and sliced it up, then peeled potatoes and carrots and put them on the stove to boil. She then went into the living room to set the table for lunch for Aunt Agatha and herself.

She alerted the old aunt when everything was on the table and sat down to await her arrival. Aunt Agatha appeared a few minutes later, took a look at the lunch and sniffed before sitting herself down at her usual place at the table.

"Everything alright, Aunt Agatha?" Thérèse inquired.

"Leftovers again," the old lady answered, fixing Thérèse with her formidable gaze.

"I was taught to not waste food," Thérèse replied hotly.

"If you hadn't been at the German woman's house, you would have had more time to prepare a more substantial luncheon."

Thérèse stared at her for a moment, then made a snap decision. She picked up her lunch and walked out of the living room without a backward glance. She went to the kitchen and ate her lunch alone, then washed up her dishes in the sink.

A little while later, she went upstairs to check on the baby who was awake and needing attention. Coming downstairs with him in her arms, she opened the door to the living room gingerly. The dining table was empty, but Aunt Agatha's dishes were still sitting at her place. She picked them up in her free hand and deposited them in the kitchen sink to wash later, then returned to sit down on the big horsehair sofa in the living room to feed little David.

"Miserable old woman!" she thought to herself. "I don't have to put up with her rude behaviour. I'm going to talk to Emmett about her tonight."

When Emmett came home that night, Thérèse whispered in his ear as he was taking his coat off,

"I want to talk to you about Aunt Agatha after supper."

He nodded, then went upstairs to change out of his suit jacket and put his slippers on. Thérèse busied herself in the kitchen preparing tea for the three of them, then went to feed the baby and give him his bath.

When the light supper was over, a rather strained meal with only Emmett and his aunt exchanging conversation and Thérèse trying not to meet the elderly lady's eye, the latter excused herself rapidly from the table and proceeded to go upstairs.

"Well?" Emmett turned to Thérèse. "What did you want to tell me about Aunt Agatha?" There was trepidation in his voice.

"She's becoming insufferable," replied Thérèse, trying to keep the emotion out of her voice. "She's always complaining about the meals I serve, she doesn't seem to like me being in the same room with her, but then she gets angry when I go out and visit one of the neighbours."

"Who did you visit?" he asked.

"Adelaide Baumgarten," she answered.

"Well, she's never liked the Germans, anyway," said Emmett.

"Why? Because Adelaide's German? She's been very kind to me and is an experienced mother who I can go to for advice about David, if I need it."

"Now, Thérèse," soothed Emmett, putting his hand on her arm and giving it a gentle squeeze. "Aunt Agatha doesn't like the Germans because of the war, and I don't think she's very approving of Adelaide and Victor's habit of tippling."

"Tippling? What's that?" she asked, puzzled.

"Drinking," he answered. She ignored this.

"They didn't even live in Germany during the war. They can't help where they came from! They're British subjects now. I'm not from England either," she added.

Emmett stared at her for a moment, and Thérèse became aware that he was grappling with whether to tell her that Aunt Agatha really didn't like foreigners of any kind. Dislike of foreigners was very common among the British, even though they had one of the largest empires in the world and a big population of immigrants. Aunt Agatha's opinion was commonplace, particularly among the older generation who had never ventured outside England.

"Try not to be angry with her, darling," Emmett remonstrated. "I know she's difficult, but she's an old lady and she's not being nasty to you on purpose. She's not herself these days, and I think it's the senility that's to blame. You should have known her when I was growing up. She was much kinder in those days."

Thérèse shrugged, then hastened to justify her friend's behaviour.

"As for Adelaide and her husband drinking, it's not that much and I don't mind," she said. "My parents used to have a glass of sherry before lunch quite often."

He stared at her for a moment. "So, she's drinking in the morning, with her children around her?"

Thérèse hesitated before answering. "Yes."

He pursed his lips.

"Well, my little rose, be very careful when you're around her. And don't let her hold David!"

Thérèse nodded, and he took her in his arms and kissed her.

"Try to forgive Aunt Agatha, darling," he murmured. "And I'll have a word with her."

Thérèse felt comforted but didn't really believe that Emmett would talk to Aunt Agatha. He held his elderly relative in high regard and didn't want to stir the waters. Little did Thérèse know that this was a pattern that was to continue throughout most of the old lady's life. Emmett always showed great respect for the women in his life, which was very gratifying for her throughout their marriage, but not easy when the two women were pitted against each other. Thérèse made up her mind to try and turn a blind eye to the elderly aunt's behaviour and ignore most of what she said. She resolved to call her mother the next day, though, when she could speak freely in French and get her advice on how to deal with the situation.

28

Six weeks had gone by and autumn was in full swing. Thérèse enjoyed walks every day with David in his pram and admired the leaves which were beginning to turn on the tall, stately trees in the neighbourhood. Birds still chirped from the high branches, and mature plants in the flowerbeds of the local houses gave each garden an array of colour. It wasn't Mauritius, but it was beautiful and Thérèse appreciated it, even on rainy days. Some days, she would stop in at Adelaide's house and have a cup of tea (often accompanied with a glass of whiskey or port on Adelaide's part) and the two of them would make noises over the baby, who would stare back at them with his big dark eyes.

Her son had gradually become aware of his surroundings and was now staying awake for much longer periods during the day. He still woke up at night for a feeding but went quickly back to sleep afterwards. Thérèse often just sat in the rocking chair, holding him against her breast and kissing his dark curls. A few days ago, she had fed him in the morning and then held him in her arms, talking to him in a soft voice. All of a sudden, she had been rewarded with a beautiful smile as he gazed up at his mother. She had laughed quietly to herself, then felt tears of love and pride welling up in her eyes. That evening, she told Emmett that David had smiled at her earlier in the day and was able to get him to replicate the smile for his father. The next day, Emmett picked up the telephone and arranged for a photographer to come to the house and take a photo of David in his bassinette, a smiling Thérèse seated beside him.

This morning, she had woken up feeling out of sorts. Her head ached and, when she got out of bed, she felt suddenly nauseous. A disturbing intuition suddenly went through her. Was she pregnant again? But David was only two months old, it was far too soon! She dismissed the thought as quickly as it came into her head, but it lingered somewhere in the back of her mind. She also knew that her mother had had several of her babies only a year, or less, apart, so it was possible.

She dressed and went downstairs to make breakfast. She noticed that Aunt Agatha's bedroom door was still closed and breathed a sigh of relief. At least she could have breakfast alone with her husband and not have to put up with the old lady's presence. Although he never admitted it to her, she thought that Emmett must have talked to his aunt after all about her treatment of his wife, because she now mostly ignored Thérèse, although was grudgingly polite if spoken to. Thérèse always hastened to finish whatever chore found her in the same room as the elderly woman, then left the room as quickly as possible. It was still uncomfortable being around her, but at least it wasn't unpleasant or confrontational any longer.

When Emmett had gone off to work, after kissing her on the cheek and wishing her a pleasant day, she woke up the baby and fed and bathed him. She dressed him in a little sailor suit and hat, then took him out to the garden where the pram was waiting. The sky was blue and squirrels were making their presence heard in the trees. She admired the roses that were giving forth their last blooms, and made up her mind to once again talk to someone about planting some hydrangeas and maybe oleanders next year.

She went around to Adelaide's house and rang the doorbell. There was a silence inside the house, which was surprising, as normally Adelaide's older children would run to the door and talk loudly before their mother arrived to open it, usually with Georgie in her arms.

She waited about five minutes, then rang again. Finally, the door opened a crack and little Sarah appeared in the aperture, her large dark eyes gazing up at Thérèse.

"Hello, darling," said Thérèse. "Is your mummy here?"

"Yes," the little girl replied, not opening the door any wider.

"Well, can I come in, then?"

"Mummy said not to let anyone in, unless it was the doctor."

"Is somebody ill?" Thérèse demanded, alarm for her friend and her children filling her.

"Georgie," answered Sarah.

"Well, let me in, sweetheart," said Thérèse firmly. "I may be able to help."

Sarah looked at her for a few moments, then decided that it would be alright to let an adult who was known to her into the house. As Thérèse walked into the habitually dark and untidy house, she could hear the sound of coughing coming from upstairs.

"Is Mummy upstairs with him?" she asked.

"Yes," replied the child.

"You stay with David, darling, while I go upstairs and see them," Thérèse instructed, removing her coat and throwing it over the banister as she started up the stairs.

The sounds of coughing became much louder as she arrived on the first-floor landing, and now it was mingled with a much more ominous sound, a deep-seated rattle. The coughing was punctuated by the sound of the child crying.

Thérèse rapped quickly on the door, then walked in without waiting for an answer.

"Come in, doctor . . . oh, it's you, Thérèse," said Adelaide, jumping to her feet as Thérèse walked in. "I told the children not to let anyone in unless it was the doctor."

"I know," Thérèse replied. "But I used to help my mother nurse the sick servants and their children on our estate back home, and I once helped her when my brother had pneumonia. I can try to help you."

Adelaide looked at her doubtfully, but then her features softened.

"Well, I don't think he has pneumonia, but you might be able to give him some relief until the doctor gets here," she said, turning back to her sick child.

Georgie was lying in a tangle of sheets, his little face pale and his nightgown tangled around him. Tears glistened on his cheeks and his eyes looked sunken. Thérèse put her hand on his forehead and found that it was burning.

"He's got a temperature," she announced. "You'll have to put cold cloths on his head and the back of his neck to try and bring it down. Do you have any Aspirin?'

Adelaide looked puzzled.

"It helps bring down temperatures," explained Thérèse. She knew that it was a medication made from salicylic acid which had been used during the Great War to give pain relief and to reduce fevers. Her mother had started using it when she was looking after sick people on the estate just before Thérèse had left.

"I've never heard of it," Adelaide answered.

"Never mind. The doctor may have some," Thérèse replied.

She could hear that the little boy's breathing sounded laboured, and she bent her head over his chest to listen to it. She could hear rattling inside and some squeaks, and she knew that the situation was serious.

"He needs help breathing," she told Adelaide. "I should make a mustard poultice for him. It helped my brother when he had pneumonia. Do you have any mustard downstairs?"

Adelaide nodded and told Thérèse where to find it.

"Ask Sarah, if you need anything," added Adelaide. "She knows where most things are in the kitchen."

"Alright," said Thérèse. "Just put cold cloths on him and keep changing them as they warm up."

Adelaide went into the bathroom to do as she had been asked, and Thérèse went down the stairs and into the kitchen. She found Sarah there, holding David, while her older brother Alastair sat at the kitchen table. She explained to the children what she needed, and they found her a pot, ladle, some mustard seed and a spoon for mixing.

As Thérèse stirred the ingredients for the poultice, she explained to the children that she would bring the contents of the pot to boiling, then let them cool down a little and put them inside a cloth or towel to place on their brother's chest. She knew that it might help to ease some of the congestion that he was experiencing there. The little girl showed great interest in the proceedings and watched Thérèse carefully. She got the impression that the child was going to remember how to do this the next time.

After the mixture had cooled, Sarah helped her find a clean kitchen towel. Thérèse ladled the contents of the pot into the towel, wrapping them firmly and tying the ends of the towel to keep anything from spilling out.

She went quickly up the stairs and knocked on the bedroom door, letting herself in without waiting for an answer. Adelaide was sitting dutifully at the side of the bed, holding cloths to her son's head as he moaned and tried to throw them off.

Thérèse went to the other side of the bed and gently pulled up the child's nightshirt, placing the poultice on his chest. He struggled against her for a few moments, but then lay quietly after that. Thérèse watched him very closely, as mustard plasters can cause burns if not watched carefully. At one point, Georgie opened his eyes and peered dimly at Thérèse. Upon seeing her reassuring smile, he closed them again.

Minutes went by, then the sound of the doorbell downstairs could be heard. A few moments later, Dr. Briggs arrived, letting himself quietly in to the room. He nodded at Adelaide, then looked surprised as he recognized Thérèse on the other side of the bed.

"Mrs. Richardson!" he said. "You know Mrs. Baumgarten?"

"Yes, we're neighbours," explained Thérèse.

"Are you helping her?"

"Yes, I used to help my mother with my family and the servants on our estate when they were ill. My mother is quite a good nurse."

The doctor nodded again, then turned his attention to the little boy. He examined him quickly, exclaiming at the poultice on the little chest and the cold cloths on his forehead and the back of his neck.

"Well, you certainly seem to know what you're doing, Mrs. Richardson," he smiled.

"Thank you, doctor," she said. "My brother once had pneumonia, and I helped my mother nurse him."

The doctor began packing his bag, then told Adelaide that he would be prescribing some Aspirin, to be crushed in a tablespoon of jam and taken at regular intervals.

"If he's not showing any progress in the next twenty-four hours, send for me again and we'll think about admitting him to hospital," he instructed Adelaide.

"Well done, Mrs. Richardson," he said, tipping his hat to Thérèse. "I'm glad you were here."

He let himself out of the room and Adelaide smiled at Thérèse.

"Thank you so much, my dear," she said, coming around the bed and giving Thérèse a warm hug. "I'm so glad you stopped by this morning."

"Well, watch him carefully, Adelaide," Thérèse replied cautiously. "The next day is crucial with the fever, so make sure you keep an eye on it.

Do you have a thermometer?"

Adelaide nodded and Thérèse squeezed her arm, then bade her goodbye.

"I'll pop by tomorrow morning," she reassured her friend.

"Thank you again!"

Thérèse let herself out of the bedroom and went back downstairs to the children in the kitchen. She hadn't heard a peep out of David the whole time she'd been with Adelaide and Georgie. What a good boy he was! She said goodbye to the children in the kitchen and thanked Sarah for looking after David, then let herself out of the house, lowering the pram carefully down the front steps.

She had a spring in her step as she walked back down the street to her house. It felt so good to be able to help her neighbour and to administer care to a sick child again. She knew that, from now on, she would always make herself available to neighbours and friends when they had a sick family member, and that she would carry on her mother's work in this new country. It was something that she would continue to do throughout her life.

29

A week went by, and little Georgie slowly recovered from his illness. Thérèse checked in on him and his family every day, and she was pleased to see how quickly he came along. She had observed from growing up in a household full of younger siblings that children always seemed to bounce back quickly from illness, unless it was something really serious, which, in this case, it certainly seemed to be. Adelaide confided in Thérèse that Georgie was prone to these episodes of colds and respiratory issues, but usually recovered from them fairly well. She said she had noticed, though, that the occurrences seemed to get a little worse each time.

Thérèse was pleased that the little boy was getting better, but she had become aware in the last few days that she was not feeling well herself. The nausea she had experienced in the last year had returned and was especially bad in the mornings. A growing suspicion lurked in the back of her mind as to what it was, but she didn't want to admit it to herself. She thought that she should pay a visit to Mrs. Dalrymple to confirm whether her suspicion was correct.

She let herself out of the house one morning on a cool and cloudy day, with David in the pram. She walked down the street, nodding at the few neighbours who were outside in their gardens pruning trees or cutting deadheads off flowers. She was slowly starting to get to know some of her neighbours besides Adelaide. Old Mr. Warren lived next door, an aging widower who had served in the Boer War. He and Emmett loved to exchange war stories when they met outside in the gardens, and he was always very polite to Thérèse, lifting his gardening hat and inclining his head respectfully to her. Mr. and Mrs. Peters lived across the road, and they loved gardening. Thérèse saw them outside in all weathers, tending to their flowers and weeding the beds. Mr. Peters also wielded a push lawnmower, one of the latest inventions, to cut the grass every week or so and, one sunny afternoon, cut a rose and presented it to Thérèse when she stopped by to say hello. She was thrilled and, when she took it home to place it in a vase, Emmett commented that it was "a rose for the rose" as she placed it on the dining room table. She had smiled and kissed him on the nose, renewing her vow to plant some more exotic flowers next summer. This year seemed to have flown by with a newborn and her visits to Adelaide's house, and had somehow got away from her.

She turned into the driveway at Mrs. Dalrymple's house and hoped that she would find the midwife at home. Perhaps she should have telephoned first? She rang the doorbell and waited a few minutes, rocking the pram gently and cooing to David, who was looking around him in the pram.

The door opened, and there was Mrs. Dalrymple, dressed in a blue blouse and skirt with an apron tied around her waist.

"Oh, Mrs. Richardson!" she exclaimed.

"Should I have telephoned first?" questioned Thérèse. "I'm sorry, I didn't think to see if this was a convenient time . . . "

"Nonsense, no, no, its fine," replied Mrs. Dalrymple. "I'm always happy to see a patient, and to get another look at one of my deliveries after a couple of months."

She ushered Thérèse in and indicated she should leave the pram on the front step and bring David in with her. They walked through the cool hallway and sat on the familiar couch in the lounge. Mrs. Dalrymple took David in her arms and admired how sturdy he was, and how alert he seemed to be as he looked around him.

"Now, what can I do for you, my dear?" she finally asked.

"Well . . . " hesitated Thérèse. "I think I may be pregnant again. Is that possible this soon after David's birth?"

"Yes, if you're no longer breastfeeding," replied Mrs. Dalrymple.

"Oh, but I am," answered Thérèse.

Mrs. Dalrymple frowned.

"Well, I have heard of it happening, although it's rare," she said. "Have you had your "visitor" at all since he was born?"

"No, but I've been feeling very queasy over the last few days."

"Hmmm," said Mrs. Dalrymple. "Would you mind being examined?"

"No," said Thérèse. "In fact, I'd be happy if you would, just so that I'll, well . . . you know . . . be sure."

Mrs. Dalrymple nodded, then led the way to her examination room. Thérèse laid David on a blanket on the floor and hopped up on the table. Mrs. Dalrymple worked deftly, looking noncommittal as she did so. When she was finished, she turned to Thérèse.

"Well, my dear, I think you are," she said. "But it may be too soon to tell yet. You should come back in a couple of weeks, and I'll be able to tell you for sure. Have you and your husband resumed relations since David was born?"

Thérèse blushed and avoided the midwife's eyes as she mumbled, "Yes."

"Well, it's unusual to fall pregnant when you're still feeding your baby, but not impossible."

"How has this happened so quickly?" asked Thérèse, bewildered.

"Your mother has thirteen children, my dear," replied Mrs. Dalrymple. "You're from very fertile stock!"

"I'm worried about what my husband will say," blurted out Thérèse. "He was rather taken aback when I told him the last time, and I'm sure that he wasn't expecting this to happen again so soon."

Mrs. Dalrymple smiled conspiratorially.

"He was there with you, wasn't he?" she questioned, patting Thérèse's arm.

"Yes," replied Thérèse, feeling embarrassed and confused. "But how do I stop it from happening again?"

Mrs. Dalrymple looked at her for a moment before replying,

"You're Catholic, aren't you, Thérèse?"

"Yes, but what has that to do with it?"

Mrs. Dalrymple winked, then looked her straight in the eye and said, "The priest has to leave the church before the benediction."

Thérèse looked at her, puzzled. What on earth did that mean? What did priests and the church have to do with not getting pregnant? Then, suddenly, as she searched the other woman's face and smiling eyes, she realized what she was talking about. Of course, that made sense! She felt herself blush to the roots of her hair as she got down off the table and picked up her baby.

"Thank you, Mrs. Dalrymple," she said to the midwife. "My mother taught me how babies were born, but never how to stop them from coming along." A thought suddenly occurred to her. "Maybe she didn't know herself?"

Mrs. Dalrymple chuckled.

"Come back and see me again in a couple of weeks, if you're still feeling the same," she instructed.

"I will, and thank you very much."

"Don't say anything to your husband just yet. You can face the music once you know for certain."

Thérèse nodded, and left the room, followed by Mrs. Dalrymple.

She walked slowly back to her house. She hoped that Emmett would be happy when she broke the news to him. She had a feeling that she was indeed pregnant again and, this time, it would be a girl.

30

October 1919

As agreed, Thérèse waited a couple more weeks before going back to the midwife. She was still feeling nauseous in the mornings but was never actually sick. She felt very tired, though, and would often fall asleep in her chair when feeding David. The baby had slowly got into a routine of taking naps in the mornings and afternoons, and she took advantage of this to lie down on her bed and sleep for a short time while he was napping.

As expected, Mrs. Dalrymple confirmed that she was pregnant, and Thérèse went home with a rather heavy heart. Although she was pleased at the idea of having another baby, she wasn't sure how Emmett would take the news. She was pretty confident that he wouldn't be too happy at the thought of having another mouth to feed. One thing that she had learned about her husband in the last year was that he was very careful with the money he earned. He kept ledgers of the household expenses and was vigilant about how much money was left over at the end of the month, and how it was spent. She was grateful that he was not a spendthrift but, having grown up in a well-to-do home in Mauritius, it was hard for her to get used to the idea of not having money to buy everything that took her fancy. She was still fond of beautiful clothes and would often stop at the village ladies' shop and treat herself to whatever caught her eye. This was frequently frowned upon by Emmett, although he often relented and told her how pretty she looked in the new outfit.

She didn't exchange any words with Aunt Agatha after she came home from the midwife, but instead turned her attention to preparing a nice supper for her husband and his elderly relative. David was now eating meat and vegetables, so she wanted to make something that he would enjoy too. She finally settled on roast chicken with mashed potatoes and carrots, and fresh peaches for pudding.

The hours ticked by interminably until supper was on the table, then it was time to bathe David and put him to bed. She enjoyed the time sitting by the side of the bathtub as her son splashed in the warm water, then wrapping him up in a big bath towel and getting him into his little nightie and socks. She read him a bedtime story, then lowered him into his cot, singing a French lullaby as she did so. Turning out the light, she tiptoed softly out of the room.

Emmett was sitting on the couch in the lounge, reading a newspaper when she went downstairs. There was no sign of Aunt Agatha. Thérèse went to sit beside him, and he reached for her hand, raising it to his lips as he did so. She smiled, and cozied in beside him, cuddling up to his warm body.

"All tucked in and fast asleep?" he asked.

"More or less," she replied. "He falls asleep quite quickly these days."

"That's good," he murmured, folding the newspaper up and turning to her.

She took a deep breath. It was now or never.

"Emmett," she began. "I have some news."

"Well, I hope it's good," he answered.

"That depends on how you take it, I suppose," she replied.

He looked at her questioningly. She took a deep breath before facing him squarely and saying,

"I'm pregnant."

He sat up suddenly, taking his arm away from around her shoulders.

"What?" he asked.

"I'm going to have another baby."

He looked shocked and sputtered, "But David isn't even a year old yet! How can that happen?"

She looked at him incredulously.

"You know how that can happen, Emmett," she said evenly.

He turned away from her. "Yes, of course I do, but . . . " his voice trailed off.

"Don't worry, I've spoken to the midwife and she told me how to avoid it happening again."

She then proceeded to explain to him how to prevent another pregnancy, using Mrs. Dalrymple's colourful analogy. He frowned at her in a puzzled way for a moment, then couldn't help but smile, and relented. He took her hand in his and put it to his cheek.

"Well, I'm sure we'll be alright," he replied. "I suppose babies don't cost much at first, and I should be getting a pay rise soon that will help. I wonder how David will take to having a brother or sister?"

"Aunt Agatha might help, if she can bring herself to speak to me," Thérèse said bitterly. "She's barely addressed a word to me since David's baptism."

"Oh, she likes babies, she'll change her mind," assured Emmett.

He leaned over and kissed her on the lips.

"Well done, darling," he said softly. Thérèse cuddled up to him and a warm feeling of contentment surrounded her. Her husband seemed to be accepting of these new circumstances, and she couldn't wait to telephone her family in Mauritius and give them the news. She knew that her mother and sisters would be happy for her.She smiled to herself. All was right with the world, for now.

The next morning, she put David in his pram once again and walked over to Adelaide's house. She could hardly wait to tell her friend her news, as she knew that she would be happy for her. She rang the doorbell and waited on the step, lifting David out of the pram and holding him in her arms.

Adelaide opened the door after a few minutes and stood there with Georgie, as usual, clinging to her. When Thérèse examined her face, she thought Adelaide's eyes looked red and swollen, and her face was pale, her hair unbrushed.

"Come on in, Thérèse," she said, after a moment, ushering the younger woman into the house. They walked down the hall after Thérèse had removed David's jacket and her own and went into the kitchen.

The place looked untidy, as usual, and the breakfast dishes were still sitting in the sink. The older children were in school, and little Georgie climbed onto his mother's lap as soon as she sat down.

"Would you like a cup of tea?" Adelaide inquired, knowing very well that tea was Thérèse's usual beverage in the morning. Thérèse nodded, and Adelaide stood up with Georgie in her arms, then busied herself with rinsing out the teapot and placing the kettle on the stove, although she had a distracted air about her.

"Anything new, Thérèse?" she asked.

"Well, yes, as a matter of fact," Thérèse replied. "I'm going to have another baby."

Adelaide looked surprised, then turned back to her tea-making. She mumbled something under her breath and Thérèse looked at her.

"Pardon?" she asked the other woman.

"I said, so am I," answered Adelaide, her eyes cast downward.

"Oh, how wonderful!" Thérèse broke out into a huge smile. "We'll be pregnant together! When are you expecting the baby?"

Adelaide raised her eyes to look at her friend, and it was then that Thérèse noticed that they were full of tears. She stood up and, still holding David in her arms, went over to her.

"Why, what's the matter, my dear?" she asked. "Isn't this happy news?"

"No, no . . . " said Adelaide hastily, turning away from her. "It's not happy news at all. I haven't even told Victor yet, and he'll be furious with me when he finds out."

Thérèse was puzzled. "Why?" she asked. "He feels he can't afford another child?"

"No, it's not that," replied Adelaide. "Look, sit down. I haven't been forthright with you about something, Thérèse. When I've made the tea, I'll tell you about it."

Thérèse was concerned. What was it that her friend could have concealed from her? She noticed that Adelaide had set out two cups for the tea. Evidently, she wasn't going to drink any liquor this morning.

After they had sat down, Adelaide took a deep breath then spoke.

"You remember when Georgie was ill, and you came over to help nurse him?"

Thérèse nodded, and Adelaide went on.

"Well, I told you that he often gets colds and bronchitis. We noticed a while ago that it seems to be getting worse each time."

She paused, and Thérèse leaned forward with a questioning look on her face.

"It's not just colds and bronchitis," Adelaide said, her eyes once more filling with tears. "It's a condition that runs in my family, and there's not much that can be done for it. We went to a specialist in Harley Street, and he said that it will only get worse as he gets older."

Thérèse felt a wave of compassion for her friend wash over her. No wonder she kept the little boy so close to her. It must be heartbreaking to have a child who is not in good health. She subconsciously put her hand over her stomach, as if to protect the little being that was growing inside of her.

"But that's not all," Adelaide went on. "The doctor told us that we shouldn't have any more children, as there would be a risk of another child having the same condition. Victor made me promise that I wouldn't get pregnant again."

Thérèse reached out her hand to her friend as Adelaide's eyes brimmed over.

"So you're feeling guilty that you're pregnant?" she inquired gently.

Adelaide slapped a tear away from her cheek.

"Guilty doesn't even begin to describe it."

Thérèse hastened to soothe her in the same way that Mrs. Dalrymple had reassured her the day before.

"But you weren't alone in this, Addie," she said. "He can't be angry with you for something you did together."

Adelaide looked at her questioningly. "But it's the woman's responsibility to make sure that this doesn't happen," she said quietly.

"Well, I know different." Thérèse told her firmly. "It's very much to do with the man."

Thérèse then went on to tell her what she had learned from Mrs. Dalrymple about how to prevent a baby's conception. Adelaide looked puzzled at first, but then suddenly understood the explanation.

"Well, I wish I'd known that," she said. "I'll remember it for the future. But it's not just that that I'm worried about. What about this poor baby? What if he or she ends up with the same condition as Georgie?"

"You'll love the baby just the same, no matter what," replied Thérèse, soothingly.

Adelaide took out a handkerchief from her apron pocket and dabbed at her eyes with it.

"Thank you, Thérèse," she exclaimed, a hopeful expression on her face. "You've made me feel a lot better. I felt so alone in all of this, but now I know I've got a friend to talk to. I'll tell Victor tonight, and I won't let him blame me for this."

"Good girl," Thérèse smiled at her. "You can talk to me any time. And it will be nice to have a friend who's expecting too, so that we can complain about the sickness and the backaches, not to mention the constant tiredness."

"It's a lot worse after the first one," warned Adelaide. "You won't be able to rest like you can when you're waiting for your first child."

"Oh, well, I'll manage somehow," Thérèse replied.

When she left, she gave her friend a firm hug and wished her luck breaking the news to her husband. In her case, Emmett had only been concerned for a few minutes, then had hugged her and made her feel happy about the new arrival expected in the spring. She once again thanked her lucky stars for having such a kind and understanding husband. The brief thought of Aunt Agatha flashed through her mind as she walked home, but then she remembered that the old aunt had been quite happy when she announced the news of her pregnancy with David and hoped that the same would be true again this time.

31

Summer 1920

Summer had come, and Thérèse had given birth to a healthy little girl, just as she expected. When the midwife laid the baby in her arms, she felt an instant connection to this child and knew that she would be very special to her, both as a little one and later on in life. She adored her little boy but felt an affinity with this baby girl right from the start.

They called her Evelyn, and she slipped easily into their family life. At first, David wasn't too sure what to make of this new little creature who had come along, but he eventually tolerated her, and then started to look for her when she was sleeping in her cradle. Emmett seemed to enjoy having another newborn, and even Aunt Agatha had once again warmed to Thérèse for presenting her with a great-niece. Although she would never be affectionate in her manner, she was less critical, and therefore Thérèse didn't have to suffer frequent disapproving sniffs throughout the day.

Nights were difficult with the new baby at first, and Thérèse found herself very tired. However, David napped in the afternoons and she was able to get the baby to go to sleep at much the same time. She didn't worry about the housework at that time, but instead tried to get a few chores done in the mornings so that she could take a nap herself. Afternoon naps, which she and her family had taken in Mauritius to avoid the punishing afternoon heat, were a habit that she tried to keep up for the rest of her life.

Thérèse didn't see much of Addie during this time, who was due to have her baby very soon as well. She comforted herself by telephoning or writing to her mother for advice on juggling more than one child. She had twelve brothers and sisters, but was determined not to follow that path in her own household. Emmett's anxiety about supporting the family was not something she wanted to incur, and she couldn't see herself taking care of a house full of children, as well as an elderly lady who was becoming senile, without any help. As far as she was concerned, there would be no more babies the next year.

The English summer weather was very appealing to Thérèse for taking the children out for long walks in the neighbourhood. With the advent of the new decade, Paris fashions had dictated shorter skirts for women, and Thérèse found it freeing to wear the new skirts that were just above the knee. She had also had her hair cut in the new "bob" hairstyle and found it much easier to manage while dealing with young children.

Emmett had received his promotion at work and had decided to invest in a Ford motor car, so that he and Thérèse could take the children and Aunt Agatha for Sunday drives to the country. The 1920s were a prosperous decade in Britain, and Emmett wanted to spend the money on his family. Who knew when another war might come along and make things difficult again?

Thérèse remembered the time that she and her husband had taken the taxi from the station to her new home and how nervous she had been at first. After Emmett had completed his driving lessons and taken his test, she was even more afraid to go in the car with him and clung to the dashboard with both hands while he ferried her around the neighbourhood. However, he was a meticulous and careful driver and she slowly allowed herself to feel safe with him. Having a car also increased their social life, and they were soon able to pay visits to some of his friends from Somerset House at their homes. Thérèse found herself getting along easily with the wives of Emmett's colleagues and her friendly and gracious manner, as well as her charming French accent, soon made them popular dinner guests.

Her life in England was becoming easier in every aspect and, although she missed her beautiful island and the family she had left behind, she was adapting very well to being a British housewife. Even the problem of Aunt Agatha seemed temporarily resolved, although Thérèse was careful not to antagonize the old lady in any way.

One day, she received a telephone call from Victor Baumgarten, who had evidently got over his distress at his wife being pregnant again. He announced in a happy voice that Addie had delivered her baby, a girl, in the small hours of the morning. Several days later, she dressed up the children for a walk and went down the street to their home, armed with a little jacket and bootees that no longer fit Evelyn.

She was met by Sarah, who answered the door and told Thérèse that her mother was sleeping and couldn't come to the door.

"Well, who's looking after the new baby, then?" Thérèse asked her.

"She's asleep, in Mummy's bed," replied the little girl.

"And who's looking after Georgie?" Thérèse inquired.

"Alastair and me."

Thérèse looked at her quizzically and asked, "Why aren't you in school?"

"Because Mummy needs help and Daddy had to go to work."

"Well, why don't you let me come in and help you take care of Georgie?" asked Thérèse kindly.

Sarah thought for a moment, then opened the door and allowed Thérèse to go into the house. She found it to be in the usual amount of disarray, or maybe a little worse than normal. Thérèse opened the kitchen door, only to see the breakfast dishes as always still in the sink and Georgie dressed in his pyjamas.

She took her children's coats off and settled them with the bigger children, then said to Georgie,

"Come on, darling, let's get you out of your pyjamas and put some clothes on."

She took the child by the hand and, with a word to Sarah to keep an eye on David and baby Evelyn, she took him upstairs to find some clothes. She passed Adelaide's bedroom on the way to the room which Georgie shared with his older brother and sister but could hear no sounds coming from within.

She found a pair of dungarees and a knitted sweater for Georgie and put him them on him, the child all the while staring at her with his huge brown eyes. He smiled after she pulled the sweater over his head but said nothing as she brushed his hair with an old wire hairbrush she found on the dresser.

They walked back downstairs and, as they passed Adelaide's room, she thought she heard the mewling sounds of an infant. She paused and knocked softly on the door but heard nothing.

"Come on, Georgie," she said to the little boy, taking him by the hand

and leading him down the stairs. "Let's go and see Sarah and Allie."

She deposited Georgie with his brother and sister then, after telling the children she would be back in a few moments, walked back upstairs and stood outside Adelaide's bedroom door. When she heard the muffled baby sounds again, she knocked once more and opened the door without being given permission to enter.

She was immediately met by a strong smell of alcohol. Addie lay in tangled heap of clothes and bedding in the middle of the bed, her newborn daughter nestled in one of her arms. The baby was moving her arms and legs, her little head going back and forth as she tried unsuccessfully to suckle from her mother. Her cries were becoming more and more agitated as she sought comfort from the comatose woman. Adelaide's mouth was open and she was snoring gently.

"Addie! Addie!" called out Thérèse. She went to the bed and began to softly shake one of Adelaide's shoulders. "Wake up, your baby is hungry. She needs feeding."

Adelaide eventually started to stir and finally opened her eyes to look at Thérèse in a befuddled way.

"Thérèse, what do you want?" she murmured, frowning and looking about her.

"Have you been drinking, Addie?" asked Thérèse sternly.

Adelaide tried to sit up and finally put her arm protectively around the baby.

"Only b . . . brandy . . . " she sputtered, looking annoyed. "The midwife told me I need it for my milk."

Thérèse spotted a half-empty bottle lying amongst the muddled sheets. She picked it up and addressed Addie firmly.

"You don't have to drink half a bottle," she said. "One glass would do. And not in the morning."

Adelaide looked annoyed but sat up slowly. "One glass wasn't helping . . . ", she began.

"Your other children are waiting for you down below," admonished Thérèse. "You need to get up and see to them, it will be lunchtime soon."

She gently took the baby out of the other woman's arms.

"You get up and wash your face. I'll go down and look after the children," Thérèse told her. "I'll take the baby with me, so don't be long."

Adelaide glared at her for a moment, then nodded and rolled slowly onto her side. Thérèse went towards the door, holding the tiny baby in her arms gently.

"Don't go back to sleep!" she warned Adelaide. The other woman grunted but moved towards the side of the bed.

Thérèse went carefully down the stairs, holding onto the banister so as not to trip with the little one in her arms. She went down the hall to the kitchen and opened the door to find the three older children sitting quietly at the table, waiting expectantly. David was playing quietly in a corner with his ragdoll, and little Evelyn was fast asleep on her blanket.

"Mummy will be down in a few minutes," she hastened to explain when they looked questioningly at her. She thought she caught a glimpse of something else in Alastair's eyes. Perhaps the young boy had an idea of what was happening with his mother? It was possible that he had seen this before.

"What's your little sister's name?" she enquired of the child. "She's beautiful."

"Victoria," replied Alastair, reaching out a hesitant hand to touch the baby's head reverently.

"That's a pretty name."

"Yes, the old queen's name," the boy said, proudly.

Thérèse sat with the baby in her arms, giving her a finger to suck on while they waited for Adelaide to join them. The baby by now was making loud sucking sounds, becoming more and more agitated by the moment. Thérèse knew that it was only a matter of minutes before she became desperate and started to cry in earnest.

The door eventually opened and Adelaide appeared, wrapped in a red dressing-gown. Her hair had been swept up into the semblance of a bun and she appeared to have washed her face, but her eyes were bleary and the smell of alcohol accompanied her as she walked into the room.

She came over to Thérèse and wordlessly took the infant from her, indicating to Alastair that he should vacate his chair at the table for her. She then discreetly started to feed the baby.

For a few minutes, it was quiet in the room, then Sarah started asking Georgie whether he was hungry and what he wanted for lunch. Thérèse got the feeling that she had been used to doing this since the birth of her baby sister. She turned to her friend.

"Well, Addie, how are you feeling?" she asked.

"Oh, you know how it is with a new baby," Adelaide answered. "It's exhausting, and the nights are bad."

Thérèse nodded. She was sure that Adelaide couldn't be feeling very well after imbibing half a bottle of brandy, as well as being up in the night with her newborn. However, she had obviously slept for most of the morning.

Thérèse turned to the older children and suggested that they take Georgie and David outside to play in the garden, then asked Adelaide what she was planning to make for lunch.

"I don't know," Adelaide replied. "Maybe some eggs?"

Thérèse nodded and went to the larder, finding a box of eggs on one of the shelves. She grimaced at the dust on the shelves in between the items of food but said nothing.

"Addie, I know it's none of my business," she said, as she found a bowl and started cracking several eggs into them, adding milk and salt and pepper. "But you really shouldn't drink alcohol while you're looking after a baby. Even if the midwife tells you it's alright."

"But she told me I should," Adelaide replied defensively. "For my milk . . . "

Her voice trailed off, and Thérèse looked at her reprovingly, all the while stirring the eggs with a beater. How could this woman be so irresponsible as to drink while she was supposed to be looking after her family? Thérèse felt an impatient annoyance welling up inside of her.

"Very well, then," she said. "But only one glass before you go to bed. You shouldn't need more than that."

There was a silence in the room, and Thérèse turned her attention to the eggs, looking for a pot to cook them in and a way to get past the awkward moment. She suddenly heard sniffling sounds coming from behind her and turned to find Addie in tears. Relenting, Thérèse put down the eggbeater and went over to her friend, enveloping her and the baby in a warm hug.

"There, there, don't cry," she murmured in a soothing voice, stroking Adelaide's head gently as she did so.

"Oh, Thérèse, it's so hard," breathed Adelaide. "I don't know if I can cope! The doctor said that he thinks the baby may have the same condition as Georgie."

"How does he know?" Thérèse asked, pushing a stray lock of hair gently behind Addie's ear.

"Just from the way she breathes," replied Adelaide. "I don't know what I'm going to do with two of them being unwell all of the time."

"It won't be all of the time, and I'll help you," Thérèse reassured her friend. Her anger at Adelaide for drinking while looking after her baby evaporated. She could see that the other woman was struggling and that this was her way of coping.

"I can come by every couple of days and give you a hand," she asserted, when Adelaide didn't reply.

Addie suddenly started to cry harder and clung to Thérèse desperately.

"Oh, Thérèse, you're so kind," she blurted out between sobs. "You have two children of your own, but you're still willing to help me? I just don't know what to say."

"I always helped my mother with the younger children at home," Thérèse replied, soothingly. "I'm quite used to it, and it's my pleasure to help a friend. Emmett won't mind, and Aunt Agatha will probably be happy to have me out of the house."

"Besides," she added brightly. "Your older two can help me with David and Evelyn while I'm here."

Adelaide finally smiled through her tears. "You're so good, Thérèse. I'm so lucky to have you as a neighbour, and a friend."

"We'll help each other, Addie," she replied.

She and Adelaide smiled warmly at one another, and then Thérèse turned her attention to the gas stove.

"Don't worry about anything, Addie," she said firmly. "But please promise me you'll try not to drink so much."

Adelaide nodded and buried her face in the tiny infant in her arms, who had finally fallen asleep. She then pulled a handkerchief out of her dressing-gown pocket and wiped her eyes and nose.

"I'll set the table for the children's lunch," she announced, getting up from her chair. "You and I can have something after they've eaten."

Thérèse nodded and began to cook the eggs in a large saucepan that was sitting on the top of the stove. She smiled to herself, feeling that she may have averted a crisis that day.

She and Adelaide began a pattern of helping each other with their children which continued for many years. Thérèse often felt like she was the older and wiser of the two, even though Addie was her senior by several years and more experienced with her own children. She struggled off and on with her drinking and with Georgie and little Victoria's illness, but Thérèse was always there to lend her nursing assistance and a calm manner. They became fast friends, and their friendship lasted until Adelaide's untimely demise in her early sixties.

32

May 1926

Six years had passed and Thérèse was now firmly rooted in London, leading a full life as a young wife and mother. Her joy was increased by the fact that her sister, Angélique, had also married a British soldier and was now living in the southern part of England. Although the journey was long, the two sisters tried to pay visits back and forth every couple of months and talk to each other on the telephone at least once a week. She also had a cousin who had come to England two years previously with his wife, and then decided to move to France, but they remained in touch. Thérèse would later tell friends and relatives that she "had a cousin in every part of the French-speaking world, and many English-speaking countries, as well".

She telephoned her family in Mauritius and exchanged news with her mother about her own growing children and her mother's children, five of whom were married and had their own families. Thérèse often wondered whether her mother would go on to have a fourteenth child but hoped she would be done with childbearing soon, as she was approaching her mid-forties. It was time her mother rested and had some time to herself.

Emmett had risen through the ranks of the civil service, getting frequent promotions, which allowed them a comfortable life. He was still somewhat frugal, but always happy to indulge his lovely wife when she really wanted something. Her French sense of style often drove her to buy expensive dresses and hats, but it brought him joy to see how smart she looked in them. She was always the best-dressed woman at church, and very often at the Civil Service balls and parties, as well. She had grown into a lovely and poised young woman who was friendly and kind to everyone. Her French accent, which she would never lose, only added to her charm.

Their social life was very busy. The first year after Evelyn's birth, Emmett had taken Thérèse to the annual Civil Service Christmas Ball. She knew several of his colleagues' wives and was very at ease about attending the ball, as it reminded her of the parties her parents used to give at the Big House, although on a much grander scale. She wore a stunning red gown, cropped just below the knee and sporting tassels and layers, flapper-style. Her hair had grown a little longer by now and she put it up in a bun for the occasion, placing an expensive gold and ruby brooch that Emmett had given her after Evelyn's birth at the base of the bun to hold it in place. She wore a long string of pearls and diamond earrings to finish off the look. Emmett had gaped at her when she came downstairs to go out to the car with him and had doffed his hat in deference to her. He wrapped her fur stole around her and extended an arm to escort her out to the waiting vehicle. Once at the ball, Emmett made it clear that he had no intention of dancing but wasn't at all concerned if his wife danced with some of their friends. Thérèse lost no time after dinner in locating a willing dance partner and stepping out on to the floor. Dancing was still one of her favourite things to do!

On the home front, she volunteered at local charity organizations, collecting clothing and household items for poor people in North London, and also for the less fortunate parishioners at St. Francis. She had made a wonderful network of women friends through the organization, and often had tea or lunch with some of them. One had even invited her to join her bridge group, so Thérèse had learned to play the game. It was to become something she would enjoy throughout her entire life. She found that the game forced her to use her natural intelligence, but she also enjoyed the social aspect of playing games with other women.

The only blot on their otherwise perfect life was Aunt Agatha. The old lady had become more and more irritable as time went by and most of the time tolerated Thérèse minimally. She was becoming more forgetful as she grew older, and Thérèse was often enlisted to help the old aunt with mundane tasks like buttoning up her coat or finding her glasses. Aunt Agatha had been somewhat kind to her niece by marriage after David's birth and had seemed pleased with the new baby. However, as time went by, she had started to show impatience with the little girl, especially when she outgrew the toddler stage and became a sweet, undemanding child. She frequently snubbed Evelyn when the little girl tried to give her a hug or talk to her, whereas David was always able to command her attention.

Thérèse had tried to intervene once or twice but was put sharply in her place. She had eventually complained to Emmett about the preferential treatment that his aunt showed to their son over their daughter, but he once again excused his aunt's behaviour, saying that Aunt Agatha was more used to little boys, since she had raised him. Thérèse was unimpressed by his defence of his aunt, but just went more out her way to avoid the old lady. She often took the children outside in the garden when the old lady surfaced in the mornings, or to Adelaide's house to play with her children.

One day, Thérèse, who had continued to help nurse the sick whenever she had the chance, had to run a quick errand to one of the neighbour's houses, an elderly widow who had taken quite ill. Much against her better judgement, she had asked Aunt Agatha to keep an eye on the children while she was gone. The aunt had reluctantly agreed but said that she would. The children were playing cards with her in the living room when Thérèse put on her hat and coat.

She left at about two o'clock, hurrying towards her neighbour Mrs. Hobson's house, where she found the elderly lady lying on the sofa in the sitting room with a fever and a very painful cough. She touched her forehead and found it to be burning hot.

"We need to bring that temperature down," she told her patient. "I'll bring you some cold cloths for your forehead and the back of your neck. Have you got any Aspirin in the house?" This had become Thérèse's preferred method of treatment for pain and high temperatures since the war.

"I think so. Look in the medicine cabinet in my bedroom," replied Mrs. Hobson, in a quavery voice.

Thérèse went upstairs and returned a few minutes later with the bottle of pills and a handful of small towels that she'd found in the bedroom. She wet two of the towels and placed them on Mrs. Hobson's head and neck, then brought her a glass of water to wash down the pills.

An hour later, the elderly lady's temperature still hadn't gone down, and Thérèse thought it best to telephone the doctor to come and see her. It turned out that Mrs. Hobson had a telephone in her house and was also a patient of Dr. Briggs. Thérèse spoke briefly with the nurse, who told her that Dr. Briggs would stop by the house on his way home from doing his rounds. Thérèse thanked her profusely and put the telephone back in its cradle.

"The doctor will be here in a little while, Georgina," she told Mrs. Hobson, who smiled gratefully.

"Now, you close your eyes and rest for a while."

Mrs. Hobson did as she was told and was soon asleep, her breathing sounding raspy as she relaxed into a deep sleep. Thérèse suspected that she had pneumonia due to a cold that she had neglected but needed the doctor's opinion to confirm this.

She whiled away the time by pulling a book from one of the shelves in the study next door to the sitting-room and trying to read it, all the while glancing at her patient to make sure there was no change in her breathing.

Dr. Briggs finally arrived at around five o'clock and awoke the old lady to examine her. He listened to her chest and took her temperature, then told Thérèse that he was going to admit her to hospital with a suspected case of pneumonia.

"That's what I thought it was," she told him.

"You should have been a nurse, Mrs. Richardson," he smiled as he spoke. "Your family and your neighbours are very lucky to have you. Mrs. Hobson could have become a lot more ill if you hadn't looked in on her."

"My mother taught me to always try to take care of the sick and ailing, doctor," she replied.

"Well, thank you for your help," said Dr. Briggs. "Now you go along back home to your family, and I'll see that Mrs. Hobson is looked after."

Thérèse found her hat and coat and left the house, after bidding the doctor a good evening. She walked briskly back to her house in the late afternoon light, aware that she'd been gone for a long time and that Aunt Agatha would probably be fretting about having to look after the children for such a lengthy period.

She let herself into the house and hung up her coat and hat, then went into the living room to find the elderly aunt and her charges. She was playing a card game with David, but there was no sign of Evelyn. Aunt Agatha looked up at her with distaste, before continuing her hand of cards.

"You were gone for a very long time, Thérèse," Aunt Agatha admonished her without glancing in her direction.

"Mrs. Hobson was very ill. I had to wait for the doctor to come. He's sending her to hospital with pneumonia," Thérèse replied.

Aunt Agatha muttered something about "looking after everyone but her own family," then challenged David to his next move.

Thérèse became annoyed. She didn't ask very much of the old lady, and here she was, once again making one of her snide comments. After all the times she had waited on the elderly woman and brought her everything she asked for, surely it wasn't too much to ask her to watch the children for a few hours?

"I'm sorry, Aunt Agatha, but I couldn't leave her until the doctor arrived. She was too ill." She looked around the room. "Where's Evelyn?"

A scowl took over Aunt Agatha's severe features. David suddenly looked very uncomfortable and buried his face in his cards.

"Evelyn has been a very naughty girl," answered Aunt Agatha. "She did something very wicked, then tried to blame David for it. She was trying to get the poor boy in trouble."

Thérèse jumped. Her sweet, well-behaved little girl did something naughty? That didn't sound right! Evelyn was a most obedient little girl who always tried to please her mother and the adults around her. She also adored her brother, and Thérèse simply couldn't imagine a situation like the one Aunt Agatha was describing.

"Evelyn was naughty?" she puzzled.

"Yes, she certainly was," replied Aunt Agatha. "She stole some sweets from my bedroom, then tried to blame her brother for it."

"Is this true, David?" she asked her son.

The boy didn't look at his mother, but quietly confirmed that this is what had happened while she was out.

"Well," demanded Thérèse. "Where is she, then? In her bedroom, waiting for a spanking?"

Aunt Agatha turned steely grey eyes on her niece by marriage.

"She's in the coal cellar," she replied coldly.

"The coal cellar?" Thérèse's heart skipped a beat. "But she's afraid of the dark . . . " her voice trailed off.

"Precisely," said Aunt Agatha. "It's a fitting punishment for stealing and lying."

Thérèse didn't even bother to reply to the old lady, or to interrogate her son any further. She ran out of the room and down the hall to the coal cellar door. As she turned the handle, she could hear muffled sobs coming from the depths of the cellar. She turned on the light and hurried down the stairs.

She found Evelyn sitting in a bundle beside the coal heap. When she saw her mother, she burst into renewed sobs and ran to her, clinging to her and crying uncontrollably.

"Poor little Evie," soothed Thérèse, stroking her daughter's hair. She knelt down and gathered the child in her arms.

"I know you're afraid of the dark, darling," she murmured into her ear. "But why did you steal the sweeties from Aunt Agatha?"

"I didn't!" breathed Evelyn into her mother's shoulder. "David did it, and he wanted me to help him. I said I wouldn't because it was wrong, and when Aunt Agatha asked us about it, he said that I did it."

She lifted her head and looked earnestly at Thérèse. "I didn't do it, Mummy, honestly I didn't."

Knowing her two children as she did, David the clever, mischievous one, and Evelyn, the sweet-tempered and good little girl, Thérèse didn't doubt that this is what had happened. It concerned her that David would steal something and lie about it but, then again, she remembered her brothers doing many naughty things as children and denying it, so she supposed this was just typical little boys' highjinks. She hugged her daughter tightly and assured her that she would talk to Aunt Agatha.

"Now, come upstairs, and we'll get you cleaned up," she said to Evelyn, taking her by the hand. She had noticed some coal dust on her daughter's little dress and brushed it off with her other hand. The girl's eyes were also red and swollen and her cheeks puffy, and Thérèse wanted to give her face a wash with some cold water. They went up the stairs and

Thérèse locked the coal cellar door after them, putting the key in her dress pocket afterwards. Aunt Agatha was not going to be able to gain access to that dark, dank place and leave one of her children in it again!

Supper had been an uncomfortable meal for Thérèse, who was fuming inwardly at Aunt Agatha, but didn't want to spoil Emmett's meal with an argument over an unpleasant situation. She planned to tell him all about what his aunt had done to poor little Evelyn and to make him swear that he would talk to the old lady about it. She felt that Aunt Agatha's behaviour had been cruel, although she had heard of Victorian parents who did such things to their unruly progeny. How lucky she was to have had such kind parents! It's true that her father had been difficult, but he never raised a hand to any of his children or punished them in cruel ways. It felt like something out of a nineteenth-century novel, and Thérèse wasn't going to have her children disciplined like that.

That night, after she had tucked the children into their beds and Aunt Agatha had disappeared to her own room, Thérèse went back downstairs to the sitting room, where Emmett was reading the daily newspaper.

"Everything alright, darling?" he asked, noticing the firm set of her mouth as she came to sit beside him.

"No, it isn't," she replied. "I had to go out to Mrs. Hobson's this afternoon because she was very ill, and I got back quite a bit later than I expected."

He put away the paper and gave her his full attention.

"Did something happen?" he asked.

"Yes. When I came home, Aunt Agatha told me that Evelyn had been a naughty girl and that she had put her down in the coal cellar."

"The coal cellar?" Emmett looked startled.

"Yes. She claimed that Evelyn had been very naughty, stealing some sweets from her room, then blamed David for it."

"And did she?" he inquired further, looked concerned.

"No, she certainly didn't! It was David who did it. He lied to protect himself from punishment."

"Oh, dear," Emmett seemed at a loss for words. For one of the very few times throughout their marriage, Thérèse lost patience with Emmett.

"Oh, dear? Is that all you can say?" she said. "Evelyn's terrified of the dark. The poor little thing was weeping and frightened in the corner when I went down there. And she's an obedient little girl. She wouldn't steal anything from anyone. She knows it's wrong."

"And doesn't David?" Emmett questioned.

"Yes, of course, he does. But he's a boy, boys do things like that. My brothers did! They thought it was a good lark."

"Well, then," said Emmett, shrugging his shoulders and reaching again for the newspaper. "No harm done."

Thérèse sprang up from the sofa, very angry now.

"No harm done?" she stared at Emmett incredulously. "How can you say such a thing? Evelyn was wrongly blamed for something she didn't do, then punished severely by being put in the place she's the most scared of in the whole house!"

Emmett looked extremely uncomfortable. "I was put in the coal cellar when I was a boy, if I was naughty," he said quietly.

"Well, maybe that was considered a fitting punishment in your day," Thérèse spat out, as though he were a parent, rather than a husband, to her. "But it's not acceptable to me. Nobody can treat my children like that, least of all an old aunt who's a guest in this house and has no business punishing my children in the first place. She should have told me when I came home and let me deal with it."

Emmett was taken aback by the vehemence of his wife's words. He looked at her for a moment, then tried to explain away his aunt's actions.

"Darling, she's an old lady, she's only doing what she knows. She saw what she thought was naughtiness and acted accordingly." He reached for one of her hands.

Thérèse batted him away angrily.

"Don't try to excuse her, Emmett," she said in a harsh voice. "You're always making excuses for her. I know you love her and promised her that you'd take care of her, but you always put her first and give in to her moods and bad behaviours. I want you to put your family ahead of her and her wishes for once. She has no right to treat my daughter like that and expect me to just stand by and do nothing!"

Emmett looked at her helplessly, then opened his mouth to say something but thought better of it.

"Promise me you will, Emmett?" Thérèse begged.

Once again, he said nothing.

In a fury, Thérèse turned on her heel and walked out of the room, telling her husband she was going upstairs and that he shouldn't follow her.

She ran up to their bedroom and threw herself on her bed, crying tears of frustration and anger. When she married Emmett, she hadn't expected to live under the tyranny of an old aunt whose nephew worshipped her and believed she could do no wrong. She had promised her husband rashly that she would help him take care of an old lady whom she had never met, but she had had no idea what she was in for. Her life certainly hadn't turned out as blissfully as she thought it would, but she knew she had to make the best of it, for the sake of her husband and children.

33

Thérèse lay in bed, wiping her eyes when another fit of crying came upon her, and she finally heard Emmett coming up the stairs to their bedroom. She turned her back to his side of the bed and lay there rigidly while he washed his face and brushed his teeth.

He climbed into bed beside her and reached his arms out to her, trying to wrap them around her body and draw her closer to him. She pulled away abruptly from him, finally sitting up when he tried again to take her in his arms.

"I'm very angry, Emmett," she told him. "Don't think you can just hug me and it will all be over."

He leaned away from her and switched the bedside light back on.

"What's wrong, Thérèse?" he asked her, looking genuinely puzzled.

"You're taking Aunt Agatha's side in this," she replied. "She's a miserable old lady, and the way she treats Evie is terrible. Don't you see that?"

"Well, don't leave her alone with the children, if you're worried about her," he answered defensively. "She's eighty-six years old, and shouldn't have to look after youngsters any more."

"You see?" she punched her pillow with her fist as she faced him.

"You're doing it again! You always put her first. Aren't the children and I more important to you? I'll be your wife forever, and your children are your future. She's the past."

"You're all equal in my regard, Thérèse," he said, trying to take her hand in his and soothe her ire. "I love all of you the same, including Aunt Agatha. She was my mother in every way."

"I know she was," she replied hotly. "But she treats your daughter in a very cruel way, and I won't have it. Evie's a good little girl with a heart of gold, and she doesn't deserve to be frightened out of her wits."

The arguing continued for the next half hour, with many tears and entreaties from Thérèse for Emmett to see things her way, but he was adamant that Aunt Agatha could discipline his children as she saw fit as long as he was in the house. Finally Thérèse, at her wits' end, threatened him with the only thing she knew that could force him to give in to her demands.

"If you don't agree to talk to her about this, I'll take the children and go back to Mauritius to see my family. My mother would never tolerate her granddaughter being treated like this!"

Emmett stared at her, his mouth open.

"Really?" he asked. "You would leave and take the children back to Mauritius with you?"

"Yes!"

"How long for?"

"Until you see reason."

Emmett rolled away from Thérèse and sat up, quiet for a moment and weighing the consequences of failing to do as his wife wanted. Agreeing to her every wish was a habit that he'd established from the moment they met, but this situation required choosing between loyalty to her and loyalty to his aunt.

He sighed, then turned back to her, his mind made up. He took both of her hands in his. She resisted him for a moment and started to pull away but, seeing the earnestness in his eyes, she thought better of it.

"Alright, my darling," he said softly. "I'll talk to Aunt Agatha tomorrow."

Thérèse felt her heart lifting in her chest. She had known that Emmett would see reason if she stood firm for long enough, and she couldn't be angry with him any longer. She leaned forward and kissed him.

"Oh, thank you, thank you, *chéri*," she replied. "I knew you'd see things the right way. You promise you'll speak to her tomorrow?"

He sighed again, then put his arms around her.

"Yes, I do. Never fear, it will be dealt with."

"Oh, Emmett," she murmured against his ear, moving closer into his arms. "I love you so much. And I'm sorry for being angry, but what Aunt Agatha did was cruel and I just couldn't stand to see Evie so upset."

She knew she had won the fight. Emmett could only hold out against her for so long, especially when she threatened to remove her presence, and that of their beloved children, from his life. His answer was to pull her against him and kiss her passionately on the mouth. As always, she felt her body strain towards him and the heat rising in her. He had no trouble persuading her to join him in a passionate reconciliation.

Two weeks had passed, and Thérèse was feeling noticeably sick in the mornings when she woke up. She kept thinking about the night that she and Emmett had quarrelled and then made up so passionately, and especially about the fact that they had been rather careless about preventing a pregnancy.

She worried about it every day, then tried to dismiss it from her mind. She knew that Emmett didn't want to add to the number of the family, and she herself had been happy with two children. However, the thought of another baby appealed to her and she started to think of herself becoming mother to an infant again.

As the days went by, her "monthly visitor" didn't appear, and the signs of pregnancy were becoming more obvious. She was tired all the time, and the nausea came and went. Emmett had had his conversation with Aunt Agatha, and the old lady was trying to be somewhat kinder to Evie than she had been before, but Thérèse found herself watching her like a hawk, looking for signs of any backsliding and becoming more and more annoyed at the old aunt.

One evening, as they were getting ready for bed, Thérèse turned to Emmett, a sudden compulsion to share her suspicions with him.

"I have to tell you something, darling," she said, looking up from the book she was reading. She had read and reread the same paragraph several times, trying to frame the right words in her mind.

"What is it?" he asked, smiling at her.

"I have a feeling I might be expecting," she said nervously.

"What makes you think that?" he asked, gaping at her.

"Well, the usual things . . . I'm tired, I feel sick, my monthlies haven't appeared . . ." her voice trailed off.

"But how can that be? We've been careful . . . " he replied, but then a look of consternation came over his face. "Oh, dear."

"We didn't allow the priest . . . " she stopped and gazed at him.

"To leave the church," he finished her sentence for her.

Thérèse nodded, then kissed him quickly.

"Don't be upset," she beseeched him. "I'm sure we'll manage. I'll be careful with my shopping, and we have lots of hand-me-downs from the children we can use, whether it's a boy or a girl."

Emmett rubbed his forehead and looked at her unhappily.

"Yes, but two children are easy to handle. Three is one more than there are parents in a family," he said lamely.

"Well, Aunt Agatha will help. You know she likes babies," she replied. When he didn't reply, she knew that he was thinking how quickly she turned the old lady into an ally, after she had complained bitterly about her a few weeks ago.

"Please don't be angry, Emmett," she begged. "I could be wrong but, even if I'm not, I'm sure we'll be alright. Addie has four, and two of them are sickly, but she manages."

He nodded in agreement, remaining silent for a moment, then turned to her.

"I won't believe it until you go and see Mrs. Dalrymple and she confirms it," he told her gravely. "Then we'll figure out how we can manage. I haven't had a pay rise in a couple of years, but maybe I need to talk to my director."

"You work so hard, Emmett," she said earnestly. "Surely he won't say no?"

"I don't know," he replied uncertainly.

"Well, I could be wrong anyway. I'll go this week," she promised. But her instinct told her that she was expecting another baby, and she was never wrong in her suspicions.

Thérèse made good on her promise and went to visit the midwife at the end of that week. That cheerful lady confirmed that she was indeed pregnant, about six weeks along, and could expect another baby in February of 1927. At first, Thérèse felt elated to become a mother for the third time but, as she walked home, she started to get butterflies in her stomach at the thought of breaking the news to Emmett. He always worried so much about providing for the family whenever she announced a new member would be coming along. She kept the news to herself when she got home and busied herself with preparing the children's tea and making supper for herself, Emmett and Aunt Agatha.

Supper was a quiet affair, as the old aunt had become somewhat chastened after being read the riot act by Emmett and was taking her discomfort out on Thérèse with a cold shoulder once again. Thérèse really didn't care, and actually welcomed the lack of comments and sniffs from the dowager's corner of the dining table.

Once the supper dishes had been cleared off and the children had been put to bed, Aunt Agatha retired to her room and Thérèse and Emmett sat on the sofa in the living room.

Emmett glanced up at her from his newspaper and raised an eyebrow.

"I went to see Mrs. Dalrymple today," announced Thérèse.

"Who?" he asked, looking puzzled.

"The midwife."

He folded up his newspaper, and when he looked at her again, there was a slight expression of apprehension on his face.

"And?" he inquired.

"I was right. I'm expecting another baby," she spoke as quickly as possible, getting the news out as fast as she could. Emmett let out a loud sigh, then took one of her hands in his.

"Well, I'm happy, if you are," he told her, smiling cautiously.

"Really?"

"Yes," he ran his hands through his hair distractedly, then nodded.

"Oh, Emmett!" she threw herself into his arms. "I thought you'd be angry."

"I couldn't be angry with you for long," he replied, kissing her gently. "I spoke to my manager, and he's going to give me a pay rise. I hinted that we might be increasing the size of the family, and he understands.

Besides, a baby might be just what we need around here. Aunt Agatha will be somewhat appeased."

Thérèse laughed and kissed him back.

"I'm so happy you're not angry," she replied. "And it's wonderful that your manager's going to give you a salary increase. As for Aunt Agatha, well, maybe she'll get over her disapproval of me for a while."

Emmett chuckled and hugged her.

"You could get around her easily, if you really tried, Thérèse," he teased her. "You just don't choose to."

"You're right about that," she countered. "Why should I put up with her being a miserable old thing in my house? She only lives here because we allow her to."

Emmett smiled, but left unsaid the thought that he had purchased the house long before he met his wife, and that he had been the one to promise Aunt Agatha that she would always have shelter with him. Thérèse really didn't have any say in the matter but, as he adored his beautiful "tropical rose" and their children, he refrained from saying anything.

34

The months sped by as Thérèse's pregnancy advanced. Evie was very sweet, frequently patting her mother's increasing belly and murmuring soft words to the baby inside. Young David was mostly oblivious but, when pressed, said that he was alright with his mother having another baby as long as it was a brother for him to play with. Thérèse would smile and say nothing, as she felt this baby was another girl.

She was young and healthy, and her pregnancy went along easily. Her initial fatigue and nausea had passed, and she was able to take up her normal activities with little effort. She supervised the children's homework when they came home from school and played with them in the evenings until they went to bed.

Her relationship with Emmett had deepened with the anticipation of the new life growing within her, and the strain of the quarrel over Aunt Agatha was forgotten. As he had promised, Emmett had made his aunt swear not to put Evie down in the cellar again, and to try to be more patient with the little girl. Evie was turning into a nervous young lady and was greatly lacking in confidence. Living in her brother's shadow wasn't helping matters, especially as David was loud and boisterous and liked to play practical jokes on other family members, especially his sister.

A beautiful summer turned into autumn and, before long, winter was approaching. The days became darker, and the weather was cool and rainy. Thérèse still found November days damp, with a chill that went right through her bones. This was why, when Emmett presented her with an early Christmas gift of tickets for a trip to Mauritius for herself and the two children, she was thrilled. He had been working very hard and had saved his annual bonus as a surprise for Thérèse. She was excited at the prospect of returning to her island home, although not sure about the logistics of travelling on the ocean when she was six months pregnant. But the thought of seeing her beloved mother and siblings again filled her with happiness. Also, the idea of escaping the cold English winter for a few weeks was a welcome prospect. She hugged Emmett tightly and thanked him over and over.

"We'll take the children out of school for a few weeks, and arrange it so we can be home in time for Christmas with you and Aunt Agatha," she suggested to him. "But are you sure you'll be alright here by yourself for that long?"

"Of course, darling," he replied. "Aunt Agatha can still cook, and I can look after myself."

"But your aunt is becoming so forgetful!" Thérèse exclaimed. "What if she burns the dinner?"

"As long as she doesn't burn the house down, it will be fine," he replied evenly. It was typical of Emmett's calm nature that very little seemed to rattle him.

"Oh, Emmett, you're so good to me," she murmured, nestling her head against his shoulder. "I'll miss you terribly!"

"But you'll enjoy being with your mother and sisters," he assured her. She noticed that he didn't mention her father. Emmett was well aware of the coolness between Thérèse and her father, and the reason for it, but she felt that, at this point, the less said the better.

The days seemed to fly by quickly after that, and Thérèse busied herself with packing valises for the children and buying herself some maternity outfits for the holiday. She knew that she always looked very pretty when she was pregnant. Her hair shone and her cheeks had heightened colour. She seemed to have an extra sparkle about her, and her mother would be pleased to see her looking so well. She marked the days off on her calendar until they would be driving to the train that would take them to Southampton.

The day had finally arrived when Thérèse and the children piled into the car with Emmett. Their suitcases filled the boot, and some were even tied onto a roof rack. Thérèse's valise was the largest of all, filled with the new outfits and Christmas presents for her family. She had started teaching the children to speak French from an early age, and now she insisted that they speak it the moment they got into the car and on the train. They were to speak to her only in French on the boat, and she warned that if they spoke to her in English ,she would not reply.

Emmett drove them mostly in silence, perhaps quietly contemplating five weeks with only his elderly aunt for company. His French was also pretty rusty, since he hadn't spoken it frequently since the war, and only occasionally used it with his wife once she had mastered English.

When they arrived at the train terminal, he supervised their luggage being put on the train and saw that they were comfortably settled in their first-class compartment. Thérèse was thrilled that Emmett had thought to send them in the most expensive fashion, as he was usually very conservative in his spending, but he evidently wanted his wife and children to be as comfortable as possible.

"Now make sure you get a porter to deal with the luggage and take you to the boat," he cautioned Thérèse. "I don't want you getting lost and missing your passage to Mauritius."

"Of course not, *mon chéri*," she replied. "I'm not going to carry the bags all by myself, but I think I can find the right dock for the boat."

"Nonetheless," he countered. "Be sure to get a porter. And don't to forget to telephone me once you arrive in Port Louis."

Thérèse assured him that she would. She knew how much her

husband worried about her safety and that of their children, and she wouldn't make him wait to find out whether they'd arrived without incident.

She hugged him hard and kissed him on the lips as he prepared to get off the train, first turning to his son and daughter to give them each a kiss and a hug.

"Have a wonderful time, my darlings," he said, his eyes misty. "Give my love to your parents and all of those aunts and uncles of yours."

He gave Evie an extra little squeeze, then blew a kiss to Thérèse. He slowly exited the compartment, murmuring "*bon voyage*" before he closed the door and walked down the corridor.

"Come on, Evie, let's play "I Spy with my Little Eye," said David exuberantly as he bounced on and off the plush seats in the compartment.

"*Français*!" warned Thérèse. "Remember what I told you. You have to practise French from now on."

David made a face, but he complied with his mother's wishes. Thérèse leaned back into the comfortable seat and closed her eyes, sighing contentedly. This would be the first time she would see her extended family in eight years, and she was excited by the prospect.

The journey took only two hours, then they were unloading their suitcases after Thérèse located a porter on the busy station platform. He promised to deliver them to the dock where their ocean liner would be awaiting them. They followed him through the station, where people were running to and fro, looking for station platforms or arriving loved ones. The smell of the sea permeated the station, and the children became very excited at the prospect of seeing the ship they would be sailing on.

The porter eventually escorted them to a dock, where a large "Madagascar, Mauritius" sign was hung, pointing the way to the boat that would be their home for the next two weeks. Thérèse looked up at the huge ocean-bound ship, remembering the vessel that had brought her to England all those years ago. The porter handed them off to a crew member who would make sure that their bags were stowed in their cabin, and Thérèse paid him generously for his trouble. He tipped his hat politely to her, before striding away into the crowd.

They followed the crew member in his sailor's uniform and jaunty hat to the gangplank, which they climbed fairly easily, Thérèse holding onto Evie's hand and helping her navigate her short legs over each step.

When they finally arrived at their cabin, the sailor threw the door open with a flourish.

"There you are, *madame,*" he bowed to Thérèse. "This is your cabin, young 'uns!"

Giggling, Evie and David threw themselves onto the bunk beds against the wall.

"I bag the top one," called out David, shoving his sister in the direction of the lower bunk.

"But that's not fair," she answered. "Why can't I have the top one?"

"Because you're the younger one, *ma chérie,*" replied Thérèse. "You'll be safer on the bottom. I don't want you falling out."

Evie pouted, but obediently sat on the lower bunk. Thérèse went over to the set of bunks by the window and placed her handbag on the lower one, glancing out the window as she did. She could only see the wall of the dock, but knew that, by tomorrow, they would be able to watch the open sea through this same porthole.

"Are you excited?" she asked the children.

"Oh, yes!" they both replied at once.

"We can't wait to arrive in Mauritius," said David. "To see our new family, and the place where Daddy was a soldier."

Thérèse hastened to assure him that he wouldn't be seeing any battlefields, just a military base, but that couldn't quell the young boy's enthusiasm.

"I'm looking forward to seeing the beach, and our grandparents' house," remarked Evie.

Thérèse smiled. She was thrilled to have the opportunity to show the children her beautiful island and introduce them to her family. She thought fondly of her husband back at home in London, sharing the house with his aged auntie, a house that was empty of the sounds of children playing and of the gentle touch of his wife. She thought for the thousandth time how lucky she was to have such a kind and generous husband.

After they had washed their hands and changed out of their travelling clothes, Thérèse took the children up on deck to watch the boat leave the dock and head out onto the sea. The air was fresh and chilly up there and gulls squawked overhead. Many other passengers had congregated on the deck as well, but she was able to find a spot for the three of them where the children could see over the railing.

"We'll wave to the people on the deck as the ship is leaving," she told them.

"But we don't know them," pointed out Evie.

"It doesn't matter. Let's just pretend we do," said the practical David.

It wasn't very long before the ship's loud foghorn sounded three times, startling Evie and Thérèse, although David laughed out loud. They began waving to the crowd on the dock, as Thérèse had suggested, and were rewarded by waves from the people on land.

With a jolt, the ship's engine started up and they began to chug slowly away from the dock. Tugboats appeared on either side of the ship and accompanied it out to the open sea as the passengers aboard watched.

Finally, Thérèse turned to the children and said,

"All right, *mes enfants*, it's been a long day. Let's return to our cabin and have a little rest."

This was met with protests by the children, who wanted to explore the ship, but Thérèse stood firm. There would be plenty of time to run around the ship the next day!

The afternoon passed quickly and then the dinner bell sounded. Thérèse had insisted that her children dress up in their best for the first dinner of the voyage and, although they had protested a little, they did as they were asked.

When they arrived in the dining room, they lined up behind some other passengers to be assigned their table by the purser. That gentleman tipped his cap to Thérèse and informed her that she and her family would be seated at table eight. He gestured in the general direction of the table and informed her that it would be their table for the rest of the voyage.

They made their way over and she saw that there was already an elderly couple seated at the table. She experienced a slight feeling of disappointment as she seated the children on either side of her, hoping that there would be some younger people, or at least a young mother like herself with children, joining them.

The elderly people nodded their heads at her but said nothing. She gave them her brightest smile and tried to break the ice with an introduction.

"Thérèse Richardson," she said, after she had sat down. "And this is David and Evie."

The lady grimaced a little, but her husband muttered, "William Dodsworth, and this is my wife, Mary."

"Pleased to meet you."

"Charmed, I'm sure."

Nothing more was said, so Thérèse busied herself putting serviettes on the children's laps and buttering rolls for them. She was pouring a glass of water for Evie when a deep voice said,

"Table eight? That's me. Alright if I sit?"

She looked up to see a very handsome young man in military uniform standing beside her, a warm smile on his face. He had large, friendly looking brown eyes and an unruly mop of dark hair. His build was generally lean but muscular.

"Of course," she replied, as Mr. Dodsworth nodded abruptly.

"Jack Quinton," the young man said as he seated himself beside Thérèse.

She shook hands with him, saying her name once again, and then introduced her son and daughter to him, after assuring them that it would be alright to speak in English to their companions at the table. He shook hands solemnly with them, even when Evie presented her left hand instead of her right. Leaning across the table, he also shook Mr. Dodsworth's hand, nodding politely at Mrs. Dodsworth.

Jack proceeded to put everyone at the table at ease by telling them he was going to Mauritius to inspect the army base with a view to dismantling it, since it was no longer needed by the British army as an outpost. Mr. Dodsworth was quite pleased to discuss the Great War with Jack, and much military talk was engaged in over dinner. Thérèse occupied herself with helping the children with their meals, showing them which pieces of cutlery they should use and instructing them as to the polite way to cut their meat. Every so often, Jack would turn to her and make pleasant small talk, inquiring as to where in France she came from (she quickly told him that she was a native of Mauritius) and asking the ages of the children. His eyes danced whenever he spoke to her, and sometimes he spoke quietly to her in order to exclude their elderly companions from the conversation. Mr. Dodsworth was always quick to draw him back into war talk, although his wife remained completely silent at his side.

The remaining two places at the table remained empty until the end of the meal, and Thérèse briefly wondered who the other two people would be. She presumed they would meet them the next day and hoped they'd be more agreeable than Mr. and Mrs. Dodsworth. It would be nice if they weren't ex-military as well so that the conversation wouldn't constantly revert to soldier talk.

After dinner, Thérèse told the children to accompany her back to their cabin and Jack stood up as soon as she arose from her seat.

"I wish you a good night," he said, saluting her and looking warmly into her eyes. "See you in the morning."

"Yes, good night, Mr. Quinton," she replied. She glanced at the couple at the table, "Good night, Mr. and Mrs. Dodsworth. Children, can you bid our dinner companions good night?"

The children responded politely, and Thérèse felt very proud of them as she shepherded them out of the dining room and down the stairs to their cabin. She couldn't help but think how handsome Jack Quinton was and how his gaze had sometimes lingered on her for several seconds too long. Try as she might, her thoughts kept drifting back to him as she watched the children playing, until she reminded herself with a guilty start that she had a devoted husband at home who had paid for her journey. What would he think if he could hear her thoughts at this moment?

35

The next morning, David and Evie awoke early and pestered their mother to let them explore the ship.

"You can't go without me, *mes chéris*," she told them. "You'll get lost! Just wait until I've had a chance to brush my teeth and dress, and then we'll all go together."

The children occupied themselves trying to look out of the porthole at the vast ocean while Thérèse busied herself in the bathroom, then they all put on their coats and hats and went upstairs on deck. The wind was cold and blustery, and Thérèse pulled her coat more tightly around her as she followed the children around in their explorations. Eventually, when they tired of running all over the boat, she suggested they go to the restaurant and see if they could find a cup of coffee for her and hot chocolate for them.

When they reached their table, there were two women sitting in the seats that she and David had occupied the night before. Evie looked rather perplexed, but Thérèse assured her it was fine to sit anywhere at the table. As they sat down, she took stock of the two women. One was a middle-aged lady, rather corpulent, but with a pleasant face, and the other a younger woman, perhaps her daughter, who was quite pretty and very well dressed.

"We're Phyllis and Georgia McIntosh," said the older woman, confirming they were mother and daughter, as Thérèse organized the children at their places and poured them some orange juice from the pitcher on the table. They exchanged pleasantries as the waiter approached and took their breakfast order, including the hot beverages that Thérèse and the children needed to warm up from their walk around the ship.

Halfway through breakfast, Georgia suddenly looked up and began to turn quite red in the face. Thérèse followed the girl's gaze and saw Jack Quinton approaching the table, this time dressed in a brown corduroy jacket and soft woolen pants. He was as handsome as ever, with his tousled hair and smiling face, and Thérèse understood why the younger woman had been blushing.

He came over to the table and seated himself beside Thérèse.

"Jack Quinton," he nodded to Mrs. McIntosh and her daughter, and they introduced themselves, Georgia turning redder than ever. Jack seemed not to notice, but instead turned to Thérèse and the children and wished them good morning. After consulting the menu, he waved the waiter over to take his order.

Breakfast was spent in fairly pleasant conversation. Thérèse learned that Phyllis and Georgia hailed from Kent in England, and had decided that they would like to visit Madagascar and Mauritius as part of Georgia's education before she went to university. She was quite an accomplished student and was going to study the classics at Oxford when she was finished with school. Thérèse estimated that she was probably about eighteen, the same age she had been when she had met Emmett. This young woman was obviously not very at ease around the opposite sex, but she did make some shy attempts at conversation with Jack. Jack addressed most of his conversation to Thérèse and the children, but he replied to the other women's questions when addressed. The older couple who had been at dinner the night before didn't appear for breakfast, and Thérèse didn't miss the conversation about military tactics and battlefields that Mr. Dodsworth had preferred the night before. She wondered briefly why Georgia and Phyllis hadn't been at dinner last night, but soon found out that Phyllis suffered with seasickness and hadn't felt up to dinner. Thérèse noticed that she mostly drank water and just picked at her toast and eggs.

After breakfast, she took the children back to their cabin and, as she had promised their teachers that she would continue some lessons with them since they were missing several weeks of school, she sat with them and did some spelling and mathematics drills.

By lunchtime, they were tired of doing schoolwork and couldn't wait to go up to the dining room. Thérèse felt a little qualm in her stomach at the thought of seeing Jack Quinton again, but she quickly dismissed it.

As soon as they walked into the dining room, she could see him sitting alone at their table. He stood up as he saw them approaching and indicated that she should sit in the chair beside him. The children quickly ran to the seats beside her and sat down, arguing noisily about who should pour a glass of water first. Thérèse silenced them gently, then turned to Jack.

"How was your morning?" she asked politely.

"Pretty boring," he replied. "It was too cold to stay up on deck, so I just read in my cabin."

"Yes, we stayed there too," she volunteered. "These two are missing school, so I've been elected their teacher while we're away."

"What are you doing in Mauritius? Do you have family there?"

"Oh, yes, my family all live on the island, apart from one sister who's married to an Englishman," she hesitated for a moment, "like me."

Jack smiled and glanced very briefly at the swelling under her dress.

"When's the little one due?" he asked, pleasantly.

Now it was Thérèse's turn to blush. It was not considered polite to refer to a lady's pregnant state, especially in mixed company. However, she answered him firmly, looking him straight in the eye, and saw only interest on his face, not prying.

"February," she answered.

"And you're alright to travel halfway around the world?" he queried.

"Oh, yes, I'm a good sailor," she told him. "And the baby's not due for three months."

"Brave woman," he answered, flashing her that warm smile before turning to David to answer a question about the army base in Mauritius.

Shortly afterwards, they were joined by Mr. and Mr. Dodsworth, and the conversation once again turned to military matters. Phyllis and Georgia didn't appear again at all.

When the meal was over, Thérèse mentioned that the children should have a nap, after which they would go for a walk around the ship to get some fresh air.

"I'll join you for the walk, if that's alright," said Jack. "I can't bear the thought of reading in my cabin all afternoon."

Thérèse could feel the colour starting to creep into her cheeks once again. A single man wanting to join her, a married woman, and the children for an afternoon walk. How was that going to look to the other passengers? She looked over at the Dodsworths. Mrs. Dodsworth looked scandalized, and Mr. Dodsworth coughed awkwardly into his hand. Jack ignored them and proceeded to ask Thérèse where she would like to meet him and at what time. She told him that the upper deck would be a good idea and that four o'clock was a suitable time. He nodded and smiled, then stood up and wished everyone a good afternoon. He winked at Thérèse before leaving and tugged his forelock to her.

"See you at four," he said, before turning and walking away.

Thérèse hurried the children away before anyone could say anything to her.

At half-past three, Thérèse roused herself from her bunk, where she had been unsuccessfully trying to fall asleep while the children napped, and went to the cabin's tiny bathroom to wash her face and comb her hair. She looked at herself in the small mirror above the sink and thought that she didn't like the way her hair looked that day. She pulled a face at her reflection.

Admonishing herself for caring about how she looked when joining a single gentleman for a walk around the ship, Thérèse reminded herself once more of the kind and gentle husband she had left at home. Flirtation was something she enjoyed since she had discovered that men found her attractive, and it was something she would continue to do throughout her life. However, she told herself that nothing but friendship could ever come of a relationship with a man outside of her marriage. She planned to always be a completely devoted wife to her dear Emmett.

Once the children were awake from their naps and had washed their faces and had a drink of water, all three of them put on their coats and went to the upper deck to meet Jack. It was now four o'clock. As they went up the stairs to the deck, Thérèse could see Jack's dark hair and recognized his soldierly carriage.

The children were chattering excitedly to one another, anticipating running around the deck and looking for land (which would be nowhere in sight so early in the voyage), and Jack turned and smiled at them.

"Hello, you two," he said to them. "Did you have a nice rest? Are you ready to look for some sea birds in the sky?"

Dashing over to the side of the deck, the children craned their necks to look for birds.

Jack smiled at her again.

"You look very refreshed," he said pleasantly. "Did you have a good sleep?"

"Not really," she replied. "I try not to sleep in the afternoons. I just rest so that I can be ready for the children when they come home from school."

"Yes, I expect they keep you very busy."

"They certainly do."

"Well, tell me about yourself," he said, steering her to the side of the deck, so that she could keep a watchful eye on the children. "I want to hear all about growing up in Mauritius."

And so she proceeded to tell him about her life on the estate, growing up with servants and a very large family. Jack listened attentively and seemed very interested in learning everything about her life.

36

The days on the ship sped by. Thérèse had initially worried that they would drag on monotonously, since she was so excited to see her family again, but each day quickly slid into the next.

They got up at eight o'clock every morning and went to breakfast in the dining hall. They were always met with warm smiles from Jack, a pleasant nod of the head from Mr. Dodsworth, and even Mrs. Dodsworth slowly thawed towards them and managed a quiet greeting after a few days on board. It turned out that she was painfully shy, although her demeanour had seemed to suggest that she was angry with the world and not disposed to waste her time on strangers. The single ladies, Phyllis and Georgia, appeared sporadically, due to Phyllis' seasickness. Thérèse suggested to her one day that she might try drinking some ginger ale and eating a few crackers when she first got up, and Phyllis remarked later that this did help her somewhat. Who knew that Mrs. Dalrymple's pregnancy advice would be of assistance to a middle-aged matron suffering from the effects of sea travel?

Georgia, on the other hand, seemed to be coming out of her shell and didn't redden as much when Jack addressed her. However, Thérèse noted with some amusement that the young lady was trying to engage his attention more often and would often look visibly annoyed when he turned towards Thérèse. He continued to seek Thérèse and the children out for daily walks after lunch, and they had fallen into a pleasant routine of walking around the deck, sometimes arm-in-arm when the sea was choppy, while the children ran around the ship chasing one another, spotting seabirds and looking out at the horizon. The adults had slipped into a comfortable camaraderie of easy conversation and frequent laughter.

One afternoon, they rounded the corner of the deck and ran into Phyllis and Georgia, who were also out for an afternoon stroll. The sun was shining brightly in the sky, but the wind was brisk and caused them to hold onto their hats to prevent them from blowing away.

"Hello, ladies," Jack greeted them warmly.

"Captain Quinton!" Georgia gushed, leaning into him.

"Good afternoon," replied Phyllis. "And how are we enjoying the fine weather today?"

"It's marvellous," said Jack, smiling pleasantly back at her.

"Captain Quinton, it's such a lovely day. Why don't you join us?" inquired Georgia, looking pointedly at Thérèse, then hopefully back at Jack.

"Oh, no, Miss McIntosh," Jack answered. "I'm enjoying Mrs. Richardson and the children's company. You and your mother carry on. Maybe tomorrow?"

Georgia was visibly annoyed and shot a dark look at Thérèse. Phyllis hastily jumped in and assured Jack that that would be just fine. She took her daughter by the arm and hurried her away, after a mumbled "Good afternoon" in their direction.

Thérèse smiled at Jack.

"You don't want to take a stroll with the lovely Georgia and her mother?" she teased Jack gently.

"No, I'm quite fine where I am, thank you," he replied, taking her arm and tucking it into his, as he was starting to do every day now during their walks. "Come on, we have to catch up with the progeny."

"They're fine,"she told him. "They always know where I am, and they can play by themselves."

She looked Jack squarely in the eye.

"Wouldn't you be happier keeping company with a pretty young girl like Georgia?" she queried. "She's closer to your age, I think."

"No, I prefer intelligent, more experienced women," Jack answered. He smiled into her eyes, and Thérèse looked quickly away.

"But she's intelligent," she countered, "and seems to be quite educated."

She looked at him seriously, "You know that I'm happily married, don't you?"

"Yes, of course I do. I just prefer to spend time with women who have something to say and don't place any expectations on me."

"Do you fear that Miss McIntosh would rush you into an engagement after a brief shipboard romance?" She couldn't help but bait him.

"I'm not looking for a romance. I'm an old soldier," he assured her quietly.

"Not an *old* soldier, just a soldier. Mr. Dodsworth is an old soldier."

They were now facing each other, Jack smiling quizzically at her, and suddenly Thérèse was feeling that she was going to blush. At that moment, David and Evie came back to them noisily, wanting Thérèse to see the ocean birds they had spotted on the waves.

"Show me, darlings," she told them, grateful for a reason to end the dialogue with Jack. "Mummy loves to see birds on the sea."

She detached herself from Jack's arm, took each of their hands and started to walk away, leaving him staring after her for a few minutes. However, he soon caught up with her and the children, acting natural once again. There was an uncomfortable atmosphere between them, however, that lasted for the rest of the day.

At dinner, Jack paid markedly more attention to Georgia, and Thérèse felt that he had heeded her silent warning. He, in fact, didn't invite her to go for a deck stroll the next day and, although she felt somewhat relieved, she missed spending the afternoon with him as usual.

For three days, Jack didn't ask Thérèse to join him on the deck after lunch. The children were puzzled as to why "Mummy's friend" didn't come with them on their walks.

"Doesn't he like us anymore, Mummy?" asked Evie, a sad look on her face.

"Oh, yes, sweetheart," Thérèse hastened to reassure her. "He just wants to spend some time with the other ladies at our table."

"He doesn't spend it with Mrs. Dodsworth," David jumped in.

"Well, Mrs. Dodsworth is much older than Jack, "replied Thérèse. "He'd rather spend his time with a young lady than with her."

"But you're much older than him too, Mum," he pointed out.

Thérèse laughed softly to herself. Jack was actually the same age as she was, but still a carefree single man. Her son always spoke first and thought about the impact of his words afterwards. She hoped this wouldn't be a character trait that would follow him into adulthood, but feared that it might.

"Yes, darling, I know," she answered gently. "But maybe Jack prefers Georgia's company?"

"No, Mummy," Evie said earnestly. "He prefers you. Maybe he thinks it's only fair to take a few walks with the other ladies."

Dear, sweet Evie! She always saw the best in everyone, and just wanted people to feel happy and cared for. Thérèse already knew that her daughter was a loving, kind soul and could see that people would often take advantage of her when she grew up. She hugged the little girl and kissed the top of her dark head.

"Thank you, darling," she told her. "Now, David, see if you can be the first one to spot land on the horizon."

She knew that he wouldn't, as they were still far from land, sailing across the South Atlantic Ocean, but it would keep her son occupied for a little while.

The next day, Jack was already seated at the table when they arrived for luncheon in the dining hall.

"Good afternoon, Thérèse. Children," he said, rising politely and nodding to her.

"Hello, Jack," she smiled warmly at him, indicating to Evie that she should sit beside him while she took the chair beside her daughter. She thought it best to keep a discreet distance between them. She told David to sit on her other side, which he did without protest. Jack turned to her immediately.

"Will you join me for a stroll on the deck after lunch?" he asked her earnestly. There was a pleading expression on his face that Thérèse felt she couldn't refuse.

Jack had told her during one of their walks that he had grown up in a military family with not much love shown from either parent, although he became closer to his mother after his father died. He had grown up with few friends, although he was always the life of the party when he was with his contemporaries. This continued throughout the war years, when he would let off steam in the officers' mess. However, he never really forged any close friendships with men, and drifted from one romantic involvement to another with women, never feeling the pull to settle down. His mother was giving up hope that he'd ever find a bride and give her some grandchildren, but he comforted her by telling her that there was "plenty of time" for that.

Thérèse didn't want to hurt his feelings, so she accepted his invitation to walk again after lunch, admitting to herself that it was a pleasant prospect. Just at that moment, Georgia and Phyllis arrived at the table and she noticed Georgia giving her another of her angry looks.

"Are we going for another walk after lunch today, Jack?" Georgia asked him eagerly as soon as she had settled herself at the table.

"No, thank you, Georgia," he replied to her politely. "I think I'll walk with Thérèse and the children today. David and Evie are going to show me how fast they can run around the deck without knocking anyone over, aren't you, chaps?"

"That's a good idea, Jack," David hastened to answer him. He turned to his sister. "I'll bet I can run faster than you!"

Evie pulled a face at her brother and reached for a dinner roll to throw at him. Thérèse held her back from making the throw and warned both of the children to settle down. She glanced up at Georgia and saw that that young lady was glaring at her furiously. There was no doubt that she was jealous of Thérèse and had thought herself successful in winning Jack's attention over from her, only to lose it again. In spite of herself, Thérèse felt a little pleased.

37

Thérèse and the children's daily walks with Jack resumed, much to Georgia's fury. She refused to address or even look at Thérèse at lunch, which often made for an uncomfortable meal. Thérèse sometimes teased Jack about his admirer, but he just looked uneasy, and told her that he was not looking for companionship from such a young and "shallow" girl.

As the days progressed, the weather became warmer and the skies more blue. They no longer needed coats and hats for their post-prandial strolls, and Jack and the children sometimes complained about the heat, which was becoming more intense every day.

They had now left the Atlantic Ocean behind and were crossing the Indian Ocean off the coast of Africa. The mainland could be glimpsed from afar, much to David and Evie's excitement. Thérèse felt stirrings of anticipation at the thought of seeing her family again. It had been too long.

On the second-to-last night of their voyage, the captain stood up in the dining hall during dinner with a megaphone and announced that he would be holding a farewell dance the following evening for all of the passengers on board. Thérèse was very happy at the thought of possibly being able to dance again (even though she was six months pregnant) and wondered whether she could count on Jack to be her partner, or whether he even danced. Emmett never danced with her and hadn't since she had forced him up on the dance floor at their wedding, and she was very excited about the prospect. Maybe even the captain, or Mr. Dodsworth would, if Jack wouldn't?

She dressed with care for the occasion in a black silk dress with white lace at the neck and cuffs. The dress was warm, but she knew it suited her well, and she was willing to put up with the heat. Even pregnant, the dress draped nicely to her body, the folds covering up her swollen belly and accentuating her curves. She dressed the children in their best outfits, a sailor suit for David and a summery flowered cotton-print dress for Evie.

They made their way to the dining hall with excitement and found their way to their table. Jack, once again wearing his military uniform, was already seated with Mr. and Mrs. Dodsworth. Mr. Dodsworth had on a suit with tails, and his wife wore a dark blue silk blouse with a high neck over a long black skirt, looking quite Edwardian and very hot and uncomfortable. However, she did smile at Thérèse and the children as they approached the table.

"I can go back to your cabin with the children when it's their bedtime, dear," she told Thérèse. "That way, you can stay longer for the dance."

Thérèse thanked her and sat down beside Jack. He looked up at her in admiration and she could almost hear him whistle under his breath.

She turned her attention to making sure the children were comfortable in their seats, and buttered a bun for each of them, trying not to look too much at Jack.

Phyllis and Georgia eventually arrived and sat down at the table with a stir, Georgia completely ignoring Thérèse, although Phyllis did smile at her distractedly. Thérèse occupied herself chatting with the Dodsworths throughout dinner, only replying to Jack when he spoke to her.

Once dinner was over, the tables were moved back and the orchestra tuned up for the dance. They began with a rousing Charleston number, and Georgia immediately claimed Jack to be her partner.

"Come and dance with me, Jack!" she cried, holding out her hand to him. Jack reluctantly stood up and accompanied her onto the dance floor, where the pair showed that they both obviously knew how to do the Charleston. Thérèse's condition wouldn't really allow her to join in that particular dance, but she couldn't help feeling a nudge of resentment towards Georgia. She loved to dance, and didn't get many opportunities at home.

When the number was over, they returned to their seats, Georgia flushed and smiling. She shot a quick look of triumph in Thérèse's direction, and Thérèse felt that it was revenge for the walks that she'd been taking with Jack for the last few days.

The music slowed down and soon became a waltz. Jack turned to her with a smile.

"Will you dance with me, *madame*?" he asked, gallantly.

Thérèse glanced at the children.

"Only if these two can come with us," she replied.

Jack looked disconcerted for a moment, but then smiled graciously at the two youngsters.

"Of course," he said.

David and Evie stood up and followed their mother and her partner to the dance floor. Thérèse showed them how to hold each other by the waist with one hand joined, and they quickly picked up the one-two-three steps of the waltz.

Once they were all whirling around to the waltz, Jack moved his head close to Thérèse's ear and whispered,

"You're the most beautiful woman here, Thérèse."

She pulled away and looked at him.

"Really? What about Georgia?" she asked, feeling the need to divert his attention.

"I've told you before, she's just a young and inexperienced girl. She doesn't know much about the world, and she can't talk about serious things, like you," he answered.

"But she's such a pretty young thing. And she's obviously very fond of you," Thérèse admonished him.

"Yes," Jack replied earnestly. "But I have no desire to spend time with her."

He once again placed his mouth beside her ear.

"There's another woman that I'm far more interested in."

"But I'm married, Jack, and I'm pregnant, for goodness' sake!" she sputtered, feeling flattered and panicked at the same time.

"I don't care! Maybe you're not looking for anything now but, who knows, in the future you might be. I'd be good to you, and we could travel the world together."

Thérèse pulled back and looked seriously into his eyes.

"I don't know what you see in me. Georgia is every bit as pretty, maybe even prettier, than me. And she's a nice girl, and available."

Jack squeezed her tighter against him.

"But you don't understand," he murmured in her ear. "You have something that she doesn't."

"What, a wedding ring?" she quizzed him in a mocking tone.

"No, not that!" He looked at her again, a frustrated expression on his face.

"Then what?" she questioned.

"I can't really explain it, darling," he hesitated. "You've got "It," that's all I can say."

"It?" she looked him square in the face, puzzled.

"Yes. It. A certain charm."

"I'm not even sure what that is."

"It's a quality that not everyone has. It's not even necessarily being the best-looking person in the room. It's a rare quality, a gift. A charisma, if you will."

"Charisma?" she repeated.

"You'll have to look that one up in the dictionary," he rejoined, then pulled away to finish the dance as the music slowed to a stop. He looked at her earnestly. "I'm really infatuated with you, I suppose, and I could easily fall in love with you. I haven't had many serious women in my life, but you have fascinated me, right from the start."

"Oh, my goodness, Jack," she said, sadly, feeling a sudden empathy towards him. "I'm a married woman. You have to understand that, please. I think I should probably return to the cabin with the children."

His eyes searched her face, disappointment showing clearly in his expression.

"I suppose, if you think so," he said, quietly. Two little figures suddenly appeared beside them.

"Mummy! Mummy! That was lots of fun!" clamoured the children, grabbing her hands as Jack released her.

"That's lovely, darlings," she said, bending down to them and encircling them both with her arms.

"Can we do this one?" asked David, as the orchestra started to play a foxtrot.

"Yes, and why don't you dance with Mummy again?" Evie said to Jack. Thérèse looked at Jack meaningfully as she took each child by the hand. She was letting him know that their dance together was over.

"Thank you, Jack," she dismissed him, as kindly as she could. He frowned, then turned around and walked towards their table.

She showed the children how to do the foxtrot and the three of them danced together in a circle. A few minutes later, she saw Jack leading Georgia out onto the dance floor and, when they passed Thérèse and the children, he glanced her way, then looked down.

Thérèse's cheeks burned. Yes, Jack had been an attractive and pleasant travel companion, but she told herself that she could never pursue anything with him, as appealing as the thought could be. Emmett was the love of her life, and she could not betray him in any way. He had very kindly given her this gift of travelling halfway around the world with her children to visit her family, and she would not abuse his generosity by making promises to another man of a future together. Besides, her strong Catholic faith required her to be faithful to her loving husband, something she knew she didn't have to remind herself of. She loved him with all of her heart and told herself she must put Jack out of her mind.

The next morning, Thérèse and the children awoke early, got dressed and washed their faces in a hurry. They couldn't wait to go upstairs to the deck and look out at the ocean, hoping to see the island of Mauritius getting closer.

Thérèse marshalled them up the stairs and they made their way to the side of the boat. Sure enough, in the distance, they could see the mountains and shores of Thérèse's home country. She felt her heart stir, and a tremor of excitement and anticipation went through her. She would see her mother again and meet the sibling who had been born while she was in England. The warm sea breeze ruffled her hair, and she could feel the heat starting to rise over the ocean. It was going to be a hot day.

Thérèse was eager to show off her children to her family. She knew that they would all love the handsome, intelligent young gentleman and the sweet little girl with the dark curls and kind heart. Evie reminded her of her sisters when they were young, and David showed signs of being similar in bearing and looks to her father, although he lacked the arrogance and proud carriage of his grandfather. She felt a slight nervousness at the thought of seeing her father again, as they had not been on the best of terms when she left Mauritius.

Jack suddenly appeared out of nowhere and approached her and the children.

"Good morning, Thérèse, children," he said, with a little mock bow, although she thought his eyes looked sad.

"Good morning," they all three chorused.

Jack continued to stand there, looking at her expectantly. She finally turned to her offspring.

"Go and see if you can spot any sea birds, *mes chéris,*" urged Thérèse. "I just have to talk to Jack for a minute."

The children turned away obediently, and Thérèse turned to face Jack.

"I didn't see you again much after our dance, Thérèse," he said.

"No, I was tired. I took the children back to the cabin for an early night. Today will be a busy day," she replied.

"You're not angry with me, are you?" he asked.

"No, of course not," she hastened to assure him. "I really was tired. Besides, I was pretty sure you would have a dance partner for the rest of the evening."

He looked briefly puzzled, but then smiled at her.

"I hope you'll forgive me for speaking so candidly to you last night," he said sincerely. "I suppose it was because it was the last night on board."

"That's alright, Jack," she smiled at him. "I understand."

"I think you've bewitched me," he said, gazing at her warmly. "I don't usually declare myself to married women who are carrying someone else's child."

"I'm very flattered," she replied calmly. "I take it as a compliment."

"Can I ask you something" he asked, suddenly seizing her hand.

She quickly pulled her hand away, glancing in the direction of the children.

"What?" she asked him, flustered. His standing this close to her was not a good idea, and she could feel the heat once again rising in her cheeks.

"Thérèse, I know that you're a married woman, and I have no right to ask you this, but I just couldn't stop thinking about you last night." He paused for a moment.

"What?" She prompted, nervous about what she was going to hear. "What do you want to ask me?"

"Just that . . . " he hesitated, then plunged in. "If ever anything goes wrong, will you please, . . . that is, . . . would you write to me and let me know? You know I'd come right away."

She looked at him, shocked. For a moment, visions of the two of them together were running through her head. Would she turn to him if anything happened between herself and Emmett? Could she see herself with this young man in the future? She took a deep breath.

"I'll always remember you, Jack, and maybe we'll cross paths again some day," she replied. "Who knows?"

He searched her eyes deeply while she tried to gather her thoughts. Emmett's face suddenly came into her head, and the moment was over in her mind. Then Jack handed her a piece of paper from his pocket.

"It's been wonderful meeting you, Thérèse," he said quietly, his voice catching a little bit. "I've written my address down for you in case you ever need me. I hope you enjoy your time on the island. I enjoyed meeting your lovely children, too."

"Speaking of whom," she indicated the two youngsters, who were running back to them. "Here they come. Look after yourself, Jack."

He nodded and held out his hand to shake hands with her. Thérèse took his hand in hers briefly, then turned to the children.

"Jack's just come to say goodbye, my loves," she said to her two little ones. "Can you shake hands with him?"

First David, then Evie, shook hands with Jack, and Evie even gave him a little hug. He turned and walked away, with one more backward glance at Thérèse.

"I think he loves you, Mummy," whispered Evie in Thérèse's ear.

"No, darling, he's just a lonely man who needs a friend," Thérèse countered.

"Well, maybe Miss McIntosh can be his friend," the little girl suggested.

"I hope so, sweetheart, I hope so," said Thérèse quietly. "Well, let's go back to our cabin and get ready to go."

They started in the direction of the cabin, the children running ahead of Thérèse. As they reached the below deck, she paused in front of a large receptacle and leaned over to throw the piece of paper into it.

As they were getting ready to leave the ship a few hours later, Thérèse caught sight of Jack with Georgia and her mother. Georgia had her arm through Jack's and was looking up at him in an adoring way. As Thérèse gazed thoughtfully at them, they both suddenly looked in her direction, and Thérèse didn't miss the triumphant expression in the young girl's eyes. Jack looked sadly at her for a brief moment, then quickly turned away.

"That's just as it should be," Thérèse told herself, then gave all of her attention to getting the children and their suitcases off the boat.

38

As Thérèse and the children walked down the ramp to leave the ship, she scanned the waiting crowd on the dock for familiar faces. She looked anxiously at the people standing there, but at first didn't recognize anyone.

When they reached the ground, she waved at a porter to come and take their suitcases, then took each child by the hand and started to look from face to face in the crowd. At first, nobody looked familiar then, all of a sudden, she saw a man who looked somewhat like her brother Rémy, but much older than the last time she had seen him. Of course, that had been eight years ago! Rémy had been a young soldier the last time she had seen him, and now he was in his early thirties, with a wife and children of his own. He wore a moustache, and there was something about his posture that reassured her that it was him. He stood looking at the people still on the boat, a slight impatience on his features, one of the estate servants standing by his side. She pulled her handkerchief from out of her pocket and started waving it in his direction.

"Rémy! Rémy!" she called out, trying to shout above the conversations of people on the dock and the milling to and fro of marine staff. She finally caught his attention and, with a big wave, he started running towards her.

"Thérèse, *ma soeur*!" he replied, gathering her up in his arms. "How wonderful to see you again after all this time!"

"I scarcely recognized you," she told him, looking into his warm brown eyes, which had suddenly misted over at the sight of her and the children.

"You haven't changed at all," he said. "Still the young bride you were when you left here all those years ago." He then turned his attention to the children. "And who do we have here?"

Thérèse, smiled. "Children, this is your *Oncle* Rémy, my oldest brother." She then indicated the children. "And this is my son, David, and my daughter, Evelyn."

David gave a little bow, and Evie reached up as Rémy bent down to look at her and planted a kiss on his cheek.

"What beautiful children you have, *ma soeur*," he commented. He turned again to the children. "You have cousins at home who are dying to meet you and show you around the estate."

David and Evie looked excited, then Rémy turned to the servant his side.

"Take the bags, Gaston," he instructed. "The car is waiting outside the dock. We have a little way to walk."

"You have a car, too, Rémy?" Thérèse asked him.

"Yes, Gaston drives me around," he answered. "I drive myself occasionally, but I prefer it when Gaston does. He's a better driver than me."

The servant smiled and started taking the bags out of the porter's hands.

"Emmett bought us a car when we went back to England," Thérèse said. "He drives it and is actually quite good at it."

"Are you one of those blue stockings who drives, as well, Thérèse?" he teased, taking her by the arm.

"Oh, no," she replied. "I leave that up to Emmett."

He laughed and patted her arm, then they proceeded to walk to the car, the children following at their heels.

Thérèse asked her brother about all of the members of the family and how they were keeping, especially her parents. He told her that everyone was well, that the older members of the family were civil to each other but didn't really cross paths much anymore. Thérèse frowned at this, and whispered to her brother,

"Does Eugénie still live on the estate?"

"She has her own house now, but no longer works at the Big House," he replied.

Thérèse tightened her lips.

"Is *Maman* happy?" she asked.

"Yes, she keeps herself busy with the younger children and, of course, the sick people on the estate. She still loves to nurse everyone."

Thérèse smiled. "Yes, she always loved to do that. Oh, I'm so eager to see her again. I've missed you all so much!"

Rémy put his arm around her and kissed her cheek.

"Well, you're about to have a reunion with everyone," he told her.

They continued to the car, then piled the luggage in the trunk and climbed in one by one. The car was a luxury German Daimler, and Rémy was very proud of it. David was quite excited as he climbed into the back seat beside his sister. Gaston put the car into gear, and they started out of the parking area and down towards the narrow highway that led to the estate.

Once they arrived at the estate, Gaston dropped them off at the Big House and helped unload the luggage, then went to park the car. Rémy ushered them through the front door of the house and called out,

"*Maman*? *Maman*? Are you here? We're home!"

After a couple of moments of silence, Thérèse heard her mother's voice from upstairs.

"Rémy? I'm coming! Do you have our visitors with you?"

"Of course, *Maman*," he replied, winking at Thérèse. She felt her stomach tighten at the prospect of seeing her beloved mother again and put an arm around each of her children. Her mother suddenly appeared at the head of the stairs, then ran down nimbly, a handkerchief in her hand.

"My darlings," she called out. "Welcome, welcome!"

She stepped off the last step, then threw herself into Thérèse' arms.

"My precious daughter!" she exclaimed. "How elegant you've become."

Thérèse noticed that her mother was rather plumper than the last time she had seen her, but her face was still beautiful and her hair lustrous and thick.

"You as well, *Maman*." She told her mother. "You look wonderful!"

Turning to her children, Thérèse pushed them gently towards their grandmother.

"David, Evie," she said. "This is your "*Grand'maman*." That's what she will want you to call her," she explained.

Madeleine put her arms around each child and hugged them warmly. When she looked up at her daughter, Thérèse noticed that she had tears of joy in her eyes. She had known her mother would immediately love the grandchildren that she had never met before, and she had been right. Children were her mother's greatest joy, and she knew that she would spoil them completely as they were her grandchildren.

"You've done well, *ma chérie*," her mother said to her, dabbing at her eyes with her handkerchief. "They're beautiful children, and such nice manners."

She then ushered Thérèse, Rémy and the little ones into the drawing-room, calling out to a servant to bring them some tea, and juice for the children.

"And bring some of the cake we made yesterday, Isabelle," she instructed the servant. The tall black woman nodded and hurried off to the kitchen.

Thérèse and her newfound family, together with the children, made themselves comfortable on the sofas in the drawing-room, and set about getting to know one another. The conversation was lively, with lots of laughter and hugs and sometimes tears, as members of the family who were lost to them were remembered.

39

They spent next few days getting acquainted with Thérèse's family, and the children enjoyed meeting her many brothers and sisters and their cousins, as well as the servants who were very kind and indulgent towards them. David enjoyed running around the estate with Rémy's sons, who were close to him in age, and the young servant, Henri, who accompanied them everywhere to make sure they didn't get into trouble. Evie enjoyed spending time in the kitchen with the new cook, Claudine, who had replaced Dhala when she retired. Claudine taught Evie to make Créole dishes, and how to bake cakes, and the little girl felt as though she were in heaven. She had always enjoyed cooking lessons at home.

Thérèse was delighted to see all of her older brothers and sisters again, except of course for Angélique, who was living in England with her husband. Marie-Anne had grown up into a slender and attractive young woman and had a husband and young daughter. The three older brothers were all married with their own children, and the children who were younger than Marie-Anne and had been little when Thérèse lived in Mauritius, had all grown up into teenagers.

Thérèse also met the youngest child who had been born after she left the island, a girl named Sabine. Her parents had thirteen children in all, and Thérèse vowed to herself once again to never allow any more children after the one she was expecting now. Three children were enough in this day and age, and she knew that Emmett wouldn't be happy with more. Children were expensive to raise in England, and she knew that her parents were very lucky to own the sugar plantation and to be able to afford their large brood, as well as servants to help run the estate. What a different life she was living in England compared to the one she had left behind! However, much as she loved her large family and the beautiful tropical island where she had grown up, she didn't regret making a new life halfway across the world.

She spent many a long hour lying on a hammock outside with her mother, discussing the past and the many friends and relatives they had in the French-speaking world. The children ran around the garden with their cousins, smelling the flowers and resting underneath the magnolia trees when it got too hot. The only cloud on the horizon was Thérèse's father, Paul.

He had only appeared on two occasions since she had arrived on the island. Once, on the night she arrived, he had come down for dinner and sat himself at the head of the table after giving her a perfunctory hug and nod of the head. He had shaken hands solemnly with David and Evie and instructed them that they could call him "*Grand'père*".

"You have grown up, daughter," he remarked to Thérèse, after they sat down. "You've become mature and matronly."

Thérèse had frowned at that.

"Mature, yes, *Papa*," she had replied. "Matronly? I'm not sure about that. I still like to dance and go out to parties with Emmett and our friends."

He had stammered somewhat as he answered her.

"I meant that you look every inch the "*mère de famille*", but still charming and full of life," he replied quickly.

"Thank you, *Papa*," she nodded her head, pleased at the compliments. However, she hadn't forgotten the tension between them when she left the island, and it was still there. Her mother had then called for everyone to say grace, so silence had descended on the table before she began.

The other occasion when she had seen her father was when her mother invited some of the neighbours around for a pre-dinner drink to see Thérèse and meet her children. Although *Papa* was a gracious host to his guests, he didn't address one word to Thérèse or her mother. Thérèse enjoyed the evening, chatting with the neighbours and their various relatives but, when she had looked up towards the end of the visit, her father was no longer sitting in his big armchair. He had apparently retired to his room without a word to his wife or daughter.

One afternoon, while sitting on the verandah with her mother, she decided to address what was obviously happening between her parents.

"So, *Maman*," she said, looking frankly at her mother. "What is the situation between you and *Papa*? I've hardly seen him since I arrived here."

Her mother pursed her lips and then looked grimly at her daughter.

"There's a reason for that, *ma chère*," she said quietly.

"What is it?" Thérèse asked curiously, although it confirmed what Rémy had told her.

"Your father and I no longer respect each other." Madeleine said, after taking a deep breath. "In fact, I don't think that we even love each other anymore."

Thérèse reached out and took her mother's hand.

"I'm so sorry, *Maman*," she tried to comfort her mother. "What went wrong?"

"It's been wrong for a long time," Madeleine replied. "Since before Sabine was born."

Thérèse was pretty certain she knew the reason and hesitated for a moment before blurting it out.

"Is it because of Eugénie?"

Her mother's mouth tightened, and she stared hard in front of her for a moment before turning back to Thérèse.

"Yes, her and the others that he parades around in front of me all of the time! And that child of hers."

"Who?" asked Thérèse.

"Henri!"

Thérèse was shocked, remembering the tall boy who had been assigned to chaperone her son and daughter around the estate and keep an eye on them while they were here.

"Henri's her son?"

"Yes, and your father's," Madeleine said, bitterness creeping into her voice. "He has others, as well, around the estate."

"How many?"

"What, mistresses, or illegitimate children?"

"Both."

"At least two mistresses, a handful of children," Madeleine put a hand to her head. "I can't keep track of them anymore!"

Thérèse went to her mother and put her arms around her.

"*Maman*?" she asked sadly. "What are you going to do?"

Madeleine sat up straight and brushed tears away from her eyes with one hand.

"As soon as Sabine is old enough, I'm going to leave him and move to the Island of Réunion," she announced. "I'm not staying here one moment after the children are old enough to fend for themselves. Right now, they need me, but I'm leaving him as soon as it's feasible."

Réunion was a neighbouring island in the Indian Ocean. It was far enough away from Mauritius for her mother to make a new life for herself, but close enough that she could still keep in touch with her other children. However, a thought occurred to Thérèse.

"How will you survive, *Maman*?" she asked her. "What will you do for food and lodging?"

"I'll make him buy me a house on Réunion, in exchange for my silence about his scandalous behaviour with the servants," Madeleine said firmly. "And he can send me a monthly stipend for Sabine's upkeep.

Besides, I've still got some savings left over from my father's legacy. I've always been careful to keep that hidden from him."

Thérèse looked at her mother with new eyes. She had always thought that Madeleine was a fragile flower who couldn't cope with the difficulties of life and of her many children, but she saw now that her mother had a lot more resilience than she had given her credit for. She was strong and wasn't going to lower herself to a man who had rejected her love and humiliated her in front of her adult children and the servants. She had formed a plan to remove herself from the ignominy that Paul had heaped on her with his affairs and to make a new life for herself. Thérèse looked at her mother with admiration, and wondered how she would cope if she found out that Emmett had had an affair and fathered a child with another woman. She silently blessed him for being such a true and faithful husband and felt a moment of discomfort as she thought of how she had flirted with Jack on the ship.

"Good for you, *Maman*!" she kissed her mother's cheek. "Why should you suffer because of him? If you ever need anything after you move to Réunion, you let me know. I'll help you with whatever it is, money, or support, whatever you need."

"Thank you, *ma fille*," Madeleine replied, her eyes once again filling with tears. "I'm so proud of you, Thérèse. You always were a good daughter, but you've grown up into a wonderful woman and mother."

"Thank you," Thérèse said earnestly to her. "It's because I had a very good example."

The two women smiled at each other, Madeleine through her tears, then hugged each other tightly.

"I love you, *Maman*," Thérèse whispered to her mother.

"I love you too, my daughter."

France

40

August 1939

It was summer and Thérèse was sitting outside in her garden in London, surrounded by the beds of roses and hydrangea that she had planted herself, watching her children entertain themselves. David and Evie were playing a version of soccer on the lawn, and Vivienne, the youngest, was sitting beside her mother, reading a book.

"We should include Vivienne in our game," said Evie, trying to be kind and involve their young sister.

"No," David replied scornfully. "She doesn't know how to play soccer. She'd ruin it!"

David had grown up into a strapping young man. Handsome and tall, he had followed in his father's footsteps and joined the army. The young women loved him, finding his dark eyes and curly black hair very attractive and his charming manner appealing, but he had decided to make the army his career, even if it meant going overseas. His childhood swagger had only increased over the years, and he still liked to get Evie blamed for his misdemeanours as much as possible.

Evie, on other hand, had grown up to be a sweet young woman who never recognized her own outer beauty. She wore glasses and was very conscious of the Gallic nose that she had inherited from Thérèse. She never felt herself to be adequate, perhaps as a result of the unkindness she had suffered at the hands of Aunt Agatha and from feeling overshadowed by her brother. Thérèse tried to make up for it by being even more loving and gentle towards her older daughter, but Evie still struggled with her self-confidence. She was a very kind person, filled with empathy, and always going out of her way to help people who needed it, never putting her own needs first.

Vivienne had been born at the end of February, two months after Thérèse returned from Mauritius. She was a bright, sunny little girl who was the apple of her father's eye. She was very clever and did well in school but also had a sense of humour and a twinkle in her eyes. She was twelve years old now and showed promise of a beauty like her mother's in her dark eyes and hair. Her older brother regarded her as a "nuisance," but she didn't seem to care about his opinions. Evie mothered her, as she did everyone, and Vivienne sometimes appeared a little spoiled.

Thérèse herself had become an adept and organized housewife, keeping the home operating smoothly during the day while her husband went to his civil service job. Emmett had been promoted several times, and was now able to afford little luxuries, like new machines for the household and pleasant holidays on the European continent. He had recently invested in a Marconi, a large contraption with knobs that sat on the floor of the living room like a piece of furniture and emitted news and music all day long, from nine a.m. to nine p.m. It was also referred to as a "radio," and he and Thérèse liked to listen to the news stories every evening after dinner.

Unfortunately, clouds were gathering once more in Europe, and the threat of war was again hanging over the western world. Germany had risen like a phoenix from the ashes of the Treaty of Versailles and a new, charismatic leader named Adolf Hitler had emerged as their leader. He had rebuilt the German economy, which had been left in tatters after the Great War, and provided jobs for the people. Their economy was now booming, and a car called the "People's Car" had been developed that was affordable enough that all Germans could own one. Hitler had inspired his people to a great sense of nationalism, but at times it seemed ominous. He harangued them with long speeches on the radio, and they loved him all the more for it, sometimes driven almost to hysteria by his words. He seemed determined to revive the German sense of national pride and to once again assert the nation's dominance over the rest of Europe.

With the renewed vigour of the country came a whole new mindset, that of growing borders for the German people, and this meant invading other countries. Austria had been first, and then Sudetenland. Hitler and his new party, "The Nationalist Socialist Party" (or "Nazis"), were fascists, despite the name of their political organization. There was talk of extreme racism being practised in the country, particularly against the Jews. Many Jewish people had their businesses raided and had been forced out of their homes. Britain had tried to negotiate with Hitler on behalf of the countries that had been invaded, and to rationalize with him that he shouldn't think of trying to invade the shores of their island. In fact, the Prime Minister, Neville Chamberlain, had gone over to sign a peace treaty with Hitler and come back, saying that he had achieved "peace in our time." Emmett felt that this was based on false hope and that Chamberlain was naïve and a fool. He wasn't alone in thinking this.

"Germany won't give up trying to dominate the world just because Chamberlain got Hitler to sign an agreement," he told Thérèse after the news announcement. "The old imperialism has never gone away. We should expect another war before very long."

Thérèse frowned, but she had to agree with him. She remembered how quickly things had changed for herself and her family in 1914. A shiver went through her at the thought of her son being in the army during a war, but she dismissed it. As a strong, fit young man, David would do his part.

Life in England had been good to Thérèse. She had a pleasant social life outside of her household, had become very good at playing bridge and often had tea with the ladies in their neighbourhood, including Addie, who seemed to have given up alcohol and now drank only tea. Thérèse had also met several wives of civil servants through Emmett and enjoyed having tea and the occasional dinner out, as well as dinners with other couples. Her English by now was very fluent, although she retained a slight French accent which most people found attractive. She was still slim, in spite of having had three children, and liked to dress as stylishly as was affordable on Emmett's government salary. Pangs of homesickness for the island of Mauritius occasionally assailed her, but she was mostly happy with her life.

Aunt Agatha had died when Vivienne was four years old, and Thérèse had nursed her until the end. After the incident with Evie and the coal cellar, the old lady had become a little kinder to the children, and she was especially fond of the youngest. Her memory continued to fade as senility set in, and she was eventually like a little girl herself. Thérèse helped her dress and even fed and bathed her, making sure she was comfortable in her armchair during the day and in her room at night. Although it was something of a relief to her when the old lady fell asleep in her chair one afternoon and didn't wake up, Thérèse always did what was expected and looked after her.

As the years had gone by, Thérèse became aware that her intuition was getting stronger. She always knew when there would be a letter from home, or a phone call, and she could usually tell when a newly pregnant young woman was expecting. She had often surprised young brides by telling them that their family was about to expand, and they would reply that they barely knew themselves.

Later that afternoon, she was standing at the kitchen sink, preparing vegetables for the evening meal. David and Evie were doing a jigsaw puzzle at the table, and Vivienne was sitting on the floor, playing a game of jacks.

All of a sudden, Thérèse had a strong feeling that someone was standing behind her. She put her paring knife down and turned around, and there stood her cousin Raoul from Mauritius, the cousin who had been in love with her and asked her to marry him. She hadn't seen him for many years, but he still looked young and stared at her with his piercing dark eyes. She was taken aback, and her heart started racing. She hadn't seen him come into the kitchen and wondered how he had got into the house.

"Raoul!" she exclaimed. "What are you doing here?"

He continued to look at her without replying, but his facial expression changed to one of sorrow and his mouth twitched a little.

"Raoul," she repeated in a faint voice, drying her hands on her apron and reaching out to touch him. Somehow, her hand missed reaching his arm and she began to question herself. Was it really Raoul, or was she going crazy?

He slowly turned away from her, then moved towards the scullery and out through the back door, which was open. Thérèse ran after him, but he was nowhere to be seen. She called his name a few more times then, confused, went back into the kitchen.

"Did you see that man, David?" she asked. "Evie, did you see him?

"What man, Mummy?" asked Evie, looking puzzled.

"The man who was just here."

"There was no man here, Mum. Is that who you were talking to?" David said. "I thought you must have an imaginary friend."

Thérèse frowned. What had just happened? Was David right? Did she imagine him? She couldn't explain the situation, as she hadn't seen her cousin for many years and she certainly hadn't been thinking about him. She decided that she must have been having a daydream, shook her head and resumed her meal preparations. She dismissed the thought and forgot about it until later.

That evening, over dinner, Emmett turned to her.

"Sorry, darling, I had a telephone call from Mauritius today and I forgot to tell you about it."

"What?" Thérèse immediately started to panic. "Is *Maman* alright?"

"Yes," he hastened to assure her. "That's who phoned. She said she couldn't reach you here."

"I must have been outside with the children."

"Yes, he said slowly, taking her hand. "Well, she called with some sad news." He hesitated slightly, then continued in a solemn voice, our cousin Raoul died yesterday."

Thérèse's hand went up to her mouth. But she had just seen Raoul in the kitchen this afternoon! She stared at Emmett for a few moments before answering him.

"I saw him today," she stuttered. "He came into the kitchen to visit me."

Emmett looked confused.

"But you couldn't have," he answered her. "I told you, he died yesterday. They're burying him the day after tomorrow. Your mother wanted me to tell you."

The colour drained from her face as Thérèse realized what had happened that afternoon. All those intuitions she had had over the years, the premonitions of people dying, of letters arriving from home, of the children she was carrying even before she started showing, were all part of a gift that she possessed. A gift that came from another world, and which she had heard about from some of the servants back home. She suddenly felt herself blessed in some way, but also cursed, as it wasn't always a good thing to know what the future holds. Obviously, Raoul had come to say goodbye to her after his passing, and she wondered whether she would receive other visitations from souls who were on their way to the next world.

Over the years, she did in fact have many visitations from loved ones when they died. They always gave her a feeling of peace, and she was never afraid of them. She learned that the gift she had was called being "psychic," and although she didn't tell many people about it, she did share the knowledge with some of her family members. Some believed her, some didn't. Emmett remained sceptical when she told him that she had seen Raoul that afternoon, but he eventually came to accept that his wife saw and knew things that most other people didn't. She had surprised him on many occasions by predicting events accurately that soon came to pass. It was just another thing about his wife that he admired.

The summer passed quickly, and Emmett's words about Germany came true. In the beginning of September, Hitler's troops invaded Poland and refused to respond to demands by Britain and France to leave. War was declared by the Allies on September third, and the British were asked by the sitting government to prepare for future air raids. A blackout was announced, and Thérèse hastened to put up dark curtains on all of the windows of the house. Prime Minister Chamberlain urged people to avoid places of entertainment and crowds, unless it was to attend church.

This was going to be a very different war for Thérèse. The Great War had been something in the distance, which she learned about only through letters and the fact that her brothers had gone away to fight. This time, the war was a lot closer and affected her and her family much more obviously. The war would be fought in neighbouring Europe and might even end up on British soil. She quickly adapted to the new rules brought in by the government and listened carefully to the news every night to learn of the day's events. Many people felt it was only a matter of time before Hitler invaded France, then set his sights on the island kingdom to the north.

41

May 1940

The war continued. After invading Austria and Sudetenland, Hitler had decided that he needed yet more "living room" for the German people. Over the course of the last six months, he and his armies had walked into Luxembourg, then Holland and Belgium, and occupied all three countries. Britain and France continued to oppose him, but the United States was reluctant to engage. They had been practising "isolationism" and preferred to sit on the sidelines and observe what was happening in the rest of the world before deciding to declare war on Germany. They had only just recovered from a devastating depression, which had lasted throughout the thirties, and weren't anxious to become embroiled in a costly war and to risk the lives of many young Americans, despite the pleas of the new British Prime Minister, Winston Churchill.

The world situation had affected Thérèse's family, as it had many others. David went off to Europe with the army and returned on a short furlough in November to announce that he and a fellow female soldier, Sylvia, who was stationed at his base, had decided to get married. It wasn't uncommon for young people to make the precipitous decision to get married during the war, but it was often disastrous. Thérèse had been dismayed when she was told, although Emmett had taken it in his stride. She felt that her handsome young son was very popular with the girls but could have done much better than to marry the first one he met overseas, especially after only knowing her for about six weeks. Evie declared her intentions of joining the W.A.F. (Women's Air Force) and, although Emmett was very proud of his daughter, Thérèse, like her mother before her, worried about her children. She felt that Evie would probably be safe working in an airport in England, but she had fears for her son out in the field. Vivienne was still only a child, and so was able to remain at home with her parents.

"It's not going to be long before the Germans march into France," Emmett told Thérèse. "It's just a matter of time. They won't be able to hold out for long against Hitler's determination and his well-trained army."

Thérèse believed him, but she didn't think that it was imminent. She was sure that the French army would have the wherewithal to fight off the Germans if they tried to invade, and her cousin who lived in Normandy assured her that everything possible was being done to achieve a peaceable arrangement for France with Germany. However, she could hear the uncertainty in her young relative's voice.

Her cousin Hélène was the daughter of her mother's youngest brother, Alphonse. During the early thirties, she and her husband had moved from Mauritius to France, where he had been a soldier in the French army. They had settled in Normandy, where she gave birth to a son.

Hélène had been writing to Thérèse and begging her to come to visit for a long time. This year, she had increased her requests to her cousin to come and see her. Her son was ailing, and she wanted the reassurance of an older and more experienced relative to care for him. Thérèse, being very fond of her cousin, was very eager to go and see her. It had been too long since they'd been together.

Thérèse talked to Emmett about going over to France in May, but he wasn't happy with the idea.

"There's a war on, darling. It may not be safe there," he told her.

"But I haven't seen Hélène for such a long time, and I really miss her," Thérèse explained, dismayed at his objection. "And I've never even met her husband and son."

"It's probably not safe over there," he repeated. "And we'll miss you here."

Thérèse was becoming impatient with his concern for her well-being.

"But it would only be for a few days, and people are still going to and from France safely," she countered.

"Well, we need you here," he replied firmly.

She had let it go for a while, but Hélène kept up her requests for Thérèse to come to France. The latter, never able to ignore an invitation, especially from a family member, wavered back and forth but was becoming more and more anxious to see her cousin.

In the middle of May, she received another letter from Hélène, once again asking Thérèse to come and see her. She felt that she had let down her cousin down, as she had implied in her last letter that she had been working on Emmett to let her go to France.

"My cousin really wants to see me," she implored him, tears pricking her eyes.

"But I told you, there's a war on," he replied in a determined tone, looking at her firmly.

"There's no war there yet," she answered him. "Please, I'll only be gone for a few days, just long enough to get acquainted with her family and spend some time with Hélène."

Emmett frowned but knew that he couldn't hold out for long against his insistent wife. She always knew how to get around him, and he knew that he couldn't change her mind once she got an idea in her head. He threw up his arms in despair, and she hugged him before rushing to sit down and write to Hélène.

"I'll be there as soon as I can," she wrote. "I'll take the ferry to Calais and can then get a bus to your village. I'll plan to buy a ticket by the end of the week."

She finished her note, signed it, then put it in an envelope and went to the post box to send it.

Her next stop was Addie's house, where she asked her friend to watch Vivienne after school for a few days while Emmett was at work. Addie agreed, but not without some hesitation when Thérèse told her she was going over to France.

"It will be nice for you to have a little holiday, Thérèse," she said, taking Thérèse's hand in hers and smiling at her. "But aren't you're risking your safety by going over there?"

"Oh, I don't think I'm risking anything, Addie," she replied. "There's no war in France yet."

"But the Germans are getting closer, and people keep disappearing. I'm always hearing about it from my family in Europe."

"I'm sure I'll be fine," Thérèse reassured her, patting her hand. "I won't stay long. I'm sure I'll be back in a week".

Addie looked doubtfully at her but kissed her warmly on the cheek.

"Well, don't worry about your little sweetheart," she assured Thérèse. "I'll take good care of her here, and you'll be back before she even starts to miss you."

Thérèse smiled. "I'll try not to worry," she told Addie. Then, bidding her friend goodbye, she went home to start the business of booking a ferry to France and letting her family members know what she was up to.

After Emmett left for work the next day, Thérèse telephoned Dover long distance and booked a passage on a ferry to Calais for two days' hence, then walked up to the nearby Underground station, which was known as the "Tube," and inquired as to what would be the best way of getting to Dover from her home. She was told that a tube to Victoria station would get her a train to Dover, and she could easily get on the train unless she wanted to travel first class. She then returned home to pack her suitcase and await her opportunity to tell Emmett about her travel plans.

As she knew he would be, he was reluctant to let her go and tried once again to dissuade her. She remained adamant, however, and he eventually gave up, especially when Vivienne joined in and started begging her mother to let her go with her.

Thérèse told her daughter firmly that this was not an option for a thirteen-year-old girl who was in school during the day, and Vivienne started to pout. However, when her mother told her that she could spend her days at Adelaide's house while her father was at work, she soon cheered up. The rules were very lax at Addie's house, and Adelaide usually let her do whatever she wanted and cooked her anything that she asked for.

With her family informed of her plans, Thérèse finished her packing that evening and, after getting ready for bed, slipped in beside a waiting Emmett, who immediately wrapped his arms around her.

"You be careful, my darling," he told her, kissing her lovingly on the forehead. "I need the mother of my children to come home to me in one piece."

"Don't worry about me, Emmett," she reassured him. "The war hasn't spread to France yet, and I know I can get back quickly, if I need to. There are still ferries going back and forth."

"Well, I'll miss you terribly," he said, squeezing her tightly against him.

"I'll be back before you've even noticed I'm gone," she teased, kissing him gently.

He pulled back and looked at her earnestly.

"I love you very much, and you're very precious to me. You know that, don't you?" he asked.

She nodded, and he began to kiss her, pushing her back against the pillows then gently rolling her underneath him. He paused for a moment, leaned over and turned off the bedside lamp, then returned to kissing her passionately.

42

Thérèse left the house the next morning at nine o'clock, having kissed Emmett goodbye as he went off to work, then seeing Vivienne off to school. She walked up to Addie's house with the child's suitcase in her hand and knocked on the front door, depositing the case on the doorstep.

Addie answered quickly and smiled at her friend as she opened the door.

"You've brought her things, have you?" she asked, taking the case from Thérèse.

"Yes, everything's there, including some puzzles and her favourite book," Thérèse replied.

"What time's the ferry?" Adelaide asked her.

"Two o'clock this afternoon."

"Well, darling, you be very careful," admonished Addie. "I know France hasn't engaged with Germany yet, but it probably won't be long, and you don't want to get caught in the middle of it."

"I'll be fine," replied Thérèse, not feeing quite as confident as she sounded. She had been aware of a niggling feeling in the back of her mind since she woke up this morning and she was starting to think that her intuition was trying to warn her of something.

"Keep your eyes and ears wide open as to any mention of troops being spotted and get the hell out of there if they are," warned Addie.

"Don't worry, I will," Thérèse reassured her, giving her friend a quick hug. She then turned back to the door. "Well, I must be going. I've got a train to catch."

Addie smiled and kissed her on both cheeks, wishing her well. Thérèse went down the steps and began the short walk to the Tube station at the end of her street.

She arrived at Victoria Station at around ten o'clock and went to the ticket booth to buy a return passage to Dover, on the coast of England. The ferry would take her to Calais in France and she would take a bus to her cousin's little village. She was excited at the prospect of seeing Hélène again and catching up with all her news, as well as meeting her husband and little son.

When the train arrived, she found an empty second-class compartment and put her suitcase up on the luggage rack. Sitting down on the hard leather seat, she took a newspaper out of her handbag and began to read about the latest developments in Mr. Churchill's ongoing discussions with the French president. A few minutes later, the sliding door of the compartment was opened and there stood two English soldiers in uniform.

"Do you have room for us in here?" asked the taller of the two, a nice-looking young man with sandy hair and blue eyes.

"Yes, I do," replied Thérèse, indicating the seats opposite her.

"Thank you," he nodded his head and then motioned to his companion to follow him. His fellow soldier was dark in complexion and had a serious, studious look about him.

They made themselves comfortable on the seats by the window, after stowing their backpacks in the luggage rack. After a few minutes, the sandy-haired one turned to Thérèse and said,

"Do you mind if we smoke?"

Thérèse shook her head. Smoking was still allowed on trains and buses in those days, and she was quite used to Emmett's smoking at home. Her father had always smoked a pipe, and Thérèse had grown up with the familiar smell of tobacco. She had once in a while been known to take a cigarette out of Emmett's packet and smoke it herself, although she never inhaled the smoke. It was considered very sophisticated for a woman to smoke cigarettes in the 1940s, and Thérèse enjoyed the air of elegance she felt it imparted to her.

She thanked the young soldier and reached for a cigarette. He lit it for her, then smiled.

"Sergeant Izzy Stornaway," he said, offering her his hand to shake. "And this is Corporal Charlie Leavitt."

He indicated his bespectacled companion, who smiled shyly at Thérèse and nodded his head.

"We're with the British Expeditionary Force," explained Izzy. "Going to join our companions in Dunkirk."

Thérèse had heard of the Expeditionary Forces. They had been stationed in northern France by Churchill to keep an eye on the German army's possible intentions of invading France.

"My husband was in Mauritius in the Great War," she told the young men, by way of explaining her own connections to the British army. Both of their faces immediately lit up with interest.

"Did he see any action?" asked Izzy.

"Oh, no," she said. "There wasn't any there. He was the quartermaster at the British army base."

The soldiers both smiled indulgently, a slight expression of smugness on their faces.

"We expect to see some action before very long," replied Izzy. "Churchill thinks Hitler will move very soon to occupy France. Why are you going there?"

"I have a cousin with a sick child who wants me to come and visit. I promised to help her take care of the little one for a few days."

Charlie spoke for the first time. He looked serious.

"Well, don't linger too long," he warned. "It could be only a matter of a few days before France is occupied."

Thérèse once again had that bad feeling deep down and wondered whether she had been foolish to take on this holiday. Emmett had tried to warn her about the dangers of visiting France, and she had ignored him. Perhaps she should have declined her cousin's requests to come and see her, considering how perilous this visit might turn out to be. She dismissed her fears and turned her attention back to the young men.

She chatted with the soldiers all the way to Dover, telling them about her family and her upbringing in Mauritius. They seemed very interested and quizzed her on her life on a tropical island and what it was like to live on a sugar-cane plantation. She went on to tell them about her husband and children and how pleasant their lives had been in England until war was declared.

In turn, they told her about themselves and their short careers so far in the army. They had up till now only been posted to an English army training base, but they were looking forward to being in Europe and seeing some action soon. They seemed eager to be involved in the fighting, and Thérèse thought back briefly on her brothers who had been in the French army, particularly the two whom she had lost and Dominic, who still suffered with shell shock. She had a feeling that these two young men had no idea what they were in for.

The train arrived in Dover at one o'clock, giving Thérèse an hour to find the dock for the ferry she was to take and to board. Izzy and Charlie offered to accompany her to the docks so that she wouldn't lose her way, and she accepted their offer gratefully. It had been a while since she'd taken a ferry to the continent and she wasn't sure she remembered how to get to the right dock. Although she was going to Calais and the two soldiers to Dunkirk, their boat was leaving later than hers and they were very gallant in offering to show her the way. They hadn't exactly flirted with her on the journey down, but they seemed glad to have her company and it certainly made the journey go faster. Izzy carried her suitcase while they walked to the busy docks from the train, and Charlie led the way, parting the crowds and indicating their path as they walked. When they finally arrived at the dock for Calais, Thérèse collected her ticket, then turned to the two young men.

"Well, thank you very much for accompanying me," she told them with a warm smile. "I'm really grateful for your help, and your companionship on the train."

Izzy smiled back and held out his hand to her once again.

"It was very nice to meet you, Thérèse," he said. "Maybe our paths will cross again. Who knows? Bon voyage!"

"And to you both," she replied. "Have a safe journey, and good luck with the Germans, if you should meet any."

"I think it's inevitable," he answered, smiling.

She smiled back and then shook hands with Charlie, who reminded her once again not to stay too long in France in case things suddenly changed. She waved to them as she turned to go up the gangway to board the big ferry boat.

Once aboard, she went below deck to the ship's café and ordered a ham sandwich and a pot of tea. All she had had on the train was cigarettes and some coffee which was brought round, and she realized that she was hungry.

She found a booth by a window and sat down to eat her lunch, making a mental note of the time and wondering how long the crossing would take. It was slated to be two hours and, once she arrived in Calais, she would look for a bus to take her to Hélène's village of Yvetot. She was curious to see her cousin after so many years, and to meet the man she had married and their little boy. She stared out to the calm sea and cloud-dotted sky, pondering what was awaiting her in France. Would it be a pleasant stay with her cousins, or a fraught need to flee the country as quickly as possible?

43

Thérèse alighted from the bus later that afternoon after an uneventful crossing and immediately started to look for the address her cousin had given her. The village was small, with many quaint little houses along cobbled streets and people wandering in and out of the small shops dotted along the way. She stopped a passerby to ask for directions and was delighted to be able to speak French once again. She used to speak it with her children, but little Vivienne had decided at the age of six that she didn't want to speak a "foreign" language anymore, so Thérèse only had the chance to speak it when she telephoned home to Mauritius.

The gentleman who gave her the directions looked like an old fisherman, with his big raincoat and weathered face, and he regarded Thérèse curiously as he recognized that she wasn't from the area. Having lived in London for so many years, she had forgotten about the curiosity of people in small villages when it came to strangers.

The day was grey and cool, and she felt a few spatters of rain on her face and head as she walked in the general direction of her cousin's house. Eventually, she came to a winding street with small, charming houses on either side, some of them with thatched roofs.

She arrived at number 42 and, with mounting excitement, rapped twice on the door that had a large brass knocker on the outside. After a few moments, she could hear muffled footsteps, and then the door was thrown open. There stood her cousin.

"Thérèse!" exclaimed Hélène, throwing her arms around Thérèse's neck and pulling her inside. "It's so wonderful to see you. Thank you so much for coming all this way!"

Her cousin had matured from the young girl she remembered back in Mauritius. She was a short, pretty woman with dark hair who reminded Thérèse somewhat of her own mother. Hélène was in her twenties now and looked very much the young matron. Thérèse thought that the family resemblance was strong.

"My pleasure, darling," replied Thérèse, looking around at the small living room area. At that moment, a tall, pleasant-looking man came down the stairs with one hand outstretched.

"This is my husband, Lucien," said Hélène. She gazed lovingly at the big man, whose height was in stark contrast to his tiny wife. He had straight brown hair and warm hazel eyes.

"Thank you for coming to visit our family," he said earnestly, clasping her hand. "But I must warn you, rumour has it that the Germans are on their way to France, with every intention of occupying us. They say it could happen any day now."

Thérèse was taken aback. Emmett had been right! Things were more precarious than she had thought they were.

"Well, what will you do, if that ends up being true?" She asked him, nervously.

"We should all leave as quickly as possible," he replied. "Perhaps we could go back to England with you?"

"I could get reservations for all for us on the ferry to Dover in fairly short order," said Thérèse, after a moment's hesitation.

"Now let's not assume it will come to that," Hélène hurried to interject. "Things may be just fine, and you'll be able to get home safely before anything happens, Thérèse."

Thérèse nodded, somewhat comforted.

"Can I meet your son, then?" she inquired.

Hélène motioned to Thérèse to follow her up the stairs. She led her to a tiny bedroom at the end of the hallway and opened the door wide, to reveal a little boy with a thatch of dark hair. He looked to be about seven years of age and was lying in his bed with a book in one hand.

"Christophe," murmured Hélène quietly. "Here's your Aunt Thérèse who's come to visit you."

The little boy turned his head and gazed seriously at Thérèse. Seeing his thin, pale face, Thérèse got the impression that this child was quite sickly and frail. She smiled warmly at him.

"It's very nice to meet you, Christophe," she said, sitting down on the bed. "How are you feeling today?"

"Oh, not very well, but I'll be better soon, I think," he told her. He had quite a mature air about him for a young child, as only children often do.

"Yes, well, we'll see what we can do for you," she replied. She looked over his head at her cousin, who had a worried expression on her face.

After they left the room, she asked Hélène if she knew what was wrong with her son.

"Just a general weakness," was her answer. "He coughs often and sometimes has a fever. We never know how he'll be from one day to the next."

"Well, we should make him some good, hearty soup and a chest poultice and see what good that does him," said Thérèse.

"Yes, but with food rationing, it's difficult to make good soups anymore," Hélène told her anxiously. "We've been very limited in what the government allows us for food."

"Yes, I suppose you have," Thérèse said. "We have rationing too in England, but it's not bad at the moment." She then added, "It's probably going to get worse, though."

"Count on it," answered her cousin with a grim expression.

After a quick *apéritif*, the family sat down to a simple meal of chicken and potatoes, then Hélène took a plate up to her son. Lucien excused himself from the table and went outside to tidy up some items in the back garden, and Thérèse took her suitcase to the little bedroom that Hélène had assigned her at the back of the house and unpacked.

She spent some more time with Christophe that evening, reading him a bedtime story and getting to know him a little better. He seemed quite reserved with her at first, but warmed towards her and was smiling by the time she wished him a good night.

The morning dawned sunny and warm, fitting for mid-May. Thérèse got up early and joined Hélène and her husband, who were already up for breakfast. The two women mostly gossiped about various members of their family and, in particular, Thérèse's mother's decision to leave her husband and move to the island of Réunion with her youngest daughter. Hélène had been somewhat scandalized when she first learned of her aunt's defection to the island, but Thérèse hastened to reassure her that there was a good reason for that. Lucien looked rather amused when he heard the details of the story, but sympathized with Madeleine when he learned of the reasons behind her actions.

After breakfast, Lucien announced his intention of going into the village to see what he could find out about the progress of the German army, and whether there was a possibility of an occupation of France coming any time soon. He thought that his friend Grégoire might be able to provide some information, as he had some connections to people who seemed to know the Germans' movements.

Thérèse offered to go up to Christophe's room and take him his breakfast, then see if she could encourage him to sit outside for a while in the warm sunshine. She told her cousin that sunlight and fresh air were good for people who weren't feeling well, especially if they had problems with their chests.

"Whatever you'd like to do for him is fine, Thérèse," Hélène told her gratefully. "I've saved the bones from last night's chicken, so we can make soup from them."

"Good," replied Thérèse. "I'll put them on to boil this morning while we're sitting outside."

Hélène nodded and began tidying up the kitchen from breakfast. Thérèse made a pot of hot tea for Christophe, then poured some porridge into a bowl and added a couple of slices of *baguette* to a tray and took it up to him.

The day went by quickly, and Lucien returned in the early evening from his friend's house, looking very worried.

"Grégoire feels that the Germans are only about a day away!" he announced, running his hand through his hair in an agitated manner. Hélène gasped and put a hand up to her mouth.

Thérèse quickly realized what would happen if they lingered too long in the little village. Things were getting dire, after all! Once the Germans arrived, there would be no leaving France. She knew they had to act fast. She owed Emmett an apology for doubting his warnings.

"Do you think it's true?" asked Hélène in a faint voice.

"You realize what this means, don't you?" Thérèse asked her, ignoring the question.

"What?" asked Hélène, looking terrified.

"We must leave as soon as possible," she told them urgently. "We'll get to Calais as early as we can, then take the first ferry back to Dover. Can you be packed and ready to go by tomorrow morning?"

Hélène and Lucien looked at each other, and Hélène's blue eyes filled with tears.

"So you'll take us with you, Thérèse?" asked Lucien, gratefully. "But what about the house? And the things we leave behind? We can't take it all with us."

"You'll just have to leave it," Thérèse replied. "Take the things that mean the most to you and leave the rest."

"I think, at this point, that the Germans can have whatever is left," Lucien said decisively. "It won't be any use to us if we can't come back here again."

Thérèse nodded, but felt helpless for the first time as Hélène threw herself into her husband's arms and sobbed openly. Thérèse patted her cousin's arm gently, then told the two of them that she would repack her suitcase, and go to say goodnight to Christophe. However, she would leave it to his mother to tell him of their plans.

She went to bed with trepidation that night, wondering what the following day would bring. She had lived through a war before but had never been this close to danger. She thought of Emmett and her daughter at home and wondered how they would receive the news if she wasn't able to return to them. She wished she had listened to Emmett and not come to France, but now she could help her cousins get out of the country before it was occupied. It might be a hazardous journey. However, at the back of her mind she felt that everything would be alright if they just kept their heads and proceeded calmly. Their lives depended on their ability to carry out the escape plan.

44

Thérèse woke at five o'clock the next morning, unable to sleep any longer. She had heard the sound of the old milk horse's hooves clip-clopping along the street, and it seemed at odds with the precarious situation that they found themselves in.

She washed and dressed quickly and went downstairs to make some tea. The house was in darkness but, after the tea was brewed, she went upstairs again and knocked on her cousin's bedroom door. She heard muffled sounds from within, then Hélène called out,

"Yes?"

"It's five-thirty, darling. I think you should get up so that we can leave as soon as possible."

"Yes, of course. I'll be down shortly," was the answer.

After Hélène appeared, they hurried through breakfast. Lucien came down soon afterwards, ate quickly, then went outside to check that everything they were taking with them was in the car. The two women woke up little Christophe, who was tired and didn't want to get out of bed. His mother coaxed him gently to get up with a promise to make eggs for his breakfast. He finally swung his thin little legs over the side of the bed and walked haltingly to the door of his bedroom.

"My legs hurt," he said, rubbing his eyes with the back of his hand.

"Here," said Hélène, putting her arm around his little body. "*Tante* Thérèse and I will help you if you can't walk by yourself."

Thérèse went on the other side of him and somehow, between the two of them, they were able to half-lead and half-carry him down the stairs to the kitchen. He looked very pale and coughed several times during breakfast, and Thérèse and Hélène exchanged a worried look between them.

"I hope he'll be alright," said Hélène quietly to Thérèse.

"We'll just have to wrap him in a blanket and carry him as much as possible," Thérèse replied. She was a little concerned that the child wouldn't fare very well on the boat to England. However, she dismissed the thought as she considered the alternative that could be awaiting them.

By 6:30 a.m., they were ready to leave the house. They went outside to a dull, grey morning with no sun. Lucien had loaded their suitcases into the boot of the old Citroën that he kept in the back garden of the house. Thérèse inspected the ancient car with a jaundiced eye. She was worried that it wouldn't survive the journey to Calais and would break down by the side of the road, but said nothing. It was the only mode of transportation available to them for the journey.

Once they installed Christophe in the back seat of the car with his blanket wrapped warmly around him, Thérèse and Hélène got into the car and waited while Lucien did a final inspection of the house, before locking the front door and returning to the car.

"Do we have everything?" he asked Hélène.

She nodded yes, tears once again filling her eyes, while her husband slipped into the driver's seat and started up the engine of the old car. It had a couple of false starts, but eventually gurgled into life, and he put it into gear to start the drive to Calais. It began to rain as they were driving down the road.

They drove through towns and countryside for most of the morning, stopping at a small village along the route to refresh themselves. Lucien announced that he was going to find a bakery and purchase some fresh bread, then proceeded to a cheese shop to buy some Camembert to eat with it. It had been several hours since they had had breakfast, and the food would be welcome. However, he emerged from the cheese shop with a frown on his face, silently opening the car door and getting into the front seat.

"What's the matter, *chéri*?" asked Hélène, concerned by the troubled look on her husband's face.

"The owner of the cheese shop warned me against going to Calais," he announced quietly.

"Why?" asked Thérèse and Hélène, in unison.

"He says that he's heard the Germans are intent on occupying Calais some time in the next week," he replied.

"How did he find that out?" Thérèse answered quickly, feeling a tightness in her throat.

Lucien shrugged. "People talk," he replied. "There's probably an underground organization keeping them informed."

Thérèse had arrived from England via Calais and had assumed they would go back that way. However, they couldn't possibly go there if the Germans were planning on marching into the town, so now they would have to alter their plans. She turned to Lucien.

"What do you think we should do, then?" she asked. Ideas were spinning around in her head, but she thought she should let Lucien voice his opinion first. There was silence.

"We could perhaps try Boulogne?" piped up Hélène. "It's a seaport as well, and we could maybe find a boat there to take us to England."

Her voice quavered on her last words, and Thérèse recognized the anxiety that was once again creeping onto her cousin's face. She was starting to feel something very similar herself.

Lucien ruminated on this for a few moments, then nodded.

"Yes," he replied. "Boulogne isn't too far from Calais. We could probably reach it in about the same amount of time, maybe less."

"Well, the sooner we get there, the better," announced Thérèse. "We need to hurry as much as we can. We should eat our lunch while Lucien's driving."

Hélène agreed, and Lucien said that he could manage to eat his bread and cheese while navigating the route to Boulogne. Once again, he put the old vehicle into gear and proceeded to drive down the road and out of the village.

They pulled into a small town not far from Boulogne later that afternoon. The clouds had cleared up somewhat, and a watery sun was shining out of a pale grey sky. Christophe had announced that he was hungry, and both women needed to use the toilet, so they looked for a hotel or restaurant where they could get food and rest for a short time.

After driving around for about half an hour, they finally located a small hotel with a café that was still open. They seated themselves at a table and, after a few minutes, a waiter approached them with a frown.

"Where are you travellers going?" he asked. "These are not good times to be driving around the country."

"Boulogne," replied Lucien. "We're trying to get to the harbour and find a boat that's going to England."

"I wouldn't do that," the waiter replied quickly.

"Why not?" asked Thérèse, now feeling anxiety starting to grip her.

"The Germans are on their way to Calais, and are marching towards Boulogne as well," he explained.

Hélène gasped and put a hand over her mouth. Little Christophe appeared puzzled, not understanding the fear in his mother's eyes.

"What are we to do?" Hélène asked, speaking in a half-whisper.

The waiter looked around him, then leaned forward and spoke in a quiet, urgent voice.

"The owner of this hotel has some intelligence through an organization that has been working against the Germans," he told them. "He gave me this information this morning. I would try Dunkirk. I believe there are British soldiers stationed there. It's possible they may have one or two boats left that will be going to England tomorrow, or later tonight."

"How far to Dunkirk?" asked Thérèse, always the practical one.

"I'm not sure, maybe eighty kilometres?" he answered. Thérèse knew that was fifty miles.

"That's a long way," said Hélène. "What do we do? Stay here and risk trying to go in the morning, or drive there tonight?"

"I think we should go there now," answered Thérèse, urgently. "We don't know whether France will be occupied tomorrow. We have to get away as fast as we can."

"If you're going to Dunkirk, you'll have to go through Calais to get there," warned the waiter. "You'd better take the back roads, not the highway."

"I know those roads pretty well," said Lucien. "But it will take longer."

"What shall we do, then?" asked Hélène, shakily.

Lucien thought for a few moments, then rubbed a hand over his eyes.

"We'll have to fill up with petrol," he said slowly. "Then try to find a place to stay overnight. I don't think we'll make it all the way there even if we leave now."

The two women looked at each other. The thought of another long drive wasn't appealing, but the idea of being caught in German-occupied France was far more frightening. Thérèse made up her mind.

"We should leave now," she insisted. "We can always find a hotel or *pension* along the way if we can't make the whole drive tonight."

"We can't risk getting caught by the enemy army," put in Hélène, in a panicked voice. "We have to get to England as fast as possible!"

Little Christophe started to cry, although Thérèse was sure he didn't understand the implications of what was happening. She was pretty certain that he could feel the tension among the adults, though, and read the dismay on his mother's face.

"Alright," sighed Lucien. "We'll fill up and get back *en route* right away. Let's just hope we can find a place to stay along the way that isn't already full, and that the old jalopy will make the journey."

They got up from the table, and Lucien told the waiter not to bother taking their food order. He instructed Lucien to wait a minute, then turned towards the hotel kitchen. He returned in short order with a tea towel in which he had wrapped some rolls and a leftover *baguette.* They all thanked him profusely for his kindness, then turned and left the hotel.

Thérèse felt her stomach somersault as they walked towards Lucien's car. The old vehicle had made it this far, but there was no telling what might happen along the road.

They drove throughout the night, the complete blackout in all of the towns along the way making it necessary for Lucien to navigate very slowly and carefully. They went past many villages and towns, and it was especially difficult for him to drive along the narrow roads between towns without any light to guide them. There seemed to be no hotels that were open or willing to take guests after dark, and Thérèse concluded that many other people had had the same idea and were trying to flee France at the last minute. Nobody knew what life would be like under the German regime, but numerous newspaper reports and radio documentaries about other occupied countries had made it sound frightening. People were disappearing, and food was scarce. Absolute adherence to army rule was expected, and reprisals were quick against people who chose to disobey.

At about three o'clock in the morning, Lucien announced that he couldn't drive any more and turned to Thérèse to ask whether she knew how to drive. She shook her head no, and he bit his lip silently. Hélène and Christophe were fast asleep, and he suggested that he should wake Hélène to see whether she could take a turn at driving.

"Why don't we just stop by the side of the road?" asked Thérèse. "If we keep driving through the night, nothing will be open when we arrive in the morning, anyway. You might as well get some sleep before we try to finish the journey."

Lucien hesitated for a moment, then nodded.

"Yes, I think that's the best idea," he replied. "It won't be comfortable, but at least I'll be able to drive again. I don't think I can keep my eyes open much longer."

Thérèse nodded in understanding.

"How much further until we're there?" she asked.

"About an hour, maybe an hour and a half," he told her.

"Well, if I wake up first, I'll wake you and we can continue," she volunteered. "The ferry terminal won't be open much before eight o'clock, anyway, I would think."

Lucien agreed, then pulled over to the side of the road and turned off the car engine. They were on an empty road and were sheltered from view by some tall, leafy oak trees. This was as good a place as any to stop, Thérèse thought. She prepared herself for an uncomfortable sleep in the back of the old car and leaned back in her seat.

"Good night," she said, rolling up her coat and laying her head against the car window, closing her eyes.

"Good night," Lucien replied.

She lay there, eyes closed, unable to sleep for a while. Lucien had fallen immediately into a deep sleep, breathing heavily but not quite snoring. Hélène and Christophe slept more quietly, but she was aware of their even breathing as she tried to quiet her mind. What if they couldn't find a ferry in Dunkirk either and had to remain in France? Would they have to go back to Yvetot? Would they encounter enemy soldiers on the journey back? How long before she would be able to get to England?

Would she ever?

45

Thérèse woke a couple of hours later, her neck and shoulders stiff from leaning up against the car window. She stirred and turned over, trying to straighten her body and bring some feeling back into her numb legs.

The other occupants of the car were still asleep but, looking at her watch, she realized that it was coming up to six o'clock, and dawn was breaking around them. It was chilly in the car, and she pulled her coat tighter around her to try and keep herself warm. Lucien lay with his head on the back of his seat, mouth slightly open and snoring gently.

After hesitating for a moment, she leaned forward and tapped him on the shoulder.

"Lucien," she whispered, then more urgently, "Lucien, it's nearly six o'clock!"

He didn't stir, but she noticed Hélène's eyelashes flutter as she began to open her eyes.

"What's the matter?" she asked, looking at Thérèse in confusion.

"We stopped by the side of the road to sleep for a while, but it's almost six o'clock, and Lucien said it would be another hour or more to reach Dunkirk," she told her cousin. "The ferry dock probably opens at eight, and we really should try to get there as early as possible."

Hélène nodded, then began to gently shake her husband's shoulder and murmur to him softly to wake up.

Lucien slowly woke up, scratching his head and yawning widely. He nodded his head when Hélène reminded of him of where they were and of the necessity for resuming their journey as soon as possible. He shook himself, then put the key in the ignition and started the car engine. The vehicle sputtered into life and, after allowing it to warm up for a minute or two, he put it into gear and pulled out onto the road once again.

The journey continued mostly in silence, all three of them still exhausted from their short sleep. Thérèse was feeling anxious about their ability to leave France at all and wondered what would happen to the four of them if they were unable to get away. Would she be able to get a message to Emmett that she couldn't return home? The possibility filled her with dread, but she dismissed it quickly from her mind. She tried to call upon her intuition to give her an idea of how things were going to go, but it seemed as though her anxiety was in the way of forming a clear picture.

They arrived in Dunkirk shortly after half past seven. The port city was very quiet, the shutters and blackout curtains closed in most of the houses, and very few people were out and about. Lucien drove directly to the docks and found a parking place for them not far from the wharf. He went to get out of the car to purchase their tickets, but Thérèse put her hand on his arm.

"Let me go," she urged him. "You two stay here in case Christophe wakes up and is frightened."

He hesitated, but then nodded, and she pulled her coat on and got out of the car.

"Thérèse, wait," called out Lucien, rolling down the car window.

"What?" she replied, stopping in her tracks. He handed her some rolled-up bills of French francs through the window.

She stuffed the notes in her pocket and began walking towards the ticket area of the port. The silence around them was eerie, disturbed only by the lapping waves and seagulls calling to each other.

Thérèse strode through the doors of the ticket station, feigning a bravado she wasn't really feeling. The building was practically empty, with just a few employees in uniforms milling around rather aimlessly and looking grim.

"*Oui, madame*?" asked a bearded, grizzly-looking official who blocked her further entrance inside.

"I would like to purchase tickets for four people for a passage from here to Dover," she told him. "Would we be able to use them to go to Dover today?"

The official looked blankly at her, then an expression of alarm crossed his face.

"*Non, madame*," he replied, gravely. "Don't you know that the German army is on its way here? There'll be no passages for civilians to England today, from anywhere."

He emphasized the last word, then stared sternly at her as she digested his words.

"But we have to get back to England!" she protested. "My husband is waiting for us there. I'm a British citizen."

"You could be the wife of the British prime minister and I wouldn't be able to help you," he replied firmly.

Thérèse stared at him, open-mouthed.

"No passage whatsoever?"

"No civilian traffic at all," he answered levelly. "The only boats leaving here will be the British army returning to England. They've requested civilian boats from England, as well as naval vessels, to come and take them back. All French boats and ferries are grounded for the moment. Haven't you heard?"

Thérèse shook her head, now very worried.

"I haven't listened to the news. We have a sick little boy with us, and we've got to get him out of France," she insisted.

The ticket official looked impatient, but she could still detect some sympathy in his eyes.

"Well, you'll have to find another way," he said.

"But all we're asking is to just get out of here," she repeated urgently.

"Well, I'm sorry," he replied, ushering her towards the door of the building as he spoke. "You'll have to find somebody else who can help you."

He pushed her out of one of the double doors of the exit, leaving Thérèse standing there, rising panic in her throat. What were they going to do now?

She walked slowly back to the car, a lump starting in her throat, not knowing what she was going to tell her cousin and her family. She had promised to help them to get out of France, and now they were stranded on the coast with no way to get across the water to safety.

She broke the news to them as gently as she could. Lucien swore softly under his breath, and Hélène started to cry again. Her sobs awoke Christophe in the back of the car, who began to wail in sympathy with his mother. Hélène got out of the car and went around to the back to hug her son and try to comfort him.

"What are we going to do?" Thérèse asked Lucien.

"I don't know," he replied, looking rattled. "Drive back to Yvetot, I suppose, and hope we get there before anyone reports us missing. We'll have to stay there for the duration of the war. At least we can be prisoners in our own home, instead of in a strange place." He paused, then added hastily, "And you can stay with us, of course, Thérèse."

They were all silent for a minute. Every prospect seemed bleak at the moment and there was nothing they could say. Finally, Thérèse pulled herself together.

"Well," she suggested. "Perhaps we could find a hotel or restaurant and have some breakfast first. I'm sure everyone's hungry after travelling all night, and the bread didn't really fill the gap. it would be nice to at least wash our faces."

"You don't think we should just start driving right away?" he asked.

Hélène spoke up from the back seat of the car.

"We should stop first," she said. "Christophe must be hungry too, and I think we need to stretch our legs a little."

Lucien shrugged his shoulders and motioned Thérèse to get into the car. They drove around the town for a while before eventually finding a restaurant that was serving breakfast to their guests. Thérèse begged the owner to serve them as quicky as possible before they started their long journey back to the village of Yvetot, and he took pity on them and agreed.

They ate in glum silence, aware that they had failed in their attempt to find a passage back to England, and not knowing what awaited them on the journey back to Hélène and Lucien's home village. The adults tried to conceal their anxiety from little Christophe, who was still blithely unaware of the gravity of their situation.

After breakfast, Thérèse excused herself and went to find the privy in the back garden of the restaurant. She tried not to think of what might lie ahead for herself and her family but concentrated on trying to remain calm.

On her way back to rejoin their table, she noticed a small group of British soldiers sitting at a table in the corner. They must have come into the restaurant while she was outside. One was considerably taller than the others, and there was something familiar about the shape of his head and the sandy hair, cut in military style. As she passed by their table to return to her family, the soldier suddenly looked up and a startled expression appeared on his face.

"Thérèse!" he called out. "It's you, isn't it? Thérèse from the train?"

Thérèse stared at him, scarcely able to believe her eyes. It was Sergeant Izzy Stornaway whom she had met on the train from Victoria Station to Dover, and his friend, Corporal Leavitt, was seated beside him. Of course, they had told her they were heading for Dunkirk. Could it be a stroke of luck to find them here? Thérèse stopped beside them, her heart thudding in her chest as she smiled uncertainly at the young soldiers.

"Thérèse," Izzy said, jumping up out of his seat and extending a hand for her to shake. "What are you doing here in Dunkirk?"

"Sergeant Stornaway," she replied, relief flooding her at finding a familiar face in this unknown town. "I'm here with my cousin's family. We tried to return to Dover yesterday, but we were told not to try and go to Boulogne, or Calais. And now we've heard that there are no boats going to England." The words came rushing out as she explained their predicament.

"Well, it's no wonder, with the Germans advancing on all sides," he said solemnly.

A thought occurred to her. She quickly voiced it before her courage failed her.

"Can you help us get back home?" she entreated. "It's our last chance to get away from here."

The soldiers all exchanged glances as she spoke. Izzy hesitated for a few moments, then turned to his companions.

"We can help this lovely lady, can't we, chaps?" he asked. A couple of them nodded enthusiastically, although one seemed hesitant. Ignoring him, Izzy turned back to her. "We can have a word with our commander, but I don't think he'd deny a British citizen and her family help during these dangerous times. How many of you are there in your party?"

"Four," she answered. "One's just a little boy."

"You go back to your family," replied Izzy comfortingly. "The boys and I are going to sort out what we can do for you."

"Oh, thank you!" Thérèse's heart jumped. To his surprise, she grabbed Izzy's hand and gave it a quick kiss, then returned to her cousin's table with a lightness in her step. This was the best news she'd received since leaving for Calais yesterday. Maybe things were going to turn out alright, after all?

Thérèse explained to Hélène and Lucien what had just happened, and that there was a possibility that the British soldiers might be able to help them to get back to England. Lucien asked her what they could possibly do, but she told him she didn't know yet. She advised him and Hélène to be patient and wait and see what would unfold. Not long after that, the soldiers settled their bill with the waiter, then got up and came over to their table.

Thérèse briefly introduced Izzy and Charlie in French to her family, and the other two soldiers then introduced themselves through her. Izzy leaned forward and, after looking around to make sure that nobody else was listening to their conversation, spoke in a hushed tone.

"As you may know, the British army has requested every able-bodied boat and fishing boat along the coast of England, as well as naval boats, to come over and take us home," he explained to them. "There have been hundreds of volunteers. It's part of Churchill's evacuation of the Expeditionary Forces from France. Apparently, Hitler has issued a stay order against any bombing of our boats."

"The reason you can't get a ferry back to the British Isles is that the French government has agreed to let it happen, in spite of the Germans marching on northern France," interjected Charlie. "No French boats will leave port until it's completed."

"I'm sure our commander will agree to let you come back on one of the fishing boats, once we explain the situation to him," added Izzy.

Huge relief surged through Thérèse and, when she translated into French what he had said to Hélène and her husband, she saw her relief mirrored in their faces. A fishing boat may not be a very comfortable mode of transport, but anything was better than being stuck here and not knowing what might be in store for them. She held herself back from jumping up and hugging the young soldiers in front of everybody, but contented herself with shaking their hands and thanking them profusely. Lucien and Hélène joined in with enthusiasm in French.

"Now, listen," instructed Izzy. "Report to the docks at noon, not a minute later, and we'll see what we can get arranged for you by then. You might have to miss the first couple of boats but, if you're alright to do that, we'll get you on one of them, I'm pretty sure."

Thérèse hastened to assure him they would be there, and she and her cousins left the hotel with a sense of relief and happiness.

46

After spending the morning walking around the town and passing the time as best they could, they arrived at the docks at around half past eleven. There was an air of anxiety everywhere as people went about their business, and Thérèse could sense that the citizens of Dunkirk were getting very worried about their uncertain future as the German army moved towards the port cities in northern France.

They parked the car where they had left it before and removed their suitcases from the boot. Thérèse noticed that little Christophe was looking rather pale, and Hélène put her hand on his forehead with a concerned look when she commented on it.

"I think he's starting one of his fevers," she told Thérèse in a low voice. She wrapped him in the blanket from the back of the car and passed him to Lucien to carry while she took the suitcases from him. Thérèse picked up one of the suitcases, and the four of them walked towards the docks looking like a rather rag-tag group.

When they reached the ticket office, the official once again came to the door and started to admonish Thérèse.

"I told you, *madame,*" he said in a firm voice. "There won't be any boats going to England today."

"We're going with the British forces," she explained to him calmly. "We're just waiting for Sergeant Stornaway. He told us to meet him here."

"Hmmm," the official looked disapproving, but shrugged his shoulders and went back inside, letting the door swing behind him. She heard him exclaim, "*Zut, alors*!" before he disappeared inside.

They waited anxiously at the dockside and, after a little while, spotted the soldiers coming towards them. Thérèse raised her arm and waved at them, hoping against hope that they would have good news. Izzy came up to them and put his hand on Thérèse's arm. He seemed to have quite a bit of pent-up anticipation and talked to her in an urgent tone.

"Our captain has agreed to allow you to come with us, but we're not going to be able to leave from the docks," he confided. "It's too difficult and dangerous for the boats to come in here, and the Germans will be watching the ports, so we're going to embark from the beaches. Are you and your family okay with that? Can you drive to the beach if I tell you how to get there, and just leave the car behind?"

Thérèse looked at her cousin and her husband. She translated rapidly and was happy to see that they were quite willing to go along with the soldier's request. Izzy then looked at the suitcases that she and Hélène were carrying.

"I'm afraid you'll have to leave those, as well," he said. "There simply won't be room on the boats. They're going to be packed to the rafters, as it is."

"Yes, that's fine," she replied. She thought of the clothes and toiletries she had packed in her suitcase but reminded herself that when they were fleeing for their lives they wouldn't be needing those things. She explained the situation to her cousins and, although Hélène wasn't happy to leave with only the clothes on their backs, Lucien soon convinced her that they had to comply or risk being refused a seat on a boat if they didn't.

"That's fine," Thérèse told Izzy. "Explain to Lucien where the beach is, and I'll translate for you, if you need."

Izzy did his best to give Lucien directions in his halting French, with Thérèse chiming in wherever necessary. Within a few minutes, they had stashed the suitcases in the boot of the car, climbed into their seats and were driving towards the beach that Izzy had specified.

After they had abandoned the car, they stood on the beach with another group of civilians. The wind had got up and was whipping Thérèse's hair around. Earlier she had removed several pound notes, a hairbrush and some lipstick from her suitcase and put them in her handbag and, at the last minute, had pulled a silk scarf out and stuffed it in her pocket. She took it out now and tied it around her head.

They waited for a long time. As the hours passed, more and soldiers arrived and formed themselves into long queues to await the passenger and naval boats that would be carrying them. Thérèse hoped desperately that this rescue mission would not be cancelled after all.

Christophe seemed to be getting more sickly as the time went by and was now very pale, lying in his mother's arms and sleeping as they sat on the windy beach. It was quite chilly, and Thérèse hoped the child didn't end up with pneumonia from the cold.

Suddenly, a cheer went up from the soldiers, and several of them pointed towards the sea. A few who had been seated on a breakwater stood up and began to shout excitedly to one another. Thérèse got to her feet and tried to shield her eyes against the sun to look out towards the ocean. Sure enough, she could spot a few black dots on the horizon.

"What is it?" she asked one of the soldiers anxiously. She hoped that it wasn't German troops arriving. But of course not! They wouldn't be cheering if it were.

"It's the English boats coming for us," he replied. "We're going to get out of here. Thank the Lord!"

She turned excitedly to Hélène and Lucien.

"The boats are coming!" she told them, breathlessly. "We're going to be alright."

She tried to see whether she could spy Izzy and Charlie among the crowded troops along the beach, but there were far too many of them and they all looked very similar in their uniforms and caps.

Hélène roused little Christophe, who cried in protest, but stood up as his mother urged him to. They made their way with the soldiers towards the edge of the water and stood patiently waiting for the boats to slowly approach them.

Within half an hour, the vessels had reached the beach, although it felt like an eternity to Thérèse as they waited their turn to be directed towards a boat that would carry them safely away from here. However, she knew how fortunate they were to have gone to that particular hotel for breakfast and that Izzy and his companions were there.

When their turn came, they were shown to a small fishing boat that looked as though it had room for only a few passengers. They were helped into the boat, Christophe carried by a burly sailor, and settled themselves on the wooden benches on the deck. The skipper, Captain Davidson, introduced himself and said they would be leaving very shortly.

"She's only a small boat," he explained, "and it's going to take a long time for us to arrive in England, but she's very seaworthy and my crew are all experienced."

"Where are you from?" Thérèse asked, wondering how far these brave Englishmen, who had risked everything to help soldiers and civilians escape from a very risky situation, had sailed.

"Gosport, Hampshire," he replied.

Thérèse nodded. She knew of the little coastal town, having heard the name being called out by the stationmaster when travelling by train to Southampton.

Lucien, who had been expressing doubts about the ability of some of the vessels to make the voyage to England, seemed relieved, and asked whether his wife and son could sit somewhere where they would be sheltered from the wind. The captain indicated that they could go down to his cabin below decks, but that there wouldn't be much room there for him or Thérèse. Thérèse knew from previous experience that it would get very cold on deck, but she could put up with some hardships now that they were on their way to escaping France. She made a mental note to check on the child every hour or so to make sure he wasn't getting any worse. Her little patient needed to survive this journey in order to make a new life in England.

47

The voyage took up the rest of that day and carried on into the night. They were surrounded by boats in every direction, some of them fishing boats like theirs, some big naval destroyers, and some only tiny tugs and trawlers. Churchill had requested as many vessels moored along the coasts of England as could be spared to lead the British Expeditionary Forces out of Dunkirk, and it would become one of the most famous escapes from the German army in the Second World War. It was code-named "Operation Dynamo" and was a very important event in the history of the war. Looking back over it many years later, Thérèse felt proud to have been a part of it. What she didn't know, and would only find out later, was that the Germans surrounded the town of Dunkirk not long after they left. They had a very lucky escape, which Churchill would later refer to as "a miracle of deliverance." To the end of her life, she always thanked her lucky stars that she had met Izzy and his friend on the train to Dover that day.

She tried to doze off and on during the night, pulling her coat ever tighter around her. She and Lucien had chatted a little at first, but gradually fell into a companionable silence. Blackness descended around eight o'clock in the evening, lit up occasionally by a half-moon that didn't shed much light. She had checked on Christophe inside the captain's cabin a few times, and Hélène reported that, at some point during the evening, he had started to sweat profusely, and that his fever had eventually broken. Thérèse felt his forehead and it was cool again, and she advised her cousin to give him sips of water as often as possible. Hélène found a metal cup half-filled with water in the cabin and was able to get her son to drink from it.

As they journeyed through the night, Thérèse fell asleep and woke up several times, her head against the railings surrounding the boat. She woke up with a stiff neck at one point and realized that she was ravenously hungry. They hadn't eaten since that morning and there was no food on the boat, which had left England in a hurry.

She turned to Lucien, who had also awoken, and asked him if he knew where they were. He pointed towards the horizon. Very faintly in the distance, she could see land by the light of the moon, which had often been shrouded in clouds. A feeling of excitement began stirring in her stomach, along with a huge relief that maybe, just maybe, the worst part of the journey was over and they had escaped occupied France. Although she regretted the risks she had taken in coming to France, she was very glad that she had been able to help her cousin's family get away and start a new life.

Thérèse woke again just before six o'clock in the morning. Dawn was breaking, but now the sky was cloudy and there was no sign of the sun. A slight drizzle was starting to fall, and she stood up and tried to shelter herself under an awning on the deck. She had been aware of the sound of planes occasionally going overhead during the night and thought they were probably British reconnaissance planes making sure that the evacuation was going smoothly.

She stared out to sea for several long minutes, trying to bring herself to full wakefulness and ignoring the gnawing hunger in her stomach. She thought she could again hear the sound of a plane in the distance and then, all of a sudden, there were several popping sounds, followed by a loud bang and a flash of light.

Panic rising, she jumped up and ran towards the sailor who was standing in the stern of the boat looking out on the horizon.

"What was that noise?" she demanded anxiously.

The sailor turned hesitatingly to her.

"It's the Jerries, ma'am. They're firing on some of our boats. It's been going on all night, getting closer now."

Dread replaced the hunger pangs in Thérèse's stomach. The German army were firing on them? But hadn't they escaped from France and were now within sight of British territory?

"Firing on us? But we were told that Hitler had issued a pause order against firing on our boats while we were evacuating! I thought we were safe."

"There's no telling what the bastards will do," the sailor replied grimly. "Excuse me, ma'am, for the language! Still, orders or no, some of them German fighter pilots are eager to kill British soldiers."

Thérèse shuddered. Had they managed to get away from occupied France only to be gunned down in the English Channel while on their way back home? A mental picture of Emmett and their children once again flashed into her mind.

"What can we do?" she asked the sailor urgently. "Are we going to have to jump overboard and swim for it?"

"No, no," he tried to reassure her. "Why don't you and the gentleman join the lady and the young lad in the captain's cabin and try to stay out of harm's way?"

"Don't worry," he added, kindly. "The planes are far away. You're just hearing the sound magnified by the sea and the clouds."

Thérèse nodded. This was cold comfort, but she aroused a sleepy Lucien and quickly explained the situation to him. He came to his senses rapidly, a look of consternation on his face.

"Are we going to get out of here alive?" he asked her, a grim expression on his face.

"I hope so," she answered. "The sailor assures me that the guns are far off, but he suggested we go below deck with Hélène and Christophe."

He agreed and followed her down the steps to the bow of the boat.

Hélène and Christophe were fast asleep, curled up together on the captain's bed, and Lucien put a finger to his lips to warn Thérèse not to wake them. She nodded her head and sat down gingerly on the end of the bed so as not to disturb them. Lucien took up a position by the cabin window and looked out, trying to gauge the distance of the land they had seen earlier.

For the first time in her life, she was mortally afraid. And to think that, only a few hours before, she had been feeling grateful for having escaped! Now, she felt guilty for bringing her cousin and her family into this situation, although she recognized that it would probably have been worse for them to stay in France. Even given the turn events had taken, she knew she would have done the same again. She couldn't leave her cousin and her sick little boy to an uncertain fate in a country occupied by an enemy, with who knows what fate in store.

They stayed below deck for a few more hours, with Hélène and Christophe eventually awakening. There were no more sounds of aeroplanes or distant bombs, and Thérèse felt herself calming down. She tried to keep herself occupied with watching the little boy for any signs of fever returning. Christophe cried when he woke up, and Thérèse felt his forehead and examined his throat. His skin still felt a bit warm to the touch, and his throat looked rather red. She expressed hope to Hélène that he seemed to be a little better than he had been during the night, but privately thought that he should see a doctor as soon as they arrived in England.

The boat ferried on, the rain growing heavier by moments, then lessening again. Lucien acted as sentry by the porthole window of the little cabin, reporting on how much closer the land that he had spotted was getting. Eventually, he pointed excitedly out of the window,

"We're getting close!" he exclaimed. "I can see cliffs in the distance and houses on the shore-line."

Thérèse jumped up to look through the porthole window. It was the white cliffs of Dover he was seeing! A huge sense of relief washed over her. They were finally coming in sight of British soil, and surely there wouldn't be any more German planes flying overhead here? If there were, they would probably be shot down on sight by British R.A.F. fighters.

Shortly after, Captain Davidson came down to the cabin and announced that they would be landing in about half an hour, and

Thérèse and Hélène hugged each other, crying out in relief and excitement. Lucien turned to Thérèse and placed a hand on her shoulder.

"We thank you from the bottom of our hearts, *cousine* Thérèse," he said. "You have saved our lives today and we would never have escaped from France without you."

"It's the least I can do for my family," she replied sombrely. "I'm so happy I was able to help you. I couldn't leave you there with the Germans moving in." She grimaced, adding, "We almost didn't make it, though."

"You risked everything to help us, Thérèse," interjected Hélène, "And we're very grateful."

Thérèse smiled and hugged her cousin again.

"Come on," she said. "Let's go up on deck and watch the landing."

They reached for their coats, wrapped Christophe in his blanket again, and proceeded up the little stairway to the deck, the child carried in his father's arms. Captain Davidson tipped his cap to them and smiled, pleased at having delivered them safely home.

Before they disembarked from the fishing boat, Thérèse thanked the captain and crew sincerely on behalf of herself and her relatives for bringing them safely across the English Channel in difficult circumstances. The captain dismissed her thanks, but looked pleased nonetheless. She told him that if he should ever come to North London, he would have a bed and a hot meal waiting for him.

"Speaking of a hot meal, can you direct us to a nice eating place here in Dover where we can find some breakfast?" she inquired.

The captain told them of a small inn located about half a mile from the harbour and suggested that they mention his name to the proprietor, who would give them a special price for the meal. He shook hands warmly with all of them and wished them well in their travels.

Within the space of about thirty minutes, they had arrived at the inn and were seated at a table in the little café inside, revelling in the warmth of the place and the delicious smell of breakfast cooking. Christophe seemed to have rallied and told his parents that he would eat some porridge if it had golden syrup in it. Thérèse suggested that he drink some hot tea with lemon and honey in it, as well, to help soothe his sore throat. She thought that he definitely looked a little better than earlier in the morning and confided so to Hélène.

After she had finished eating, she excused herself and went in search of a telephone to ring her family. The lady at the front desk of the hotel offered the house phone when Thérèse explained their circumstances and what they had gone through in order to get back to England.

"You don't mind the long-distance charges?" she asked the lady.

"Anything to help the war effort," the lady graciously replied.

Thérèse smiled and picked up the receiver, dialling her telephone number at home.

The phone rang several times, but there was no answer at the other end. She glanced at her watch and realized that Emmett would have already left for work and Vivienne would be on her way to school on her bicycle by now. She dialed Adelaide's number and, after only about three rings, heard her friend's voice on the other end of the line.

"Thérèse?" Addie said, in an anxious tone. "Where have you been? We've all been so worried! There have been reports of the Germans marching into northern France and the ports being closed along the coast of France!"

"It's all true," replied Thérèse. "We managed to escape with the British forces, and some boats even got shot at on the way over."

"Oh, my God, Thérèse!" Addie gasped. "Don't you tell Emmett that! He'll never let you out of his sight again!"

"We're all fine," Thérèse reassured her. "We're going to take the train as soon as we've finished breakfast here, and will be back some time this afternoon."

"Where are you now?"

"Dover."

"Well, you be careful. I'll tell Vivienne and Emmett you're on your way. They'll be so relieved."

Thérèse hung up the phone and walked back into the restaurant to rejoin her family. They finished their coffee and tea and paid the hotel proprietor for their meal, which he duly discounted when hearing Captain Davidson's name. Then they hailed a taxi to the station to await the first train back to London. Fortunately, Lucien had, like Thérèse, thought to put some money in his pockets when they left their suitcases behind, and they were able to pay for the taxi and four train tickets.@@@The train journey seemed to go on forever, but they finally arrived back at Victoria Station. Thérèse herded her family together amongst the crowds on the platform and towards the Underground. There were many soldiers among the civilian passengers at the big station, and Thérèse briefly wondered whether any of them was going to France, or whether they were all returning from Dunkirk, like herself and her family. She searched again for Izzy and Charlie's faces but didn't spot them.

Little Christophe slept as they travelled on the Tube towards her home in North London. She made a mental note to phone Dr. Briggs the next day and get her little cousin seen by the good doctor. She knew he would be in good hands with him, and that he could maybe diagnose Christophe's condition.

Thérèse wondered whether she would be able to find work for Lucien and a place for the family to live in London. It wasn't easy to get work in wartime England, although she thought that Lucien might be able to work in one of the aircraft factories. His lack of English wouldn't be too big a problem if he was doing manual labour. She also thought that maybe Emmett might be able to find him employment with his Civil Service connections. The first priority, though, would be to get the family back to her house and installed in the bedrooms that had been vacated by David and Evie. She knew Emmett would welcome her cousins, and that Vivienne might be happy to have a little boy to play with, although he was quite a bit younger than she was and not very healthy at the moment.

She had a great sense of satisfaction that her mission had been accomplished, and that she could tell her mother in Mauritius that she had been able to rescue Hélène and her family from an uncertain fate in German-occupied France. Thérèse knew she had taken a huge risk in going over there to visit them, but she had no regrets at all, now that it was all over. She recognized that it had been a close shave and, if they hadn't made the decision to leave as soon as they had, things could have turned out very differently. She hoped that someday she would be able to reconnect with Izzy and his friend Charlie to thank them for their assistance in getting out of France. Perhaps Emmett would know how to contact them, once the war was over. After all, that should be within a year, and they surely wouldn't have forgotten her by then!

That night, back home again, as she snuggled against a grateful and happy Emmett, she promised herself that she would never leave his side again. As for Emmett, he had been listening to the news every night and was extremely relieved to have his wife safely returned to him. Nothing except for helping family was worth taking such a big risk, jeopardizing both her safety and her life in England. Little did she know, however, that she would not keep her promise to herself for long.

The German army marched into Dunkirk and put up their Swastika flags over the town on June 4th, 1940. Hitler had conquered France and was now turning his sights to the island kingdom to the north.

48

The bombing had begun.

It had started with several random planes flying over the south coast of England, dropping bombs mostly on fields and pastures. However, as time went on, they became more precise and slowly moved further northward. Wherever possible, the Royal Air Forces retaliated with attempts to shoot the bomber planes down or deliver carefully aimed bombs over Germany. However, the German bomber pilots were learning to become more accurate in their aim, possibly with the help of a new radar weapon, and began to drop bombs over English towns and countryside.

Churchill delivered his famous speech to the British in the House of Commons:

"We shall fight on the seas and oceans, we shall fight with growing confidence and growing strength in the air, we shall defend our island, whatever the cost may be. We shall fight on the beaches, we shall fight on the landing grounds, we shall fight in the fields and in the streets, we shall fight in the hills. We shall never surrender! "

The House roared its approval, and the British people followed suit. They were greatly emboldened by his words and met the slowly approaching German air raids with courage and determination. No one was allowed to gather in public places after dark, and every citizen had a designated air raid shelter to go to. Thérèse's family would be able to go to the local Tube station and descend the escalator to the tunnels below the surface.

Thérèse carried on with her life as though nothing untoward were happening and tried to ignore the sound of the air raid sirens, which could be heard in the distance from various parts of London. Emmett, on the other hand, was growing increasingly concerned for the safety of his wife and the daughter who remained at home.

"It's getting more and more unsafe for you and Vivienne to stay here, darling," he would say, a deep crease across his forehead as he gazed at her anxiously. "The bombs are getting closer to us all the time, and I really don't want you both here if they drop one close to our house."

"What about Hélène and Lucien? Aren't you worried about them too?" she quizzed him one night when they were tucked up in bed, reading.

He looked uncomfortable but answered her question immediately.

"Yes, of course I am," he hastened to assure her. "I can probably find Lucien a job somewhere out in the country where it will be safer for them."

Lucien had been working at Victoria Station as a porter since arriving in London. He was quickly picking up English, and Thérèse was quite impressed with his progress.

"Maybe you could find something for him in a factory?" she asked. "His English is getting quite good, and I'm sure he could do some assembly-line work."

"Yes, yes," murmured Emmett, seeming to dismiss it. "But I want you to go up to the north of England, darling. Many in Churchill's party seem to think that the Germans will try to bomb London to get at him. They know that he's the brains behind the war effort. It's just not safe for you here."

"But what about you?" she searched his face with a concerned expression.

"I've got to stay here, for my job," he replied. "We've got bomb shelters at Somerset, and I'm sure I'll be fine. I'm not so sure about here, though. This house isn't far off the flight path from the coast."

Thérèse bit her lip but didn't reply. She had made herself a promise that she wouldn't leave Emmett again after going off to France and nearly not being able to get back, but for once she felt that she wasn't going to be able to exert her influence over him. His anxiety came out of a place of love and concern for her and Vivienne, and she couldn't argue with that.

"Well," she said. "Let's not worry about it for now. We can talk again when the bombs start getting closer."

Emmett looked at her with exasperation, but turned away and closed his book, preparing to turn out the light.

At the end of August, a raid was conducted by the Germans over London on a Saturday night. It was actually a mistake, as it was intended for an aircraft factory east of the city, but the bomber pilots lost their way and the bombs fell on central London neighbourhoods. There was minimal damage, and few casualties, but it struck real fear into the hearts of Londoners for the first time. The war had suddenly become very personal to many of them, including Emmett, who was sure there were other raids coming, ones much closer to where they lived in the north of London.

He confronted Thérèse about it once again after breakfast one day, when Lucien and Hélène had gone out to the garden with Vivienne and little Christophe. The latter was thriving these days and seemed to be much better since coming to England, perhaps because of Thérèse's vigilance over him.

"I think I want to send you and Vivienne up to Liverpool, darling," he told her. "I have some relatives who live in Southport, and I think you'll like it there. It's a nice little town, and Vivienne can go to one of the schools there. I'll come up and visit wherever possible, and you'll be safe from the bombs."

"You don't think the Germans will bomb the north of England, then?" she asked him.

"No, at least, not for the time being. It depends on how far they're able to advance on this part of the country. I hope that they won't, at all," he added.

"Alright," she answered. "But what am I going to do all day, while Vivienne is at school?"

"You can join the Women's Voluntary Service," he told her. "They're sure to want a clever lady who can speak French and has excellent nursing skills."

She smiled. "Well", she answered. "It's certainly something I should think about. We all need to do our bit for the war."

"You've already done a lot by rescuing a family out of occupied France," he reminded her.

She gave a little laugh, then started to clear up the breakfast things. She had survived the Great War but hadn't been living in a country that was being bombed by the enemy. Perhaps going somewhere to be out of the line of fire wouldn't be such a bad idea, after all. She wasn't ready for it yet, though.

Two weeks later, the beginning of September, there was a huge air raid on London, and this was one was very serious. Houses were levelled, and people were killed. The attack on England had started in earnest, and the enemy was very serious this time. This wasn't intended to bomb aircraft factories but rather, civilians and their homes and places of business. There was no question that they were also targeting the Prime Minister of England, who had succeeded in resisting their efforts so far.

Thérèse and Emmett had hurried the family out of the house as soon as the sirens started, and they all walked as quickly as they could to the Tube station. They stepped carefully down the steps of the inactive escalator and eventually came to the bottom platform of the Northern line.

There were many other people down there, and it was quite cramped. They looked for a space that would fit six people but, after realizing that that probably wasn't feasible, they agreed that Hélène and her family should find their own space, and they would meet up again once the all-clear sounded.

Vivienne seemed frightened so, after she and Emmett had staked out a spot on the train platform that would fit the three of them, Thérèse took her in her arms and hugged her.

"Don't worry, *ma cherie,"* she whispered in the youngster's ear. "It will be alright. The bombs won't be able to reach us down here."

Vivienne looked up at her mother with questioning brown eyes.

"But what if they hit the Tube station, and we're buried alive?" she asked.

"That won't happen," replied Thérèse. "The Germans are looking for the Prime Minister. They'll be bombing Westminster, which is far from here. We'll be going home again in a couple of hours."

As it turned out, Thérèse's reassurance was incorrect. The bombing continued throughout the night, and they had to eventually make themselves as comfortable as was possible on the hard station floor. People came around handing out blankets and hard pillows, and Thérèse gratefully took some for her family.

Vivienne fell asleep around eleven o'clock, and Emmett and Thérèse took turns watching over her throughout the night. Emmett was able to go to sleep during the small hours of the morning, but Thérèse remained awake, nervousness and discomfort denying her slumber. She struck up a whispered conversation with a lady who was with her family on the platform beside them, and they did their best to pass the time talking about their children and their experiences during the Great War.

The all-clear finally sounded at around dawn, and Thérèse leaned over and gave Emmett's arm a shake. Vivienne stirred on her pillow, then smiled up at her mother.

"We're all alive!" she beamed.

"Yes, darling," Thérèse replied. "I told you we'd be alright here. The Germans didn't come to our part of London."

Emmett opened an eye and frowned at his wife.

"Wait until we get outside before you say that," he admonished her.

"Emmett, don't frighten her!" she scolded him. "I'm sure everything will be fine."

Sure enough, when they emerged from the station, everything looked exactly as it had when they went down the night before. However, Thérèse was sure that she caught a whiff of an acrid smell in the air and, towards the southern part of the sky, she saw what looked like smoke.

As they walked home, Emmett clutched her arm and said softly to her, "I'm going to start making some telephone calls as soon as we get home, my dearest. I want you and Vivienne to go up to the north as soon as possible."

She looked at him with reluctance, but she knew that he was right. The time had come to get out of London.

49

Four days later, Thérèse and Vivienne boarded the train at Victoria Station early and found themselves an empty compartment in first class. Emmett had driven them to the station and insisted on buying them first-class tickets. When Thérèse protested, he remained firm.

"My girls should travel in comfort," he said when she pressed him. "It's a long way to Liverpool."

He had hugged them both many times as they waited for the train to arrive and gave them advice on where to shop for food, what times of day telephoning London would be cheaper, and what to do about obtaining ration coupons. He had got in touch with a cousin in Southport, just outside of Liverpool, who he hadn't seen since he had left London before the Great War and who was willing to billet two family members, sight unseen. Emmett had been very grateful and was happy that he didn't have to worry about his "girls," since they would be living in a warm house with adequate food. As the train pulled into the platform, there were tears in his eyes as he kissed his wife and daughter goodbye.

"Take care of yourselves, my darlings," he said in a broken voice. "I'll miss you terribly, but make sure you ring me often."

Thérèse clung to him for a few moments before taking Vivienne by the hand and leading her to the steps going up to the train. This would be the longest time that she and Emmett would be away from each other, and she knew she would miss him terribly. Vivienne was excited by the adventure of a long train ride but blew kisses to her father as she stepped up into the railway carriage.

The journey was expected to last for most of the day, so Vivienne had brought along a sketch pad and some sharpened pencils to keep herself occupied during the train journey. She had shown a talent for drawing in the last little while, and Thérèse encouraged her to do more of it. She herself had brought along a romance novel to read but found herself watching the hypnotic countryside with its patchwork of yellow and green fields and pastures instead, before drifting off to sleep to the rhythm of the train's wheels.

While Thérèse slept, Vivienne contented herself with drawing until she felt hungry. She woke her mother and the two of them walked to the dining-car for some lunch. Thérèse was impressed with her daughter's good manners towards the white-gloved waiter who served them their food. She was pleased that she and Emmett had done a good job of impressing politeness on their children.

After their return to the carriage, Vivienne chattered to her mother about various things, asking many questions about the north of England which Thérèse couldn't really answer. She had never been there and had to rely on Emmett's descriptions of the town of Southport to satisfy her daughter.

"Well, sweetheart," she said, when Vivienne asked her how many people lived in the town and which school she would be attending. "We'll be there soon, so you'll be able to find out for yourself."

They arrived around four o'clock in the afternoon, and Thérèse hailed a taxi after they had departed from the train and found their way out of the big station in Liverpool.

Liverpool was a sprawling city, not as big as London, but just as busy at this time of day. The weather was cool and windy, with a grey sky and clouds that looked as though they threatened rain. The cab journey to the address that Emmett had given them turned out to be about half an hour. Eventually, the driver stopped the car outside a small, brown semi-detached house in a street full of identical houses, then carried their luggage up the garden path. Thérèse and Vivienne followed him and Thérèse rang the doorbell after giving the taxi driver a generous tip, for which he tipped his cap to her.

They heard a dog barking from the interior of the house, but waited for a few more moments before the door rattled from the inside and was opened by a middle-aged man in a pair of tweed pants and a bulky grey cardigan. He was slender and of average height, with thinning grey hair, and wore wire-rimmed glasses.

"I'm Eustace Braithwaite." He offered his hand to Thérèse politely. "Emmett's cousin. Pleased to meet you." He turned to Vivienne, smiling. "And who do we have here?"

"I'm Thérèse, and this is my daughter, Vivienne," Thérèse replied, shaking the proffered hand.

"This is Fred," he indicated the big border collie. "He's a friendly chap, if you just let him sniff your hand and get to know you."

Vivienne giggled, then bent down to hold out her hand to the animal. His tail immediately started wagging, and he snuffled, then licked the child's hand.

"He likes you!" pronounced Eustace. "That's a good start! Well, come on in and meet the wife."

Eustace picked up the heaviest of the suitcases, and Thérèse and Vivienne followed him down the narrow hallway of the house. It was rather drab inside, with dark wood and shabby brown carpeting, and it smelled a little musty. There was yellow wallpaper on the walls, but somehow, it did nothing to cheer up the aspect of the house.

"Oh, well, it's a safe haven," thought Thérèse, as she dwelled briefly on the night in the Tube station and the smell of smoke after they had emerged into the daylight.

Eustace opened the door at the end of the corridor and revealed a cheerier kitchen with white walls and blue and white checked curtains. An oak table with four chairs sat in the middle of the room, and there were rather worn-looking wooden cupboards with brass knobs along one wall. A few paintings, mostly of the Dutch school of art, hung on the walls, and a large wood stove dominated the furthermost one. A small, neat woman in a green housedress and a colourful headscarf rose from one of the chairs.

"Hello, there," she said enthusiastically, seizing Thérèse's hand and pumping it up and down. "I'm Martha."

She smiled at Thérèse, and Thérèse knew instantly that she would be friends with this woman. Martha had the kind of open face with a permanently pleasant expression that people automatically trusted. Her smile was warm, and she had a twinkle in her eyes.

"Would'st tha like tha tea?" she asked as she shook hands with Vivienne, who looked puzzled. The girl looked up at her mother, a frown on her face.

"We're from Yorkshire," Eustace explained. "Martha's accent's stronger than mine, and sometimes she's a little harder to understand for southerners."

Martha beamed.

"Tha tea, luv," she said to Vivienne. "Art tha hungry?"

She pronounced it "hoongry" and Thérèse hastened to answer her.

"We ate on the train," she explained. "But I'm sure Vivienne would be able to eat again."

"Aye, then," Martha answered. "Well, sit thaselves down, and I'll make us some sardines on toast."

Eustace held out chairs for Thérèse and Vivienne and they made themselves comfortable at the table while Martha busied herself at the stove, opening a large can of sardines and toasting large pieces of brown, homemade bread. She poured them each big mugs of tea and added milk and sugar without asking whether they took it or not. Thérèse preferred her tea just as it came out of the pot but thought this was not the moment to point that out.

Eustace told them about Southport, telling them about the highlights of the town and assuring them that so far there had been no bombing here. He also explained his connection to Emmett through their mothers, and how they had often played together as boys. Finally, he touched upon meeting Martha when he had gone to York to train for the army during the Great War and how, like Thérèse and Emmett, they had got married as soon as the war ended.

They ate their sardines and toast, followed by Yorkshire Eccles cakes washed down with the strong and invigorating tea, chatting in a familiar fashion. Already, Thérèse liked this couple and their cheery, open dispositions. Finally, she suggested that she and Vivienne go to their rooms and unpack their suitcases. Martha nodded and got up from the table, collecting their plates as she did so.

"Go up and unpack tha cases while Eustace and I wash the tea things," she said. "Then coom down and we'll sit in the drawing room until it's time for bed."

Eustace showed them where the staircase was, behind a door in the long corridor that ran the length of the house. They climbed the narrow stairs until they reached the attic, which contained the guest bedroom. Eustace and Martha slept in a bedroom on the main floor.

The room was cold, with a narrow window on one side and two small cots against the wall. An attempt had been made to cheer it up with some framed needlepoint pictures and a flower in a small vase on the bedside table. A large walnut wardrobe stood on one side, and Thérèse opened their suitcases and began hanging up their few items of clothing. She noted with relief that the beds had warm eiderdowns on them and speculated that they might be needing those once winter came.

When they were done, they went back downstairs and joined Eustace and Martha in the small drawing-room, which contained a fireplace and rather dull brown furniture. They spent the evening chatting with their hosts before washing their faces in the little bathroom off the kitchen and then ascending the staircase once again.

After Thérèse had tucked Vivienne into bed, she gave her daughter a book to read, then kissed her on the forehead.

"Sleep tight, darling," she whispered.

"It's cold in this house, Mummy," Vivienne complained, huddling down under the blankets.

"Well, it's colder in the north of England than the south," Thérèse explained. "But the people are lovely, and I'm sure you'll come to love cousins Eustace and Martha."

Vivienne wrinkled her nose briefly, but then she smiled.

"I'm sure I shall," she replied, burrowing down further. "'Night, 'night, Mummy."

Thérèse blew her a kiss, then climbed into her own small bed. The sheets felt chilly at first, but her body heat soon warmed them up and she turned her face to the wall before falling into a deep, uninterrupted sleep.

50

They had been staying with Eustace and his wife for about a month and continued to get along with them very well. Both were very kind people, and Emmett must have known this when he approached them about hosting his wife and daughter for the duration of the war. Thérèse and Martha became friends very quickly, and Vivienne enjoyed playing with the dog, Fred, and taking him for walks throughout the town with Eustace when he returned from his job at the local post office.

Thérèse enrolled Vivienne in the nearby girls' school, where she wore a blue and grey uniform. At first she had trouble understanding the other pupils and teachers, but she quickly caught on to their northern accent and soon began to speak in the same fashion. Her teachers were pleased with her quick ability to learn, and she was soon near the top of her class in most subjects. Thérèse had herself always been good at her lessons when she went to school in Mauritius, but she hadn't excelled. She felt that Vivienne's intellectual capabilities probably came from her father, but perhaps she was selling herself short on her own quick wit and ability to learn new things and adapt to new environments.

She spent her days helping Martha with the cooking and housework, accompanying her to the shops to cash in their ration coupons and listening to the radio every night for news on the war with Germany. However, much as she enjoyed chatting with Martha, she soon found herself missing her active social life in London and the friends that she had met in the neighbourhood and through the Civil Service. She telephoned Emmett regularly for news of himself and their various friends, as well as the bombing situation in the capital city, but she soon found herself complaining to him that her life felt rather empty.

"Why don't you ask Martha if there's a wing of the Women's Voluntary Service in Southport?" he suggested to her during one of their telephone calls. "I remember I'd mentioned that to you before."

"What is it, exactly?" she asked him.

"It's an organization started for women to help in the war effort," he replied. "You can help with sending supplies to the army or finding housing for displaced families. They do a lot of good here in London. I think you'd enjoy it, darling, as you love to help people."

It sounded like just the ideal thing for Thérèse, both to relieve her boredom and also to satisfy her desire to be of service to others.

"I'll speak to Martha about it tomorrow," she assured him, before going on to inquire about Hélène and Lucien.

Emmett told her that they had found a billet in Surrey, where Lucien had got himself a job working on a farm and little Christophe seemed to be benefiting from the country air. She was happy to hear that her cousins had managed to get out of London and hoped there wouldn't be a lot of bombing in the southern countryside. Perhaps they might be able to join her in Southport after a while, if things got any worse in the South.

The next morning, she approached Martha about the Women's Voluntary Service, asking whether she knew of a chapter of the organization in Southport.

"I'm sure there'll be one in Liverpool," Martha replied. "But tha could look in Southport, as well."

"Where would I go to inquire?" asked Thérèse.

"Maybe t' town hall?"

Thérèse nodded, concluding that she'd have to find out for herself. She didn't think that Martha was all that interested in doing charity work outside of her home. After all, billeting two people she had never met before was a charitable job of its own.

After lunch, Thérèse put on her wool coat and hat and started the long walk to the centre of town where the Town Hall could be found. She had walked for about a mile, stopping to ask directions of strangers on a couple of occasions, when she finally saw the classic building with the tall spire on Lord Street.

She went through the main doors and approached a young woman seated at a desk in the main lobby. She was plainly dressed and had brown hair, worn in two plaits on either side of her head and wound around into buns, Tyrolean style. She looked up from her work and smiled.

"How may I help you?" she inquired in a pleasant voice.

"I was wondering whether you could tell me if there's a branch of the Women's Voluntary Service here in Southport?" Thérèse asked her.

"Yes, there is," nodded the young woman, opening a drawer in her desk and searching through some papers. "I've got a name and address of the lady in charge somewhere here if you don't mind waiting a minute."

"No, of course not," replied Thérèse.

"Just have a seat over there," the woman waved at a row of chairs by the far wall.

Thérèse sat herself on one of the wooden chairs and studied the framed photographs of various Southport locations on the walls in the lobby. After several minutes, the young clerk waved her over and handed her a piece of paper.

"That's the lady's name," she informed Thérèse. "You can probably ring her up or stop at her house and talk to her. She might be having a meeting there now."

"Thank you very much," smiled Thérèse, taking the paper and reading the name and address on it. The name was "Edna Gorman", but she was unfamiliar with the address. She thought she would telephone the lady the next day and ask about joining the volunteer group.

After breakfast the following morning, Thérèse made the call. The phone rang several times, then a brusque voice answered with the exchange name and number.

"Mrs. Gorman?" asked Thérèse, tentatively.

"It's *Miss* Gorman," replied the terse voice at the other end.

"Oh, excuse me," Thérèse hastened to add. "Thérèse Richardson here. I was just making some inquiries about the Women's Voluntary Service. I understand that you're in charge of the Southport branch?"

"Yes, that's correct."

"I was wondering whether I might volunteer. I'd like to become part of the war work, and I've always had a love of helping people, especially in a nursing capacity."

"Well, you'll mostly be packing blankets and supplies to send to the armed forces, but we do help families who've been displaced, too," replied Edna. "There may be illness among them," she added.

"I'm willing to do anything you need me to do," Thérèse said fervently. "When and where do you meet?"

Edna told Thérèse that she could come to her house the next morning at ten o'clock, and she would walk with her to the depot where the supplies were kept. Thérèse thanked her and told her that she looked forward to meeting the next morning.

She arose early the next day, had breakfast and saw Vivienne off to school. After sharing one last cup of tea with Martha, she put on her coat and hat and set off towards the address that Miss Gorman had given her.

The wind was blustery, and Thérèse felt several raindrops fall on her as she walked along. She regretted not bringing an umbrella but managed to arrive at the right house before the rain started. It was a small white bungalow with a red-tiled roof and yellow curtains adorning the front windows. She rang the doorbell and stepped back from the door to wait patiently. After a few minutes, a tall young woman with bright red hair and intelligent green eyes appeared. She was wearing a pair of brown work pants and a red wool jersey and sounded nothing like the gruff voice from the day before. She held out an enthusiastic hand to Thérèse.

"Pleasure to meet you, Mrs. Richardson," she said. "I'm Edna Gorman."

"The pleasure is mine," replied Thérèse. "I'm so pleased to be able to help out."

"We're grateful to have you," came the answer. "It's always good to have more hands on deck."

The young woman reached for a long grey gabardine coat and rainhat hanging in the hall, then picked up a large black umbrella and went out the front door, indicating to Thérèse that she should follow her.

Thus ready to meet the weather, she set off down the street at a very fast pace, with Thérèse struggling to keep up with her. After twenty or so minutes, they reached a large grey building with a sign that said "Chesterfield & Sons".

"Well, here we are," said Edna. "Old warehouse, no longer needed by the owners. The two boys went off to join the services, and the old boy decided to retire. Donated the place. It's perfect for storing supplies."

"I would think so."

It was cold inside the building, but Edna offered to make tea and had soon lit an old stove off the main area, so it started to warm up slowly.

Before long, the two women were drinking their tea, and Edna had shown Thérèse the long rows of supplies for the army that were housed in the depot. Several other women would be arriving shortly, and they would find, fold and pack the various items of bedding and clothing in boxes to be sent away to army bases all over the country.

The women started arriving shortly afterwards, and Thérèse was introduced to them. Before long, there were about two dozen of them, and Thérèse knew that she would never remember all of their names. She did remember Shirley and Ruth, though, as they were assigned to work with her. They were both middle-aged women, solid and cheery in their dispositions.

The three of them worked tirelessly, gathering items from the shelves and packing them into large cardboard boxes. They chatted as they worked, and Shirley and Ruth told Thérèse about themselves. When it was Thérèse's turn, they were fascinated to hear that she had grown up on a tropical island, and that her first language had been French.

"But you speak English so well, dear," exclaimed Shirley. "Did you just learn it when you came here?"

She was amazed when Thérèse said yes.

"You speak it better than some English people!" proclaimed Ruth. Thérèse smiled to herself. She knew that it was true.

At lunchtime, the women filed into the small kitchen, which was presided over by a lady named Grace, who served up a lunch of cold tinned beef and salad and the usual cups of tea. They stood around, plates in hand, gossiping and laughing while they ate and then taking turns to wash up their dishes before returning to work.

They continued to pack supplies and the afternoon passed by quickly. At five o'clock, Edna declared that it was time for everyone to go home.

"You can walk back with me, Thérèse, if you like," she said, as they were putting on their coats.

Thérèse nodded, and they followed the last of the women out of the door. Edna once again locked it with the enormous keychain and Thérèse fell into step with the younger woman.

"Well, how did your day go?" Edna asked her as they walked briskly along the road.

"Very well, thank you," smiled Thérèse. "I enjoyed meeting Ruth and Shirley."

"Any sore muscles?" inquired Edna. "Sometimes the women find that they're pretty tired after a day of packing."

"Oh, no," Thérèse told her. "I'm used to doing housework and gardening. I like to keep occupied."

"Well, we'll have plenty for you to do, if you'd like to join us," said Edna in a pleased tone.

"I'd be delighted!" answered Thérèse, sincerely.

When they reached Edna's house, the two women once again shook hands, and Thérèse assured Edna that she would be at the warehouse again the following morning, and that she could find her way there without assistance.

51

The days melted into one another, as Thérèse continued to assist the Women's Voluntary Service by day, and in the evening helping Martha make the tea and wash dishes upon her return home.

She supervised Vivienne with her homework each evening after tea, then would sometimes listen to the radio news with Eustace. Things weren't going well with the war. The Germans kept up their heavy bombing and, little by little, were creeping closer to their planned invasion of Britain. The Royal Air Force did their best to give as good as they got with their bombing of Germany, but it often seemed like a losing battle. Word had it that Churchill was desperately hoping to bring the United States into the war, but so far had only succeeded in getting some used warships donated by the American President, Roosevelt. "FDR," as he was affectionately called, was very sympathetic to Europe's needs, but he still had to convince his people that they wanted to engage in another large-scale war.

Things were bleak in France, from what Thérèse could learn on the radio. Food was scarce, and the French were being kept under control by German troops. Curfews were put in place, and anyone caught out after dark was either arrested for questioning or shot on sight. There was more talk of people disappearing, and no one knew where they were being taken. They were herded onto cattle trains and never heard from again.

One day while she was working at the depot with the Women's Service volunteers, Thérèse saw a pretty young woman with dark hair and a rather serious expression come through the main door and stand there hesitatingly, an uncertain look on her face. Edna caught sight of her and immediately went to greet her. They talked quietly. Then Edna looked around the room, her eyes alighting on Thérèse, and she took the young woman by the arm and brought her over to Thérèse.

"Theresa," she said (she had taken to calling Thérèse by the anglicized version of her name). "This is Lucille Dumais. She has arrived recently from France. Perhaps you could show her around and tell her what we do here."

"Of course," Thérèse replied, smiling warmly at the young woman who was regarding her seriously. She was dressed in very shabby clothes, a faded brown skirt, dingy white blouse and homespun blue cardigan that looked to have some tiny holes in it. Nonetheless, she had a respectable air about her and carried herself well.

"Your name is Lucille?" inquired Thérèse, in French.

"Yes," replied the young girl, suddenly looking much happier. "I'm so grateful to meet someone who speaks my language! I never paid much attention in English classes at the *lycée* before the war, and it's been difficult."

"I imagine it would!" exclaimed Thérèse. "When did you come here?"

"Just a week ago," Lucille replied.

"How did you get out?" Thérèse was confused. "Isn't the country occupied by the Germans?"

"Yes, of course," Lucille told her. "But I knew a Resistance member who helps spies leave France and travel safely to England."

"Who are the Resistance?" asked Thérèse, curiously.

"They're also known as the Free French," answered Lucille. "They spy on the Germans and try to smuggle people who are in trouble with the enemy out of France."

Thérèse's eyes opened wide.

"You were a spy?" she asked this innocent-looking young woman, who nodded and blushed.

"Well, not exactly a spy," she explained hesitatingly. "But I did pass information from the Germans to the Resistance whenever I could. I had a connection at the army headquarters in my town."

"Well, I think that's called spying," Thérèse answered her, respect for this young woman growing in her mind. "That's very brave of you. Where are you from?"

"Rouen, in Normandy," replied Lucille.

Thérèse nodded. She knew from listening to the news, and also from Emmett explaining the situation to her, that the Vichy government under Marshal Philippe Pétain in the southern part of France had been Nazi sympathizers and worked closely with the Germans to facilitate the occupation of the northern half of the country. It didn't surprise Thérèse that there were now Resistance workers in Rouen quietly opposing the government.

"Well, if there's anything I can do for you, if you need anything at all, you let me know," Thérèse assured the young woman, patting her arm. "My cousins and I escaped France in a boat just before the Occupation, and the enemy were even firing on some of us."

Lucille opened her eyes widely.

"Well, you're brave, too," she told Thérèse.

They smiled at one another, each seeing an ally in the other.

"For now," said Lucille, "you can show me what to do here. Anything I can do to help the war effort is very important to me."

It didn't surprise Thérèse that this earnest young woman would want to repay her escape from France by doing volunteer work in England. It was just the sort of thing that she herself would have done.

Several weeks went by, and the pleasant September temperatures moved into late autumn. The trees were losing their leaves, and evenings were becoming darker earlier than before. Thérèse and Vivienne were now well accustomed to the cool, damp weather in the north of England, and their ears had become used to the dialect that most people used in this part of the country.

Emmett telephoned them regularly on Sundays and, although Thérèse felt safe at his cousin's home, she missed him very much and worried about him every time she heard that there had been yet another bombing raid on London.

There were now some bombing raids on nearby Liverpool too but, so far, none had come close to Southport. On a couple of occasions, Thérèse had heard the loud "boom" of the bombs being dropped on the city, but looking out the window during the night she hadn't really been able to see anything. A curfew had been imposed in Southport, and nobody was allowed to be out after dark. She always made sure to return to the little row house by five o'clock, in time to help Martha get the tea ready and to discuss the daily news reports with Eustace. She was careful to make sure that Vivienne was in the kitchen doing her homework before she discussed the bombing of various British cities with him, though. She didn't want to frighten the child.

Her friendship with Lucille at the Women's Voluntary Service had grown over time, and Lucille looked towards her as something of a mentor. Lucille's English was improving daily, and she was regarded as a willing worker at the W.V.S. warehouse. No task was too difficult or daunting for her and, as she seemed to have a lot of physical strength and stamina, the older women would often ask her to lift the heavier boxes or climb up on a ladder to reach the highest parcels on the shelves.

One morning, Lucille arrived at the depot looking very upset. Thérèse watched her from afar, noticing that when someone greeted her, Lucille got tears in her eyes and reached for a handkerchief in her pocket. Filled with sympathy and wondering what was wrong, Thérèse immediately went over to her.

"What's the matter, *chérie*?" she asked, putting her arm around Lucille's shoulders.

Lucille looked up at her, tears spilling down onto her face.

"It's my brother," she replied. "He's been injured fleeing from the Germans from a factory in Rouen. They were trying to sabotage the manufacture of guns for the enemy. He was able to get to a Resistance safe house, and they're trying to get him out of France, but they're afraid he may be recognized by the German soldiers."

"Oh, my dear, I'm so sorry!" said Thérèse, folding Lucille in an embrace. What a terrifying experience for this young woman - she was basically all alone in a foreign country, and now her brother was in danger.

"Can your family get him out?"

"It's just me and my brother," Lucille explained. "Our father died when we were very young, and *Maman* passed away just before the war."

This was even worse. Lucille had told her, during one of their many conversations about the situation on the continent that, without family members to help organize a rescue, there was a possibility that Resistance fighters might never be able to escape.

"Don't worry," she reassured her friend. "I'm sure they'll be able to make the connections to smuggle him out of the country."

"But he's injured!" sobbed Lucille inconsolably. "He'll need a nurse to go with him."

"They'll arrange something," Thérèse soothed her, stroking her hair, then handing her own handkerchief to wipe her eyes and nose. Lucille nodded her thanks.

"Do you want to go home, Lucy?" asked Edna, who had come up behind them.

"No, no, I'd rather be here and keep myself occupied doing things," replied Lucille. "If I stay at home, I'll just think about my brother and worry even more."

"Of course you will," said Thérèse. "I'm sure we've got lots for you to do, haven't we, Edna?"

Edna smiled. "Oh, yes," she agreed. "We can always find plenty of jobs for you to do."

Lucille smiled through her tears, and then Edna gave them their list of tasks for the day.

Thérèse thought about Lucille's brother for many days after that. She kept hearing the young woman's voice saying he needed a nurse to help him if he were to come to England safely. Something told her that she was meant to play a part in this rescue and, although she tried to dismiss the little voice whispering in her head, she kept returning to the idea, unable to let it go.

52

Thérèse couldn't stop thinking about her friend at the Women's Voluntary Service and what she had told her about her brother. A plan was hatching in her head and, once it had put itself there, she wasn't able to oust it. The fact that Lucille had said he needed a nurse to accompany him back to England to be with his sister kept calling out to her, and she was finding it harder to drown out that voice.

She felt she could help the family reunite, and that this could be another way for her to contribute to the war effort. Her ability to speak French and fit in with the locals, as well as her nursing capabilities, would come in handy in any attempt to rescue this young man. She tried to ignore the thought in the back of her mind that she had promised herself to never leave Emmett's side again. However, he had sent her here to the north of England, and now they were apart. Would it make any difference if she undertook a rescue mission to help an injured Frenchman while she was here?

Every day she quizzed Lucille as to whether a nurse had been found, and each day the answer was no. Lucille often got tears in her eyes when she spoke about it to Thérèse, and Thérèse could see that she was losing hope.

She weighed the pros and cons of her plan, urged on by her feeling that this was something she was meant to do, and found them to be about equal. Vivienne was by now very comfortable staying at Martha and Eustace's house, and her schoolwork kept her busy in the evenings, so she would barely miss her mother if she suddenly found it necessary to make a journey. The biggest hurdle would be Emmett, who would certainly forbid her to do anything but stay put.

The Germans had begun to bomb the north of England more frequently, and several raids had been made on Liverpool. So far, Southport had escaped any bombing, probably because it was a seaside town and didn't have any wartime factories. Thérèse was relieved that Emmett had decided to send her and their daughter somewhere out of harm's way, but it didn't stop her from mulling over the rescue of the young Frenchman.

Finally, one day, as she was packing bedding into a large cardboard box at the W.V.S. depot, she could no longer contain herself. She turned to Lucille, who was working with her, and blurted out,

"What if I went over to France and helped to bring your brother back? I have nursing experience."

Lucille stared at her open-mouthed, an expression of incredulity on her face.

"You would do that for me? For my family? Go into France and help him come back here? You'd be risking your life, Thérèse!"

"Yes, I know," Thérèse replied quietly. "But I've done it before, for my cousins, and we got out safely. I just can't get rid of the feeling that I'm supposed to help you and your brother. It's why we met."

Lucille's expression changed from doubt to one of fierce joy. She threw her arms around Thérèse's neck and hugged her hard.

"Oh, you're so kind!" Lucille exclaimed. "You're such a wonderful, brave woman. I never thought I'd meet someone in England who was willing to help my family. I was hoping that someone from the Resistance would eventually help us."

"They're probably stretched thin and can't spare anyone," Thérèse told her. Her mind began racing at once as to how this could be done.

"I'll need some help to get into France in the first place," she mused. "You know some of the Resistance here in England, don't you, Lucille?"

"Yes, it's how I got out myself," Lucille answered. "They gave me a new identity while I was in France, with papers, and put me in touch with the people who would help me get to the boat that brought me here."

Thérèse nodded. "Well, I'll need to know who the primary contact is here," she replied.

Lucille hugged her tightly once again.

"I can't believe you're willing to do this for me," she murmured against Thérèse's ear. "I honestly believed that my brother would die in France, or that the Germans would capture him."

"I don't think that will happen," Thérèse soothed her. "A little voice keeps telling me that I'm supposed to do this, and that it will be alright."

Lucille stepped back and looked searchingly into her face, "What little voice?".

"Never mind," Thérèse replied. She didn't want Lucille to start thinking that she was an insane woman who heard voices and then change her mind about accepting her help. She knew that it was just her intuition speaking, the same voice that had accurately told her things that were going to happen in the past. She quickly changed the subject.

"Can you give me the name of the person who arranged your passage here?" Thérèse asked Lucille. "Are they in France, or here in England?"

"It's a woman, and she goes back and forth as much as possible. However, she's here at the moment, working with MI6 in London." Lucille explained. "She has a spy network all over France and arranges for people who are under suspicion from the Germans to escape."

"What's her name?"

"Marie-Madeleine Fourcade."

Thérèse looked intently at Lucille. That name had a ring of familiarity to it.

"And you can put me in touch with her?"

"I'm pretty sure I can," confirmed Lucille.

"Good! Well, let me know when you hear from her," she said.

The young woman clasped both of Thérèse's hands in hers. "Thank you, thank you so much," she beamed, tears once again welling up in her eyes. "I'm so grateful to you."

Thérèse smiled at her, a feeling of anticipation filling her being. She knew that she had taken on something that would probably be dangerous, and perhaps very foolish, but she also knew it was the right thing to do.

And now she would have to conceal her plan from her adoring husband. She knew that would be the only way she could go ahead with her project. Once again, she briefly considered her promise to never leave him, but quickly rationalized that this was something she needed to do, much like the rescue of her cousins from France.

A few days later, Lucille arrived at the old warehouse and came over to Thérèse with a folded piece of paper.

"It's from Marie-Madeleine," she told Thérèse in a low whisper. "She's coming up to Liverpool in the next two days and she'd like you to meet her."

Thérèse felt a quiver of excitement go through her.

"Yes, of course, I'll go and see her," she said quickly. "I'll have to make arrangements for my husband's cousin to look after my daughter, but I think she'll understand."

Lucille nodded.

"I'll leave you with it then," she replied. "Edna has some translation work she wants me to do for her in the office, so I won't be packing with you today."

"Alright."

After Lucille had walked away, Thérèse opened up the sheet of paper. The name of a hotel was scrawled on it in large, round handwriting, with the address in Liverpool and the time, "1600 hours" written underneath. The date was for the day after tomorrow. A note had been added at the end indicating that the writer of the missive would be wearing a red hat.

Thérèse realized she would have to come up with a reason for going to Liverpool that would convince her family members that her journey was just something mundane, rather than the cloak-and-dagger excursion it might turn out to be. She thought that she could maybe take Martha into her confidence but would not worry Vivienne or Eustace with the details.

As she was walking home that evening, she hit upon the idea of telling them that she had to go to the city for a job with the Women's Voluntary Service. They probably wouldn't even inquire as to what the job was, as war work took many shapes and forms. As she turned the corner to their street and walked up to the semi-detached house, she felt her resolve strengthening to go ahead with her plans.

After tea, Vivienne went into the study to do her homework, and Eustace announced that he was going to take Fred for a walk. As they washed and dried the tea things in the tiny kitchen, Thérèse at first hesitated to broach the subject with Martha, but then decided to take the plunge.

"Martha . . ." she began, hesitantly.

"Yes, luv?" asked Martha, scouring a pan in the washing-up water with a Brillo pad.

"The W.V.S. has asked me to go to Liverpool the day after tomorrow. Would you mind looking after Vivienne for me if I don't get back until late?"

Martha agreed easily, smiling at Thérèse.

"Yes, of course, dear," she told her. "That young 'un's never any trouble at all. Such a good girl!"

Thérèse smiled, pleased with the praise for her youngest child.

"Thank you so much," she said. "You're a dear."

She leaned further towards Martha and dropped her voice conspiratorially.

"It might involve a special project." She was dismayed at how easily the words tumbled out of her mouth. "I can't say too much, but will you promise me for now not to say anything to Eustace or Vivienne?"

Martha opened her eyes wide.

"Why?" she asked. "Is tha going to be doing some type of secret work?"

"I really can't say much now, Martha, but will you swear not to tell them anything, except that I've gone to Liverpool for the afternoon?"

Martha looked undecided for a moment or two, but then shrugged her shoulders.

"Of course, luv, if that's what you want," she acquiesced. "But promise to tell me about it after you get back?"

"Of course," affirmed Thérèse, patting her arm companionably. "It will be our secret for now, alright?"

Martha smiled, eyes sparkling. Thérèse had judged her accurately. Martha loved receiving and keeping secrets, and Thérèse knew that she could count on her to keep quiet about the details of her visit to Liverpool.

Two days later, she boarded the train to the city and made herself comfortable on a seat in second-class, checking to ensure that the piece of paper from Mme Fourcade was still in her pocket. The day was chilly, typical of late autumn and, even though she'd become accustomed to the cooler temperatures here in the north, she had dressed in a warm camel wool coat and a new navy blue hat. Emmett had sent her some money to pay Eustace and Martha for rent and the cost of food, but there was a little left over for her to spend on herself and Vivienne. She wore the hat at a jaunty angle and knew that it suited her well.

The train journey went by quickly as Thérèse gazed out the window at the passing countryside. Cows and sheep dotted the hills, and country lanes could sometimes be seen from the train. The little villages and hamlets along the way showed pretty cottages with thatched roofs, amid older farm buildings that were sometimes rundown in appearance.

Before too long, the train was pulling into Liverpool. Thérèse could see evidence of bombing on some of the streets, and she silently thanked Emmett for having had the foresight to send her and Vivienne to Southport. Imagine escaping the inferno in London only to be bombed in Liverpool, where they would be far from home and possibly have nowhere to go! She was fortunate that her husband had relatives in the little seaside town.

But now she was about to embark on a much bigger adventure, and it could end up being even more unsafe than escaping bombing in England. She asked herself for the hundredth time why she felt so obligated to perform this rescue mission but knew that it was something she couldn't really explain, so it was pointless to try.

On arriving at the central station in Liverpool, Thérèse disembarked from the train and headed to the ticket gate, where she handed the porter one-half of her return ticket. She asked him where the taxi rank could be found and he pointed her in the direction of the exit.

After flagging down a taxi, she settled herself in the back seat and gave the driver the address of the place where Mme Fourcade would be staying, the famous Double Tree Hotel. She glanced at her watch and was happy to see that it was half-past three, well in time for her appointment.

After a short journey, the taxi pulled up in front of the beautiful nineteenth-century hotel. Thérèse paid the driver and got out.

Sure enough, as Thérèse entered the hotel lobby and walked towards the café, she could see a young woman seated at a small table, wearing a red hat and an elegant grey suit and smoking a cigarette in a holder. Thérèse approached the table and leaned forward, addressing her in French.

"Are you Mme Fourcade? May I join you?"

The young woman looked up at her and smiled.

"Yes, I am," she nodded. "*Mme* Richardson?"

Thérèse smiled and affirmed her name.

"Cigarette?" the woman asked her. Thérèse nodded and took one from the package that was offered to her. A lighter was obligingly held up for her.

Mme Fourcade was much younger than Thérèse had thought she would be, and very beautiful. She had wavy brown hair that was swept up on her head under the red cloche hat, and her piercing brown eyes seemed to peer into Thérèse's soul as she spoke. Thérèse didn't know what she had expected, but she hadn't thought the head of the French Resistance would be quite as fashionable and chic as this young woman. But, of course, what better way to keep her identity a secret than to look like a woman of society? Thérèse felt confident that she was in capable hands as she exchanged pleasantries with this charming woman.

"Would you like some tea?" Mme Fourcade offered.

"Yes, please," Thérèse answered her, realizing she was quite hungry.

"And perhaps some scones?"

Mme Fourcade waved over a waiter and gave him the order, then turned once again to Thérèse.

"I understand you would like to help our friend Lucille Dumais by accompanying her wounded brother out of France."

Thérèse nodded her agreement.

"What makes you feel qualified for this mission?" Mme Fourcade asked her, those piercing eyes gazing at her.

"Well . . . " Thérèse hesitated. "I have nursing experience, and I went into France last summer and helped my cousins to escape England, just before the German occupation."

"So you've done this type of thing before?"

"Yes." Thérèse didn't mention that they had been helped by some British soldiers, and that the Germans had allowed the boats to escape from France. However, she felt the fact that some of them were fired upon was proof of the precariousness of the mission.

"You're aware that there will be danger, then?" questioned Mme Fourcade. "My compatriots will do their best to help you, but if you get caught by the Germans, we will not be able to rescue you."

Thérèse hadn't thought of that, but that little voice in the back of her head once again sounded, telling her that she wouldn't have to worry.

"It will be very fast, though, won't it?" she asked Mme Fourcade. "I just have to arrive in France, meet Gaston, and bring him back here?"

Mme Fourcade gazed at her for a moment before she spoke.

"It might not be as easy as you think," she warned. "Of course, we will have connections there from the Resistance to assist you with the return journey, but you have to be very careful not to arouse any suspicion from the Germans."

"I'll be careful," Thérèse assured her, perhaps more confidently than she felt. "We could say that he has been injured in a farming accident and I'm helping him get to a hospital."

"Tell them anything you need to say to convince them that you're just going about your business, nothing more suspicious," replied Mme Fourcade. She leaned back in her chair. "I like you, *Madame* Richardson. May I call you Thérèse?"

Smiling, Thérèse nodded her assent.

"You have courage, Thérèse, and are, I'm sure, very resourceful," Mme Fourcade continued. "By the way, we should find a code name for you, so they'll know who you are when you arrive."

"Code name?" asked Thérèse, feeling excitement mounting in her. "Do you have one?"

"Of course," Mme Fourcade smiled at her as though she should know that. "It's 'Hedgehog'. What would you like to be called?"

Thérèse thought for a few minutes, stirring her tea with her spoon. Then something occurred to her.

"My husband has sometimes called me his 'Tropical Rose,'" she told Mme Fourcade. "Would that do?"

Mme Fourcade nodded and smiled.

"That's perfect," she said, taking a notebook and pen out of her handbag and opening it to a page covered in the same large, round handwriting that had been on the piece of paper with the hotel name on it. She scribbled something down quickly.

"Now," she continued, after she was done writing. "I'm going to give you the name of a contact at the Liverpool harbour. Can you be there in three days' time?"

"Saturday?" asked Thérèse.

"Yes."

Thérèse felt a shiver of anticipation go through her.

"I don't see a problem," she replied. "What time do I have to be there?"

Mme Fourcade leaned forward and, opening her notebook to another page, started explaining to Thérèse how things were to proceed. When she had finished, she tore the pages out of her book and handed them to her.

"Any questions?" she asked.

"No, I don't think so," Thérèse answered.

"If you think of anything before Saturday, just give me a ring at the phone number that I've put at the bottom of the page."

"I will," Thérèse agreed.

The two women chatted pleasantly for a few more minutes, then Mme Fourcade picked up her handbag and stood, announcing that she had to leave to attend another meeting with a contact from the British government.

Thérèse shook her hand, and Mme Fourcade wished her well.

"Good luck, Tropical Rose," she said in a sincere tone. "I hope to see you back in Liverpool in the next few days."

Thérèse nodded her head in farewell, then watched the woman walk quickly out of the café with a business-like step. She felt that it was no coincidence that this intelligent, intense woman was leading a major resistance movement during a terrible war against a powerful enemy. But why did she have the strange feeling that she had seen her before somewhere?

53

After Thérèse's return to Southport, the family had their tea. Thérèse helped Martha wash the tea things and, as they were finishing up, she turned to Martha with a somewhat hesitant look on her face.

"Martha, can I talk to you about something?" she asked timidly.

Martha dried her hands on the tea towel that was hung on a hook at the side of the kitchen counter and turned to her.

"Aye, lass," she said. "What's on tha mind?"

Thérèse swallowed, and hastily decided that she might as well come out with it.

"Remember that I told you I might have to go away for a few days?" She said. "Would I be able to leave Vivienne in your care while I attend to some business?"

"What sort of business?" Martha looked curious.

"Well . . . " Thérèse began, then took a deep breath. "I can't really say at the moment. Will you trust me, and I'll explain it all to you when I get back?"

"Well, I think tha ought to at least tell me where you're going," Martha stared at her, a guarded look on her face.

Thérèse searched for a suitable answer, then came up with the first thing that she could think of.

"I have to go back to Liverpool for a few days. I have some things that I have to see to, and I don't want to take Vivienne out of school," she explained quickly, feeling very guilty about lying to this kind woman who would never suspect that she wasn't being truthful.

"What sort o' things? Are they that pressing? There's a war on, and Liverpool's being bombed almost every week," Martha said.

"Yes, that's true, but I have some things to sort out that need my signature, and I can't do it here."

Martha hesitated. "Hmm, well, I don't know what anyone can ask that's worth risking tha safety for, but I'll take it on good faith," she finally said. "It's none of my business, I suppose. Go on, lass, I'll look after t' young 'un. Don't tha fret."

Thérèse hugged her warmly.

"Thank you so much, Martha!" she breathed, relieved that she hadn't had to make up a story about the "pressing things" she had to do while there was a war going on in the country.

"And please, promise me you won't tell Emmett you know about any of this, if he should ask," she added. "Come to think of it, don't tell Eustace or Vivienne, either. Just say I had to go to Liverpool."

Martha chucked her under the chin.

"Alright, lass," she affirmed. "Tha'rt being right mysterious, but I won't let on I know anything."

"Thank you, thank you, Martha! You're such a good friend," Thérèse gushed gratefully.

"We're *family*," emphasized the older woman. "And t' little 'un's a good girl that doesn't need much caring for. She's got a good head on her shoulders."

"Yes," Thérèse agreed, adding, "Make sure she makes her bed in the morning and helps you with the tea things, and does her homework every night."

"She's a right conscientious little thing, I know I won't have to remind her. She's such a clever girl."

Thérèse nodded, then Martha asked,

"How long does tha think tha'll be gone?"

"I don't know," Thérèse responded. "It really depends on how long it takes to do everything . . . appointments, et cetera . . . you know." She knew she was scrambling now, but Martha seemed satisfied.

"That's alright, lass. Tha can take as long as tha needs."

Thérèse once again hugged her cousin by marriage, who had really become a surrogate sister during the time they'd been together.

Later that evening, Eustace was a bit more anxious to find out the details of Thérèse's sudden trip to Liverpool, but Martha assured him that it was "family business" that he didn't need to know about, and he soon acquiesced with a nod. Thérèse also thanked him for his understanding and for looking after her daughter, and he assured her that Vivienne was no trouble at all and could help him to take care of Fred during her absence.

The next morning, just as she was getting ready to leave the house for the W.V.S. centre, the telephone rang and Martha called up the stairs to her that the telephone call was for her. She picked up the receiver and a male voice was on the other end.

"Tropical Rose?" he queried.

The code name that Madame Fourcade had assigned to her!

"Yes," she replied quickly.

"This is St. Tropez Harry," answered the voice at the other end, mysteriously. "I understand that you're going to help our uncle?"

"Oh, he's your uncle?" Thérèse asked, somewhat confused.

"You're going to get him to where he needs to go, isn't that right?" asked the man, shortly.

Thérèse realized that he was speaking in a sort of code, and that Gaston probably wasn't his uncle at all.

"Oh, yes, yes," she hastened to assure him, now that she understood the situation. "Have you got the address of the place and where he's staying now?"

"Yes, I have. Can you come to the Liverpool docks, Departure Area B tomorrow at noon? We'll have all of the details for you."

"Yes, I can do that," she told him. "I'll be there and I'll be wearing a navy blue hat."

"Alright, then," he replied. "You'll know me by the dark moustache and brown trench coat."

"Very well," Thérèse affirmed.

They rang off and she hurried to get herself ready to leave for the depot. Things were happening a lot faster than she expected.

Lucille was thrilled to hear that Thérèse had made all the arrangements and was leaving for France as early as the next day. She had almost given up hope of her brother ever being rescued and had seriously been thinking of trying to get back into her country of birth herself, even though she knew it was very dangerous for her as the Germans knew who she was.

She hugged Thérèse tightly again and thanked her many times over for being brave enough to risk everything for her brother. Thérèse again briefly asked herself why she was doing this and what Emmett would think if he knew about it, but she quickly dismissed those thoughts and told herself it was something that she needed to do.

The next day dawned quite sunny and warm for late October, and as Thérèse threw a few clothes into a rucksack that she'd borrowed from Eustace, she wondered whether she would be back in this house once more a few days from now, or whether she would have to remain in France for the rest of the war. She knew Emmett would be very angry with her if that were the case, and that she'd eventually have a lot of explaining to do to the kind cousins who had trusted her, and to her young daughter.

Donning her wool coat and the navy blue hat, she walked to the local bus stop to await the bus that would take her to the Southport station to catch the train for Liverpool. It occurred to her that she had done this journey twice in the last week, and she wondered if it would be something she would start to do frequently. Perhaps the Resistance would have other work for her to do once she had completed this mission? Don't get ahead of yourself, Thérèse, she told herself as the bus approached and she opened her handbag to find change for the bus fare.

Not long after that, she was sitting in the train that was due to pull out of the Southport station shortly, and she laid her head against the seat cushion and closed her eyes for what was supposed to be a few minutes.

When she awoke, the train was already pulling into Liverpool station, so she collected her rucksack and handbag and prepared to step out.

She was able to find a taxi to take her to the docks fairly quickly. Her heart beat rapidly as she thought about her meeting with "St. Tropez Harry," and she wondered what plans he had in store for her. Presumably, since they were meeting at the docks, she would be boarding a boat for France.

The taxi ride was short, and she was soon stepping onto the wharf at Departure Area B. It was about ten minutes to twelve, and she realized that she had timed her journey very closely, but she really didn't want to wait around on the wharf longer than necessary. It was quite breezy by the water's edge and she pulled her coat tighter around her.

At noon on the dot, she spotted a tall man in a brown coat walking towards her. He was looking in her direction and, as he got closer, she could see the dark moustache on his upper lip. This must be St. Tropez Harry.

He walked up to her with a purposeful step and smiled at her as he approached.

"Tropical Rose?" he asked.

"Yes, but my name's Thérèse," she answered him.

He looked furtively around him.

"Just stick to your code name," he whispered. "You never know who might be listening or watching through a telescope, or binoculars."

This was true spy stuff, out of the radio programmes that Thérèse had listened to at home with Emmett! She felt a little shiver go through her.

"Alright," she said. "So, what are the plans you have for me?"

"Get a hotel room anywhere you can find that's close to here," he told her, "then check out again at nine o'clock tonight. Meet me here again, and we'll have a boat waiting to take you to France. We'll smuggle you into Normandy, then someone will take you to Rouen by car. Always use your code name when talking to our operatives and, if you're stopped by the Germans, use the name that's on these papers and tell them you're a citizen."

He handed her a sheaf of papers and Thérèse leafed through them quickly. Her name was supposedly Madame Florence Albert and she lived in Elbeuf, Normandy.

"Are they stolen papers from a real citizen of France, or are they forged?" she asked Harry.

"They're forgeries, but they've really perfected the identity cards and birth certificates that the French are using these days," he answered her.

"The Germans won't know the difference."

"Thank you," she said, opening her handbag and depositing the papers inside. "Do you have any suggestions for hotels?"

"There are a few close to here," he replied. "Just start walking back to town and you'll soon come across one."

"Will they wonder why I'm checking out on the same day that I arrive?" she questioned him.

"You'll think of something." He smiled at her warmly. "I'm sure you've got lots of initiative."

Thérèse frowned. These days, she was getting far too good at thinking up lies quickly. She vowed to herself that, once this rescue mission was over, she would always tell the truth. That is, unless this mission was successful, and she was tempted to take on another.

54

Thérèse checked out of the Morrison Hotel at half-past eight that night, using a flimsy excuse about meeting a relative in town. It was the cheapest hotel close to the docks and after checking in she whiled away the afternoon, sitting at a table in a tea shop watching the passersby. A young man had at one point asked to join her, but she told him that she was "waiting for her husband" and he left her, tipping his cap in a disappointed fashion.

As she walked towards the docks once again, excitement mounted in her stomach, though outwardly she appeared calm. She had stashed her forged papers in her rucksack and purposely left her handbag in the hotel room, as she knew she wouldn't need a handbag where she was going. It was already dark outside, and she tried not to make eye contact with anyone she encountered along the way.

As she approached the docks, she saw a tall figure walking towards her. As he came closer, she recognized the dark hair and moustache and wondered again what his real name was.

"Good evening," he raised his hat politely to her. "Are we all ready to go?"

"I think so," she replied nervously, then added, "As ready as I'll ever be."

He nodded and indicated that she should follow him.

They walked for about twenty minutes along the wharf, and she looked inquisitively at the dark shapes of boats moored to the various landings. She assumed that most of them were fishing boats, as not too many people were taking pleasure boats out while there was a war going on.

Eventually, they took a left turn down one of the docks, and Harry turned to her, holding his arm out. She could make out a small fishing boat, not unlike the one she and Hélène's family had taken when they left France.

"This is your ferry, madam," Harry bowed with a flourish. "Captain Sinclair should get you safely to the other side. He knows all the spots to land so that the Germans won't be watching on the other side, and he has orders to take you to your contact once you land on the beach."

Now Thérèse was getting really excited. She felt once again like a real-life spy on a mission. A surge of confidence suddenly went through her and she felt that, with the impeccable organization of the Resistance, she was going to return Gaston safely to his sister in Southport.

"Thank you so much," she said to Harry.

"Let me introduce you to the captain," he said, taking her arm and leading her to the edge of the dock. He stepped down into the boat, then extended a hand to help her to climb in. She half-jumped, half-stepped in and felt the boat rocking precariously as she steadied herself.

"Careful, now," admonished Harry. "Are you alright?"

She nodded, and he led her down the small deck to the captain's cabin.

A middle-aged, bearded man was at the helm. He smiled pleasantly as Harry introduced them and then turned and introduced his ship's mate to her, André, a slender young Frenchman with dark blond hair.

"It's just the two of us on these night missions," the captain explained. "I try to involve as few of my crew as possible. You can never be too careful, you know."

Harry nodded in agreement.

"The fewer people know what we're up to, the better."

Thérèse smiled and sat down on the bench that Captain Sinclair indicated to her along the side of the cabin. André smiled at her and regarded her curiously.

"Well, Tropical Rose, I'll leave you here in the care of the captain and his mate, and I'll see you again on the other side," Harry said, holding out a hand to her. She shook it solemnly, then thanked him again for showing her to the boat.

As soon as Harry had disembarked, Captain Sinclair fired up the motor and the engine roared into life. Thérèse was glad she seemed to be a good sailor. She caught the young sailor eyeing her with a questioning look.

"Tropical Rose?" asked André, in French. "How did you come by that name?"

As the little boat made its way into the open water, Thérèse explained how Emmett had come up with his affectionate name for her. Then the captain changed gears and the engine became quieter.

"How long is the crossing, would you say?" Thérèse asked.

"Several hours," he replied. "You should try to get some sleep if you can."

Thérèse nodded and leaned her head back against the wall of the cabin. She knew that sleep wouldn't come easily - she was far too nervous and excited about this adventure. However, she thought she should at least try, as it would probably be a long day tomorrow. She took her rucksack off her back and made it into a makeshift pillow, hoping it would help her sleep, along with the rocking of the boat.

The time went by quickly and Thérèse managed to squeeze in a couple of hours' sleep. She awoke to pitch black, with only the small lantern in the cabin to help her distinguish the features of her shipmates. The sea was as calm as a millpond, with only the odd wave slapping the sides of the boat. She stood up and stretched, going to the porthole to look up at the night sky.

The stars were obscured by clouds, and even the moon had disappeared behind them.

"It's a good thing it's a cloudy night," remarked Captain Sinclair. "It will be a lot easier to land and get you to where you need to go."

Thérèse nodded.

"Have you done this a lot?" she asked him.

"Only when we have to bring someone across, or to get somebody out of France," he answered.

"How many times have you done it this year?"

"Oh, a dozen times or so," he told her.

This reassured Thérèse. The captain obviously knew what he was doing, and she didn't need to fear she would become a prisoner of the Germans, ending the mission before it started. Once again, she felt confident, and the little voice in her head told her not to worry about anything.

A half-hour later, the captain cut the engines and they slowly drifted towards the shore. The moon had reappeared, and Thérèse watched out of the porthole as the boat approached the empty beach. Dark shadows of tall trees bordered the shore, and she thought to herself that this looked like as safe a place as any to land.

Finally, they had come as close as they could to the shoreline without beaching the boat. André indicated that he would lower the rowboat from the side of the fishing craft and would ferry her the rest of the way.

When he returned, he nodded to her, and she held out her hand to Captain Sinclair.

"Thank you for a safe passage, Captain," she smiled as he shook her hand. "I expect I'll see you in a day or two once I have Gaston with me."

"Oh, no," the captain shook his head. "You'll be going back by plane. I think the gentleman is too frail to travel by boat. They want him to get back to England as quickly as possible."

This was the first that Thérèse had heard anything about coming back in a plane. She had never been on a plane before! But there was always a first time for everything. The thought occurred to her that she hadn't been told very much about this rescue mission. It seemed to be unfolding as it went along, and she just had to obey instructions. In retrospect, this made perfect sense as, if she were captured by the enemy, she wouldn't be able to reveal very much information. The thought of being captured sent a cold feeling down her spine, but she tried not to dwell on it. She picked up her rucksack and put it on her shoulders.

As they went out onto the deck, André stepped down into the rowboat waiting in the water and turned to help her get in, just as Harry had done back in England. The rowboat was far more unstable, though, and it started to rock quite violently as she stepped into it. She suddenly fell against André.

"*Mon Dieu,* watch out!" he said, grabbing hold of her and steadying her. "You don't want to end up in the water."

Thérèse laughed and removed herself gently from his grip.

"I haven't been in one of these since I was a young girl," she explained.

André nodded, then pointed to the wooden seat at the bow of the boat and told her she should sit there. She lowered herself very carefully onto it, trying not to rock the boat once again.

As soon as she was settled, André started to row and, in a few minutes, they felt the boat scraping sand. André put down his oars and jumped out quickly, pulling the boat up onto the beach until it was docked far enough in for Thérèse to alight while the boat stayed put in the water.

He once again held out a hand to help her out of the little vessel, then signalled that she should follow him. Thérèse stepped out on to the soft sand and started to walk towards the treeline while André pulled a flashlight out of one of the pockets of his windbreaker to light the way.

He motioned with his hand that she should stop walking once they reached the trees, then pulled a new-fangled machine that he called a "walkie-talkie" out of his other pocket. Thérèse had never seen such a thing and watched in awe as he flipped the switch and it crackled ominously.

"Come in, *Racine*," he spoke softly in French. "This is *Lumineux*. Over."

After a moment, the walkie-talkie came to life.

"*Ici, Racine*," a voice rasped on the other end. "Where are you?"

"On the beach, at the usual spot," André answered.

"Just stay put, I'll be there in a few minutes," came the answer.

André turned off the walkie-talkie.

"Now we just have to wait a moment," he explained. "Your contact, *Racine*, will be here to take you to base and Rouen, then you'll meet Gaston. We'd better shelter in the trees so we're not too obvious to anyone who decides to take a midnight stroll."

Thérèse nodded and followed him into a little thicket among the trees, where they found a log to sit on. She pulled her jacket around her against the cool breeze that was blowing off the sea. After all, it was late autumn in the North of France, and therefore, not exactly warm. The trees were rustling softly as they sat there waiting.

Before long, they heard a vehicle pull up in the distance. Shortly afterwards, a man about Thérèse's age appeared through the trees. He was wearing a flat cap and was dressed like a farmer in dungarees and boots, with a brown woolen jacket left undone in the front. She couldn't help but notice that he was very handsome. Under the flat cap, he had thick dark hair and his eyes were piercing and black, fringed by long lashes. His face was chiselled, with a cleft in his chin and high cheekbones. He reminded her of one of those French film stars that all the young women swooned over.

They stood up quickly, and the two men greeted each other. André then turned towards Thérèse.

"This is Tropical Rose," he indicated her. "And this is your contact, *Racine*."

The other man smiled and held out his hand to shake hers.

"Pleased to meet you," he told her politely, shaking her hand firmly. "I'll be driving you to Rouen, but first we have to stop somewhere outside the nearest village. We don't want to get arrested by the Germans for being out after curfew."

Thérèse nodded in agreement, smiling at him. Even in the dark, she could see that his eyes were warm and friendly.

"I'll be leaving you now, Rose," said André in a business-like tone. "Have to get back to the boat before dawn arrives."

Thérèse thanked him for the safe passage, and they wished each other good luck. He turned back to get into the rowboat, and Racine took her by the arm with a nod of his head. They walked in silence for a few moments, then she saw a break in the trees along the beach. There was an old farm truck parked there in the clearing.

As they got into the truck, Thérèse turned to him.

"Why did you pick "Racine" for your code name? she asked him, curious.

"He grinned mischievously.

"I was a novelist and playwright in my other life," he explained. "And you? Why Tropical Rose?"

"I was grown in the tropics and transplanted to England," smiling at her own wit. "So where are we going now?"

Racine started up the motor of the truck and navigated the way through another glade of trees. He seemed to know where he was going, and Thérèse relaxed a little.

"We'll spend the night in a farmhouse just outside the village, then leave by about eight o'clock tomorrow morning to drive to Rouen," he explained to her. "The plan is to pose as a farmer and his wife bringing fruits and vegetables to the market in the city. We'll meet at the house of the people who are sheltering the subject."

"Do I look like a farmer's wife?" asked Thérèse anxiously, gesturing towards her smart woolen jacket and shoes.

"Don't worry," he reassured her. "The lady at the farm will have some clothes for you."

She nodded and started to feel more relaxed in this man's easy company.

"Gaston is the subject?" she asked.

"Yes," he answered her. "But we'll refer to him in code, as well. His name will be *Colombe*."

"Dove."

"Yes, but in this case, he's a wounded dove."

"How is he?" she asked solicitously.

"He's in a lot of pain, and his fever comes and goes. He was shot by a German soldier as he was escaping from the factory. A doctor removed the bullet, but in less than favourable circumstances, and he's not recovering very well. We think there may some infection in the wound."

"Well, I'm not a nurse," replied Thérèse. "But I know how to treat infections."

"Oh, you're not a nurse?" Racine shot a sideways glance at her, looking a bit nervous.

"No, but I volunteered for this because nobody came forward, and my friend is very anxious to get her brother back. I have enough nursing experience from helping my mother on the estate where I grew up and from raising my own family. I know what to do for an infection."

"Even from a bullet wound?" he asked, incredulously.

"Oh, yes," she replied confidently.

She thought back to the time when one of her brothers had accidentally shot himself in the foot with a gun before going hunting with some friends. The wound hadn't been serious, but her mother had shown her what to do to heal it. Her brother had recovered quickly and was walking around the house again in just a few days.

"Well, that's good," he said in a somewhat hesitant tone. They emerged from the trees, and he turned the old truck onto the narrow road that would take them to their rest stop for the night.

When they arrived at the farmhouse, the farmer's wife gave them a bowl of hot soup and some homemade bread. Thérèse hadn't realized how hungry she was until she tasted the delicious onion and potato soup. It was wonderful what some people could do with food rationing, but she supposed that a farmer's household would have better access to fresh food.

They were shown to their respective bedrooms, and the farmer's wife, Mme Blais, found a flowery cotton dress and headscarf for Thérèse to wear in the morning. The dress was too big for her, but Mme Blais gave her a cheap fabric belt to tie around it. She also found her an ancient raincoat that looked like it had seen better days. However, Thérèse knew that she had to look the part of an agricultural worker, not a fashion model, so she was content with it. A thought occurred to her.

"What should I do with my clothes after I leave?" she asked Mme Blais.

"You can leave them here until you come back," replied the farmer's wife, smiling. "I'll keep them safe for you."

Thérèse smiled back at her, then thanked her and went to the little bathroom and washed her face. Returning to her little room, she finally lay down on the narrow bed. The oil lamp illuminated the wooden panels in the walls and made the room look cozy and inviting. It was pleasantly warm in there, unlike the cramped little room she shared with Vivienne in the attic of Eustace's house. She reached over and turned down the lamp, realizing that this was the first sleep she'd had in twenty-four hours, other than the couple of hours of napping she had stolen on the boat. She quickly fell into a deep and dreamless sleep.

She was awakened by the sound of knocking on the bedroom door.

"*Madame* Rose?" inquired the farmer's voice, in a stage whisper. Racine had told the farm couple that her name was Rose, but she hesitated for a moment at the unfamiliar name before answering.

"Yes?"

"It's six o'clock. Would you like to get up and come to the kitchen for some breakfast?"

Thérèse acquiesced and jumped out of the bed. She quickly washed and dressed, then went down the hallway to the large, comfortable kitchen of the farmhouse. Racine was already seated at the table, a large cup of *café au lait* and a plate piled high with food in front of him. The farmer sat across the table from him reading a two-day old copy of what Thérèse took to be the local newspaper. They both smiled at her and nodded "Good morning" as she seated herself between them at the table.

"*Les Bosches* are bombing London again," *Monsieur* Blais announced, by way of conversation.

Racine pursed his lips, and Thérèse's heart skipped a beat as she thought of Emmett. The men discussed the war situation while Mme Blais brought her a plate of porridge, ham and fruit, with two thick slices of freshly baked bread. Thérèse was reluctant to eat such a large plate of food, but the farmer's wife said that it might be the last time she would eat for many hours, so she complied.

By seven o'clock, Racine and *Monsieur* Blais had loaded up the old farm truck with fruits and vegetables, and Racine and Thérèse were bidding the famer and his wife a grateful farewell.

Mme Blais gave Thérèse a warm hug and chucked her on the chin as she said goodbye.

"*Adieu, ma petite,*" she told her. "I wish you the very best of luck and do be careful."

"Thank you, *madame,*" answered Thérèse, "for everything you've done for us, and for the war."

"I do it for France," came the smiling reply, although Thérèse thought she could glimpse a worried look on the woman's face.

Racine once again put the truck into gear and they pulled out of the farmyard, sending chickens and a few crows protesting and flying out of their way.

They arrived in Rouen around noon, approaching the entrance to the city slowly. Racine showed their papers to the German guards who were stationed at the outskirts. Thérèse felt very nervous handing over papers that were false, but she tried to mimic Racine's outward confidence towards the guards.

Thérèse examined their faces. They wore cold, haughty expressions, but their faces were so young that she couldn't help thinking to herself that these were just mere boys doing the job of much older men. She supposed that a lot of it was bravado as they exerted their authority over the people who came and went throughout the day. She was very aware of the guns that they carried by their sides and knew they probably wouldn't hesitate to use them if the opportunity arose.

After the guards had conducted a perfunctory search of the back of the truck, Racine pulled away and started driving down the main street of the city. The street seemed quiet for a busy metropolis, and not very many people were going about their business even though the day was half done. Occupied France showed a sombre face to the conquering enemy, one that masked the lively undercurrent of resistance going on beneath the surface.

After driving through the city for a while, they arrived at the safe house where Gaston was staying. Racine parked the farm truck on the street in front of a small white house which had all of its shutters closed, even though it was broad daylight. Getting out of the truck, he came around to the passenger door to help Thérèse out.

"Ready to meet your patient?" he asked her.

"Yes, I am," she replied, smiling, ,as they went up to the to the house, which looked quite deserted.

Racine knocked three times on the door, waited a few seconds, and rapped three times again. The door opened abruptly and a face peered out.

"Are you coming to see the customer?" said the middle-aged man who answered.

"Yes, is he at home?" asked Racine.

"He is. Come in," the man replied.

He held the door open just wide enough to let the two of them pass, closing it after them as they stepped inside. Thérèse assumed their words had been a code allowing them access to the safe house.

She looked around her. The house was shabby and dimly lit inside, with sparse furnishings that looked as though they had been hastily arranged in the rooms as an afterthought. The man who let them in then turned and introduced himself to Thérèse.

"*L'Epine*, the thorn in the side of the enemy," he said, shaking hands with her firmly. He was an averaged-sized man with greying brown hair and lively brown eyes, who looked like he could be a schoolteacher. Thérèse suspected, however, that he did something altogether different in his everyday life. A schoolteacher would not be staying in a safe house during the day when school was normally in progress.

"Pleased to meet you, I'm Tropical Rose," she told him.

"I know that. We've been expecting you. Would you like something to eat, or would you prefer to meet your patient first?'

"I'd like to meet him, if that's alright," she replied.

"Racine? Are you hungry? You can help yourself to some food from the larder," l'Epine addressed her fellow traveller.

"No, I'm not hungry. The wife of our farmer friend gave us more than enough to eat for breakfast," Racine assured him. L'Epine turned again to Thérèse.

"Follow me," he said, indicating the stairs that went to the upper part of the house. Thérèse felt a quiver of anticipation in her stomach at the prospect of meeting the reason for her journey to this house. She followed the older man as he strode purposefully up the stairs.

They went down a corridor, and L'Epine stopped at the door of the very last room and knocked.

"Yes?" a weak voice answered.

"It's l'Epine. Your nurse has arrived," 'L'Epine announced, with a wink at Thérèse.

He pushed the door open, then stepped back to allow her to go into the room.

55

The room was darkened, and Thérèse recognized the smell of infection as soon as she walked in. She went straight to the window and opened the curtain a little so she could get a better look at her patient.

He lay supine on the bed, his eyes closed and his face ashen. She took in his features and thought how like Lucille he was. She knew that he was a little older than his sister, but he could have been her twin. He had the same dark brown hair and fine features, except that his were pale and he looked ill.

Crossing over to him, she laid a hand on his forehead, which was burning with fever.

"I'm Rose," she said softly. "I'm going to look after you until we can get you to England."

He opened his eyes slowly and smiled faintly as he studied her face.

"Pleased to meet you," he said. "I'm a little banged-up, but I can still appreciate an angel in my presence."

She smiled back at him, then picked up the arm that was closest to her and placed two fingers on his wrist. His pulse was quite quick, and a little irregular.

"Will you permit me to take a look at your wound?" she asked him, taking hold of the blanket that covered him.

He nodded, and she pulled the covers back gently. His trousers had been cut above the knee of his left leg, and she unwound a bloodstained bandage from his left thigh, revealing a large, deep wound. It had been a bullet wound, but the bullet had been roughly removed from the leg and it was now infected.

She probed the wound gently, which elicited some soft groans from her patient, but he bore her ministrations mostly with a brave face.

"Well, we'll wash that wound thoroughly and apply a poultice and maybe a little iodine," she told him. "Then I'll give you some Aspirin for your fever."

He grimaced at the sound of the word "iodine," but she knew he would bear the pain of the treatment courageously. Here was a man who had risked everything to sabotage a German facility, even though he knew he could be arrested and executed.

"I'll be back in a few minutes," she advised her patient. "Just rest while I'm gone."

He closed his eyes again and she left the room quietly. She went downstairs to the kitchen, where l'Epine sat drinking a cup of coffee. She assumed that Racine must have gone on to another mission but asked after him.

"Oh, he'll be back," L'Epine assured her. "He just went to Headquarters to see if anything new has come in from London."

"This isn't Headquarters"? Thérèse asked.

"No, this is just a safe house," he replied.

She nodded.

"Well, would you be able to get me some iodine, mustard plaster and a bottle of Aspirin from a pharmacy?" she asked him. "Or willow bark, if they don't have it?"

He stood up.

"Certainly," he answered her. "I know an apothecary who can help us and who won't report it to the enemy. They'll come sniffing around if they hear that somebody is looking to treat a wound not long after they shot one of our operatives."

Thérèse nodded in agreement, and l'Epine walked out of the room. She heard the front door close quietly as he left to discharge the errand.

He returned after about twenty minutes, a brown paper parcel in his hand. She had gone back up to Gaston's room and was sitting by his bed, watching him sleep. He moaned softly in his sleep occasionally, but his eyes remained closed until l'Epine walked into the room.

"I hope that everything is in order," said l'Epine, as Thérèse opened the package and looked through the contents.

Thérèse nodded and told him she would need to boil some water for mustard plaster, and also for dissolving the willow bark. Aspirin was apparently inaccessible in the pharmacies at the moment, as most of it had been commandeered by the German army for their soldiers. She let her patient know that she would get everything ready to treat his wound, and he closed his eyes again.

As they descended the stairs, l'Epine asked her if she thought that Gaston would be well enough to travel soon.

"Yes, I think so," she replied. "We should probably wait for his fever to break, though. How will we be travelling? He won't be able to do much walking."

"Racine will drive you in the farm truck to the place where we can land a plane, about forty kilometres from here," he explained. "Do you think he'll be alright in the back of the truck?"

"It may be uncomfortable, but I'm sure he's endured worse," she answered him.

"Oh, yes," said l'Epine. "The doctor had to remove the bullet without anaesthetic. He was very strong about it. It must have been terrible."

Thérèse couldn't imagine how anyone could bear the pain of having something removed from a limb without anaesthetic, and she had given birth to three children without any pain relief. She gained a whole new respect for this brave young man who had done so much to help his country in a war against tyranny without complaint.

"When do you think we'll be flying over to England?" she questioned l'Epine.

"It depends on how quickly he recovers and when our operatives can organize the flight with London," he told her as they entered the small kitchen. "It could be as soon as tomorrow, or maybe later in the week. You should keep us informed as to how your patient is coming along, then we'll make the arrangements from there."

"Well, why don't you ask them to start making the arrangements now, and we can keep them up to date as to how soon we'll be ready?"

L'Epine looked at her with a whole new respect.

"I admire your optimism," he said, patting Thérèse on the shoulder. "That's just the kind of spirit we need in our operations."

She smiled and turned her attention to filling up a kettle to put on the wood stove.

Gaston was very stoic with Thérèse's ministrations, even when she applied the iodine to his wound. After she had cleaned and re-bandaged the wound, she plumped up his pillows and suggested that he try to sleep once more. As she turned to leave the room, he reached out and put his hand on her arm.

"I just want you to know how grateful I am to you," he told her quietly, his dark eyes gazing into hers.

"My sister is lucky to have such a good friend, and so am I, to meet a woman who's willing to risk everything to save my life."

Thérèse patted his hand gently.

"I will do whatever I can to help someone who has fought so bravely for all of our liberty," she said warmly, smiling at him as she spoke. "The Allies need people like you."

This young man reminded her of her two brothers who had been lost in the Great War. He was about the same age as her favourite brother, Philippe, had been when he died, and in some ways made her think of him. Perhaps that was some of her motivation in being so determined to help her friend's brother. She patted his hand again.

"Get some rest," she urged him. "I'll check in on you in a couple of hours to see if there's anything you need."

He closed his eyes and turned his head to the wall. She watched him for a few moments, then, seeing his chest rise and fall evenly, silently slipped out of the room.

In the kitchen, she made herself a pot of tea and sat drinking it alone at the little wooden table, her mind lost in thought.

The front door of the house opened after a few minutes, and Racine walked in.

"There you are, Rose," he greeted her. "How's the patient?"

"Well, I've cleaned his wound and given him some willow bark for the pain. He's asleep right now, and I'm going to check on him later this afternoon."

"Do you think he'll be ready to travel by tomorrow night?" he asked enthusiastically.

"I don't know," she replied. "Perhaps we'll know better by the morning."

He nodded.

"Alright, then," he said. "I've been in touch with HQ in London and they're going to send out a plane tomorrow night to bring you both across the water."

Thérèse nodded but said nothing. It was still too early to tell how her patient would be feeling by tomorrow. Racine came closer to her.

"Do you think he'll be ready?" he pressed her.

"I really can't say," she answered. "I'll check in on him this afternoon and again tonight to see if his fever's come down at all. If so, he may be alright by morning."

"Good!" pronounced Racine. "I'll radio them tomorrow if you give me the A-OK. It's a very tight timeline, I know, but the longer he stays in France, the more likely the Germans will be to find him."

Thérèse frowned. She felt very pressured by his insistence but knew he was doing it for the right reasons. She prayed quietly to herself that Gaston would respond to the infection-killing iodine and the powers of willow bark to reduce fever and inflammation. It wasn't the first time that she had provided treatment for an infected wound, though, and the results were usually favourable.

When she looked in on Gaston later that afternoon, he was still asleep, but his body was bathed in sweat. She knew this to be a very good sign and awoke him briefly to give him some sips of water from the cup she had brought with her. When she returned that evening, his forehead was cooler to the touch, and she administered another dose of willow bark to make sure that the fever didn't climb higher during the night.

She reported back to Racine and l'Epine, who had returned to the house to share the dinner that a Resistance volunteer had come to prepare for them. It was a simple meal of vegetable soup and bread, but it tasted delicious to Thérèse, who had barely eaten all day.

"Well, that's good news!" enthused Racine, his handsome face beaming. "We have a clever nurse here who knows what she's doing."

Thérèse felt herself blushing, and l'Epine smiled at her in an avuncular fashion.

"We'll radio Headquarters in London tomorrow morning," he told her. "At this rate, Gaston will be safely away from here by tomorrow night. Excellent!"

"Barring any relapses," Thérèse reminded him.

"I'm sure there won't be any," Racine declared. "I'm confident that he'll be feeling better by this time tomorrow."

"God willing," she added fervently.

The two men nodded.

"God willing," l'Epine echoed.

Before Thérèse lay down on the small cot that had been provided for her beside Gaston's room, she knelt and said a fervent prayer that Racine's confidence in her would be justified and that her patient would be on the road to recovery by morning.

56

Thérèse woke up early the next day. The small clock in the bedroom showed five o'clock, and daylight was starting to creep into the room. She lay there for a few more minutes, then got up and went down the hall to the bathroom. After washing her face and combing her hair, she returned to her room and dressed quickly in the clothes she had worn the day before. She then tiptoed lightly back to Gaston's room, cracked open the door quietly and looked at her patient.

He was lying on his side, his hair slicked across his forehead, but his face now had some colour to it. He was breathing evenly, and she tiptoed up to him and took his wrist in her hand to check his pulse.

It was beating slowly and evenly, which was encouraging. She briefly brushed her hand across his forehead, and found it cool to the touch. This action caused him to stir slightly as he registered her touch, but he murmured softly and turned over in the bed. The sheets were soaked through and his shirt stained with sweat, which meant that the willow bark had done its job. Satisfied, she turned and left the room.

Thérèse went down the stairs and into the kitchen, in search of some tea or coffee and something to eat for breakfast. She was startled by a voice as she looked around the pantry for some bread or eggs and turned around to see Racine watching her.

"Good morning, Rose," he greeted her with a smile. "How are you this morning?"

"Very well, thank you," she replied, once more impressed with how handsome he was. Again, she thought how much he looked like a French film star.

"And do I dare to ask how Gaston is today?" he asked, tentatively.

"Well, his fever seems to have broken," she told him. "And I think he has a little more colour in his face."

"That's what I wanted to hear! I knew I could have confidence in you."

"A little prayer helped, as well," Thérèse replied modestly. "Do you think you'll radio London today to see if they can come and get him tonight?"

"Yes, the sooner we get him out of here and into a British hospital, the better. Not that I don't trust your nursing skills," he added, hastily.

Thérèse smiled and inquired what they should eat for breakfast.

"Just make some coffee for now," he replied. "A volunteer will be coming in to make breakfast for us in a little while."

"I can get breakfast," she insisted. "I'm a housewife at home, you know, and quite used to preparing food for my family. Just show me where everything is, and I'll do it."

"Practical, as well as beautiful!" smiled Racine, his eyes glancing admiringly over her. "And an excellent nurse, too. Your husband is a lucky man, Rose."

Thérèse blushed at this, warming to his attention.

"If I didn't know better, I'd think you were flirting with me, *monsieur*," she countered.

"That's for you to guess and me to know, *madame*," he grinned.

They held each other's gaze for a brief moment, then Thérèse dropped her eyes, blushing deeply as she did so. She thought back on the promise that she had made to herself years ago about not flirting with other men and turned her attention to finding the coffee and putting the pot on to boil. She had to be careful with this man, she felt, as he was obviously very aware of his good looks and his effect on women.

They ate some poached eggs and a baguette in a rather awkward silence, then Racine spoke in a business-like voice.

"We'll have to check with l'Epine and see if things are ready for the return mission," he told her. "With any luck, we'll have Gaston in England by midnight tonight."

"How are we going to get him out of here without the German soldiers seeing him?" she asked.

"We'll stow him in the back of the farm truck surrounded with fruits and vegetables," he replied.

"Well, what if they decide to search the truck?" she asked, her pulse quickening at the thought.

"Let's hope they don't," he answered her. "It's a risk we'll just have to take."

Thérèse pondered the plan for a few moments. It was very risky, and she knew that it could end up being disastrous. She knew she had her own courage, and that she could lean into it to get her through this, as well as the intuition which was still telling her that it would be alright. However, she hoped that she could count on the ingenuity and courage of this man who would be accompanying them.

They finished their breakfast, then Racine got up and went to find l'Epine. Thérèse washed up the breakfast things, her heart fluttering nervously as she thought about the events that would be unfolding later that day.

Racine returned later that morning to tell her they would be departing at five o'clock that evening. He explained that they had to leave the city before the curfew was declared; otherwise they would be stopped by the Germans and questioned. If they left during daylight, the soldiers would just assume they were a farming couple returning to their home in the country after a market day. They would then drive for a while to some woods outside Rouen, abandon the truck and walk for a couple of kilometres to a clearing in the woods where, with any luck, the plane would be able to land successfully and pick up Gaston and herself.

The plan seemed fairly simple, but it could all go terribly wrong with one false move. The German soldiers wouldn't hesitate to shoot Gaston on sight and to arrest her and l'Epine as spies and Resistance fighters. She knew that would be a terrible fate, as she'd heard tales of people being arrested and never seen again. Torture and death would probably be a part of the picture.

She dismissed these fears and told herself optimistically that the mission would proceed flawlessly. After all, Lucille had escaped from France, hadn't she? She decided to go upstairs and see whether Gaston was awake so that she could fill him in on the plan.

The day dragged by. Racine and l'Epine came and went to the little house, and Thérèse played cards with Gaston, who was feeling much better. His colour now looked healthier, and he was able to get out of bed and walk around a little, limping on his bad leg. Thérèse wondered how he was going to be able to walk "a couple of kilometres" to the plane tonight, but she dismissed the thought, hoping that it would all miraculously turn out as planned. She crossed her fingers and once again offered up a silent prayer.

After a light meal of boiled potatoes and salad with Racine at around four o'clock, Thérèse once more donned the farmer's wife's clothing. She went upstairs to take Gaston his supper, then helped him to dress in the peasant clothes that l'Epine had provided for him. He struggled to put them on, but the operation was finally accomplished and she started to help him down the stairs.

He winced and groaned as he took the first few steps, holding onto the banister, then she offered him her shoulder to lean on. He did so gratefully, but his weight proved to be too much for her. She called out to Racine, who came and took most of the man's weight on to his own shoulders. They limped down the stairs and once again she wondered to herself how Gaston was going to make it to the plane tonight.

Shortly before five o'clock, Racine announced that it was time to leave. The farm truck had been hidden in an old garage just down the street, and he would bring it to the alley behind the house so that they could hide Gaston in the back without anyone seeing him. Thérèse nodded, certain that Racine had done this sort of thing many times before and that it wouldn't be a difficult task for him.

He returned several minutes later, and they all shook hands with l'Epine, who had arrived at the house to wish them well. He kissed Thérèse on both cheeks.

"You're a brave woman, *ma chère,*" he told her. "I'm sure that our friend will be safely restored to his sister without incident by tomorrow morning."

Thérèse nodded, swallowing hard and hoping against hope that he was right. The time to go was finally here, a feeling of dread was growing in her stomach. The operation had to go smoothly, it had to! She smiled at l'Epine and tried to look more confident than she felt.

The evening was cool and, thankfully, there were clouds in the sky. There wouldn't be too many people out strolling on a dull evening like this. As they made their way out to the back of the house, Gaston leaned on Racine and l'Epine for support and limped along stoically. They crossed the little garden and went out into the alley.

L'Epine wished them goodbye and good luck once again, and Racine opened the back of the farm truck and helped Gaston to slide onto the truck bed. He groaned on a couple of occasions when Racine pulled too hard on his body in an effort to pull him to the back of the truck and surround him with the copious piles of fruits and vegetables that had been loaded in there. Thérèse assumed this was what Racine had been doing all afternoon during his many trips back and forth to the house.

Once the operation was complete, Racine told Thérèse that she should get into the front seat of the truck and got in beside her, a grim expression of concentration on his handsome face. She suspected that he was as nervous as she was but didn't want to show it in front of her.

He turned the key in the ignition and the engine started up grudgingly. He edged the truck out of the alley and started down the street.

As they turned the corner, Thérèse glanced backwards and thought she saw a curtain in one of the neighbouring houses close quietly, as if someone didn't want to be seen observing them.

57

They drove in silence through the streets of the city. People were hurrying between the little shops, trying to get their errands accomplished before curfew struck. German soldiers could be seen walking in groups of two, their guns held closely to their sides in case of any signs of troubles. Occasionally, they could be seen questioning a nervous-looking citizen, but nobody was arrested. Thérèse was eventually able to relax a little and hope that they would get away easily with Gaston stashed away in the back of the truck.

They reached the city limits within a short time, and Racine started to rummage around in one of his pockets, the other hand firmly on the wheel.

"What are you looking for?" asked Thérèse.

"Our papers," he replied shortly. Thérèse had given hers to Racine earlier for safekeeping. She worried for a moment that he might have misplaced them, but he suddenly pulled them out of his pocket and pushed them into her hand.

"Have a look at them. Familiarize yourself with the details."

She looked over the papers, which were printed on thin white paper with rather runny blue ink. They were identified as "Monsieur Hector Albert of the village of Elbeuf, Normandy, farmer" and "Madame Florence Albert, citizen of Elbeuf, Normandy." Thérèse smiled to herself. Interesting that the gentleman was identified as a farmer where his wife, who probably worked just as hard on the farm as her husband, was only recognized as being a citizen. Nonetheless, she hoped that the forged papers would hold up to the scrutiny of the German guards at the edge of the city.

Racine rummaged in another pocket of his jacket and pulled out a revolver, which he laid on his lap. Thérèse stared at it with a queasy feeling. Racine looked over at her.

"We have to have it," he explained, seeing her trepidation. "If they suspect us, we have to make a run for it."

He hid it under his jacket, but close at hand, then drove slowly up to the check stop at the city's edge.

Thérèse could see the little booth with a German soldier stationed in it. Another one stood outside, his gun slung over his back. As they drove closer, she scrutinized their grim faces.

Racine rolled down the window, and the young soldier in the booth came out and thrust his hand out.

"*Papieren,*" he demanded.

Racine silently handed him the papers. The soldier looked them over, examining each of their faces as he read the appropriate paper.

"Do you have cargo in the truck?" he questioned Racine, in halting French.

Racine nodded.

"*Was ist es?*" When Racine didn't respond immediately, he repeated in French, "What is it?"

"Fruits and vegetables left over from the market," Racine replied.

"So", barked the young soldier. "Get out of the truck and open the back for me."

"Why? I've already told you what's inside," countered Racine. Thérèse's heart started to race.

"Just do as I say," the soldier raised his voice, beckoning to his fellow guard, who started to walk towards the truck.

Looking back, Thérèse couldn't really remember what transpired, it all happened so fast. Racine suddenly pointed the gun at the young German soldier, fired it, then stepped on the accelerator of the truck as heavily as he could and sped through the check stop.

Thérèse gasped in horror as she saw the first soldier fall to the ground, then his colleague come running towards them, gun aimed and shouting at them loudly,

"*Halt! Halt!*"

Racine kept on driving, the wheels of the truck screeching around corners in the road at every turn. Thérèse felt as though she was outside of her body, terror pulsating through her. As she looked back, she could see the second soldier jump into a jeep and start it up, following them down the road, his gun aimed out the window.

He fired two or three shots at them, but they all missed. Next he leaned his hand on the horn of the jeep, but Racine continued driving. As frightened as she was, Thérèse couldn't help but notice how calm and determined he looked. She felt hot tears come to her eyes and let out a little gasp of fear.

"Just keep quiet, *chérie*," he urged her, grimly. "I'm going to try to get us out of this."

She wondered whether he'd ever actually been in a situation like this before, and her racing mind spared a thought for poor Gaston, who was probably being bumped all over the place in the back of the rickety old truck and was wondering what was happening. She glanced back and saw the army jeep behind them in hot pursuit. She sent up a little prayer to Saint Mary to deliver them from this dire situation, then clenched her fists together and closed her eyes.

She heard Racine fire two shots at the jeep that continued to follow them closely. From what she could see in the rear-view mirror, the German soldier was gripping the wheel with stubborn determination. She prayed again that Racine would be able to outrun him in the old truck. If he caught up to them, Racine would have to be very quick with his gun before the soldier aimed his rifle at them.

They continued down the road, careering along and veering dangerously at every turn. She heard two more shots coming from the jeep, but once again the soldier missed his mark.

A few more minutes passed, and Thérèse suddenly realized with a sinking feeling that he seemed to be gaining on them.

"He's getting closer!" she hissed at Racine, the feeling of dread once more possessing her.

He nodded, told her to grab the wheel, then started to turn in his seat, leaning further out the window.

"B - but . . . but . . . I've never driven before!" she stuttered.

"Never mind, just hold it straight for a minute," he spat out, turning his attention to the jeep behind them. She obeyed him, although with mounting fear. She fervently wished now that she'd taken those driving lessons Emmett had offered her when they were first married!

Racine fired another shot with his pistol, and Thérèse heard a loud bang, followed by the screech of brakes.

"Got him!" pronounced Racine, a look of satisfaction crossing his face. He took the wheel back from her, and Thérèse looked back once again. She saw that the jeep was zigzagging all over the road, one of the front tires blown out, and the German soldier was trying desperately to keep it from going off the road.

"*Oh, mon Dieu*!" she gasped out. "You did it, Racine! You did it!"

She watched as the jeep slithered inevitably into the ditch, down the embankment and into the woods, finally crashing into a tree. There was no movement from within and she realized that Racine had probably killed or seriously injured the enemy soldier. He eased up his pressure on the accelerator and they slowed down gradually once again. She looked squarely at him.

"The Germans will be looking for us now," she told him in a scared voice. "They'll be wanting to capture a Resistance fighter who shot at two of their own, and his accomplice."

"Yes," Racine answered her grimly. "We'll just have to detour around all of the small towns on our way to our rendezvous point and make sure that no enemy troops spot us."

"Do you know the way around the towns?" she asked.

"I have a compass," he replied. "But it will add time to our journey."

"We should check on Gaston," she pointed out. "All that twisting and turning in the back of the truck couldn't have been good for his injuries."

"Let me get us a little further away," he told her. "Just in case our friend comes to and radios for help."

She nodded and tried to calm herself with a few deep breaths while Racine continued down the narrow road, seemingly unaffected by what had just happened. She shot him a glance. She was realizing that he was one cool character and had to admire his quick thinking and ability to handle the situation.

A little further down the road, when nothing more was heard from their pursuer, Racine slowed the truck to a halt, pulling onto some grass by the side of the road. He nodded at Thérèse, and she quickly got out of the vehicle and went around the back. She pulled open the doors and glanced inside.

Gaston was lying on his back towards the rear of the truck, surrounded by raw fruits and vegetables that had been scattered all over the place by their chase.

"Are you alright?" She climbed into the truck bed and examined his face anxiously.

He nodded.

"What happened back there?" he asked her, as she checked his pulse and felt his forehead.

"We were pursued by a German soldier in an army jeep after we ran through their check stop," she said in a voice that sounded much calmer than she felt.

"I heard shots," he answered. "What happened?"

"Racine managed to shoot one of his tyres out and he went off the road."

"Good old Racine!" grinned Gaston. "I knew I was in good hands when they assigned him to my rescue."

He then looked at her and smiled.

"And, of course, you as well, Rose," he added, his eyes resting warmly on her.

Thérèse smiled back at him.

"I did nothing," she said. "Just held the wheel for a minute or so while Racine took aim. How's your leg feeling?"

"It hurts like the devil, and I had to hang on tight to prevent being rolled around the inside of this old jalopy, but I'm feeling much better than I was."

Thérèse nodded. His pulse seemed to be normal, and his forehead was still cool.

"Racine said our journey to the meeting place is going to take longer, since we have to avoid the towns on the way. We don't want to run into any more German soldiers," she told him.

"I'll be alright," he replied bravely. "Just bring me some water, if you can."

Thérèse nodded once more, then went back to the cab of the truck to find a water canteen for Gaston. She took it back to him, then helped him to drink from it.

"Will you be alright now, do you think?" she asked.

"Yes, as long as we don't have any more high-speed chases," he replied.

"Let's hope not," she answered grimly.

They continued with their drive as daylight waned and gave way to dusk. The trees on either side of the highway became taller and thicker, and she marvelled at Racine's ability to navigate through the countryside while avoiding the towns and villages along the way.

Her nervous fear had slowly dissipated and, for the first time since they had left the German soldiers behind them, she began to feel confident that they would pull off this mission without any more hitches. However, a little niggling voice kept whispering in her ear that their ordeal wasn't over yet.

58

Their journey went on for several more hours. Racine stopped twice more to add fuel to the old truck from a jerry can, and to pass out some baguettes and cheese that they had brought with them. Thérèse had packed the food at the last minute before they had left the safe house, anticipating that they would get hungry throughout the night. She once again checked on Gaston and gave him something to eat, and removed a few pieces of fruit that were stashed in the back of the truck for later consumption, if they needed it. He accepted it gratefully, and she was pleased to see that he had an appetite, further proof that he was getting better.

After their second stop, darkness had completely set in, and Racine had to keep the headlights on in order to see the road.

"Do we have to travel much further?" she asked him, shifting in her seat and feeling stiff from the prolonged hours of sitting.

"Just about another hour or so," he replied. "I'm not sure what time the plane is landing, so we may have to wait for a while. I hope your coat is warm," he added, glancing dubiously at her.

This was not something that Thérèse had thought of. She looked down at the old coat and wished she had asked the farmer's wife for a thicker one. She hoped it would keep her warm.

Roughly an hour later, Racine started to slow the truck down, telling Thérèse that they had almost reached their destination. She looked around her at the trees in the darkness and wondered how he could possibly know that they were nearly there, since everything looked pretty much the same as it had for the last few hours. However, she knew she had to trust that he knew what he was doing. After all, he wouldn't have been put in charge of this mission if he wasn't capable of getting them successfully through it. She acquiesced with a nod. He followed the edge of the road with the truck for a few more yards, all the while slowing down, then finally let out a little satisfied sound.

"There's our landmark," he announced, pointing to the side of the road. Thérèse peered into the distance, then noticed a streak of white paint on one of the trees at the side of the road.

"What's that for?" she asked.

"One of our *compatriotes* painted that earlier today," he told her. "He said it would be somewhere along this part of the woods."

"Well, it's surprising that you were able to find it all," she replied admiringly. "How did you know it would be at this particular spot?"

"He told me to count kilometres from the last crossroads, and that's what I did," he said, as if it was the most obvious thing in the world.

Thérèse was very impressed. She was pretty certain she wouldn't have been able to keep track of the kilometres and notice a landmark like the one he had seen, but that's why Racine was doing this job. He obviously had some very sharp tracking and observational skills. She looked at him with a new respect.

"So what do we do now?" she asked him.

"We get Gaston out of the back, and then we have to walk about two kilometres through the woods until we get to a clearing where the plane will land," he advised her.

She stared at him with alarm. "Do you think he'll be able to do that?" she asked.

"He'll have to," he rejoined. Then, seeing her worried expression, he added," he can lean on me if he has trouble walking."

She shrugged her shoulders doubtfully, but then followed him around to the back of the truck.

With Gaston leaning on Racine's shoulder, they started to limp their way through the woods. It was deathly quiet in there and extremely dark. The trees were thick, and they had to step carefully as they picked their way through. Racine carried a compass and a torch and shone the way for them, but once again, she was amazed at how he could possibly find his way. He seemed to know where he was going and, while keeping her eyes to the ground to avoid roots and anything protruding from the trees that might cause her to trip, she followed trustingly. She noticed the chill starting to creep in and wished again that she had a warmer coat.

Something suddenly flew out of one of the trees, passing close by Thérèse's face before flying up to the sky and causing her to let out a little scream. The two men turned to look at her, and she exclaimed,

"It startled me! What was it?"

Racine shrugged.

"Probably a bat," he replied. He turned to Gaston.

"How are you coping, *mon ami?*"

"I'm alright," answered Gaston in a weak voice. "I'm not sure how much longer I can keep this up, though."

"Not much longer now," Racine encouraged him, but Thérèse could hear the uncertainty in his voice.

They plowed on, Thérèse keeping an anxious eye on her patient. She hoped fervently that he would be able to make this trek through the forest and that they wouldn't have to wait too long for the plane to arrive.

Half an hour later, they emerged at the end of the trees. Thérèse could see fields by the light of the moon and, at some distance away, a building of some sort. Racine turned back to her and saw the questioning look in her eyes.

"It's an old barn," he explained. "I was told that we were to stay there while we await the plane. At least it will be a little warmer, and our friend can rest."

She shot a quick look at Gaston. His face was looking pinched and he drew a weary hand over his eyes. She was quite sure she could see a sheen of perspiration on his forehead and started to worry about his fever returning.

"How are you feeling, Gaston?" she asked, going over to him.

"I've felt better," he answered in a shaky voice, lowering his eyes.

"Can you make it to the building over there?" Racine asked him, pointing in the direction of the barn.

Gaston nodded, but then swayed slightly, causing Racine to tighten his grip on him.

"Let me help," said Thérèse, coming to Gaston's other side and putting her arm around his waist so that he could lean on both her and Racine.

They limped along in the dark and every pace seemed to be agony for Gaston. He never murmured, but Thérèse noticed that he was gritting his teeth and occasionally closing his eyes as he walked between them. She hoped against hope that he would be able to make it to the barn, as she didn't think that she and Racine would be able to carry him should the need arise.

Finally, they arrived at their destination, and Thérèse thought it was not a moment too soon for Gaston. He groaned as Racine pushed open the door of the building and shone his torch inside.

It was a derelict old barn, with hay strewn around the floor and a strong smell of mould. Luckily, there were no animals inside. A rickety ladder led to the loft, which was also filled with hay, but Thérèse doubted that the ladder was in good repair. She set about piling up some of the hay on the floor, then indicated to Gaston that he should lie down. He did so gratefully, with Racine's help, closing his eyes and remaining inert. Thérèse sat down beside him and checked his pulse once again, finding it to be elevated, and noted his pallor and the sweat on his face. She thought he had been very courageous to walk all that way without complaint and hoped he'd be up to the plane journey.

She glanced at Racine, who had done a brief inspection of the inside of the building, then asked him,

"Now what?"

"And now we wait."

"How long?"

He shrugged.

"We don't know," he said. "We wait until we hear a plane engine. This is definitely the building they told us to wait in, so it should be landing fairly close by. Why don't you lie down and try to get some sleep while we're waiting?"

"What about you?" she asked.

"I'll be alright," he said. "I'll keep a lookout and let you know if I hear anything."

Thérèse nodded and lay down not far from Gaston. She cushioned her head with a handful of hay and hoped she'd be able to go to sleep. Their mission was almost over and not a moment too soon!

She was awakened by Racine shaking her shoulder.

"Rose, Rose, wake up," he said, shining the torch in her face. He wore an anxious expression.

She rubbed her eyes and sat up, staring at him in confusion.

"What's the matter?" she asked.

"I thought I heard voices," he told her urgently. "You have to help me get Gaston up the ladder."

"The ladder . . . ?"

Racine reached out a hand and helped her up.

"I'm pretty sure I heard voices outside," he said again. "But there was no plane, so I don't think it's our colleagues. We have to hide in the loft. I'm afraid that they'll see us if we go outside."

She stared at him, aghast. The feeling of panic she'd experienced earlier suddenly lodged itself in her stomach, and her heart skipped a couple of beats. Was it possible they could have been discovered now, after they had almost accomplished their mission?

"Rose, hurry up!" Racine hissed. "Help me get Gaston up. I'll get on the ladder, then you can push him up from the bottom while I pull him."

"But . . . but . . . that won't be good for him," she stuttered. "He's so weak. I don't think he can go up the ladder, and . . . and what if it breaks?"

"That's just a chance we'll have to take," he answered. "If we stay here and they come in, we'll be caught."

The thought of this terrified her even more, and Thérèse sprang into action. She and Racine went over to Gaston, whose eyes were now open at the sound of their voices, and Racine quietly explained his plan to him.

"Can you climb the ladder, *mon gars*, if we help you?" he asked the wounded man.

Gaston swallowed, then nodded his head. Racine quickly put his arms around his waist and lifted him to his feet.

"Rose, help me walk him over to the ladder," he instructed.

She did as he said, a sense of foreboding enveloping her. Oh, why had she given up safety and security in a comfortable home in England in exchange for this wild scheme, which now seemed to be fraught with danger? However, despite her misgivings, she got behind Gaston when they reached the ladder. Racine quickly scaled halfway up, pausing to check one of the steps and cautioning them that it was rickety.

Thérèse stood behind Gaston as he put a foot on the ladder then tried to pull his other leg up on to the next rung. It was his bad leg, and he moaned as he put his weight on it. Thérèse put her hands up and tried to push him from behind, while Racine reached out a hand and simultaneously pulled him. She was soon sweating and struggling with the weight of Gaston and the effort of trying to push him up the ladder.

Between the two of them, they were able to get him halfway up, but then he put his foot on a rickety rung. Racine called out a warning and Gaston removed his foot just as the rung gave way and split in two. Thérèse let out a muffled scream, which earned her a stern look from Racine. He reached out and grabbed Gaston to steady him on the ladder.

"Now try to get up to the next rung," instructed Racine.

With much effort, they were able to get the injured man up the ladder and into the loft, all the while listening for the sound of voices. Thérèse's shoulders were aching from pushing and bearing Gaston's weight, and her legs were shaking as she pulled herself up the ladder after him while Racine helped them both from above. She struggled over the broken rung but was finally able to get herself past it.

Finally, she heaved herself up the last rung and fell into the loft with a gasp. She sat for a moment, trying to catch her breath, then Racine shone the torch at her and motioned her to assist him.

"Help me get Gaston covered up with hay," he told her.

"What? We have to hide under the hay?" she questioned him, panic rising again.

"Only if you don't want to be found," he replied grimly. "We can't risk anyone seeing us."

She nodded reluctantly then set to the task, making sure that Gaston was well covered, his head last of all.

"Can you breathe alright?" she asked him.

"Yes," he mumbled from beneath the hay. Racine nodded, then turned to her.

"Now you lie down and I'll cover you," he instructed.

Reluctantly, she lay down on the cold hay and Racine began covering her up. The hay scratched and poked at her body, but she didn't protest. When her head was completely surrounded, she was enveloped by a profound sense of claustrophobia and felt that she couldn't catch her breath. She forced herself to relax and take some deep breaths and, after a minute or so, the feeling subsided.

"Now, not a word, either of you!" cautioned Racine.

Thérèse listened to the rustling of the hay as Racine then concealed himself beneath it. The minutes ticked by. She felt herself heating up with the pressure of the hay on her body, and the tickling and scratching became worse. At one moment, she thought something was crawling across her face, but she bit her tongue and pressed her lips together to prevent herself from crying out.

After several long and uncomfortable minutes, she was convinced that Racine had been mistaken about hearing the voices earlier. She was just about to tell him exactly that when, all of a sudden, there was a commotion.

They heard the sound of the barn door being flung open and loud voices speaking in German. Dread filling her, she wondered whether the soldier that Racine had shot at had alerted his superiors and they had sent out a search party. Terror and regret filled her as she once again cursed herself for taking on this mission instead of staying comfortably and safely at home. Now they could very well be found by the soldiers who had entered the barn. The consequences of being captured by the enemy didn't even bear thinking about!

The voices sounded like two younger men and an older one. The latter had a gruff and rasping voice and seemed to be barking out the orders. She could hear them moving about downstairs in the main area of the barn and wished fervently that she could be far away from here, back home in her narrow bed in Southport or, better still, in her big double bed with Emmett in London. She held her breath.

After a few moments, the gruff voice barked out another order and she thought she could hear footsteps climbing up the ladder. Then there was the sound of cursing, followed by a thud, and she wondered whether the soldier had slipped on the broken rung and fallen back to the floor. After some more muffled whispers, the sound of footsteps could be heard again.

Seconds later, she was aware of light flooding the loft, even though her eyes were squeezed tightly shut. The person climbing up the ladder must have shone a torch on the upper level where they were hiding. Thérèse felt her body breaking out in a sweat as she continued to hold her breath.

The straw scratched her neck and face, and she prayed that she wouldn't suddenly need to sneeze and give away their hiding place. Her heart pounded and felt as though it was going to leap out of her chest, but she somehow managed to stay quiet. The blood rushing in her ears sounded to her like thunder and she was half sure the soldiers would hear it.

A few more minutes ticked by, but they felt like an hour to Thérèse as she lay there in terror, fearing discovery. Then, the gruff voice spoke again.

"*Sie sind nicht hier,*" it announced.

The footsteps descending the ladder could be heard, then a mumbled conversation between the three men, followed by total silence. Thérèse continued to lie underneath the straw, too afraid to move in case this was a trick and the enemy soldiers would pounce on her as soon as she stirred.

She felt a hand seize her shoulder. She screamed and rolled over, sitting up abruptly, straw in her hair and panic on her face.

It was Racine.

"*Oh, mon dieu*!" she exclaimed, huge relief surging through her. "You frightened me!"

He smiled and held out a hand to help her up.

"They're gone," he replied. "They gave up on us. *Sie sind nicht hier*. It means 'they're not here'. They certainly didn't look very hard."

"Thank God for that!" she breathed. "I don't know whether they would have shot us on the spot or dragged us back to Rouen for torture and death."

"The former would have been preferable," he answered. "But we're alright. Give me a hand to get Gaston down the ladder."

She nodded and stood upright, following Racine as he shone his torch to where Gaston was lying, still half covered by the straw, his eyes closed and his face once again looking pale in the harsh light. She bent down and touched his forehead with the back of her hand. Gaston stirred slightly and murmured something unintelligible but didn't open his eyes.

"I think his fever has returned," Thérèse said. "We have to get him back to England and to a hospital as quickly as possible."

He murmured his assent, then consulted his watch by torchlight.

"It may be a few hours before the plane arrives," he told her. "Do you think you can manage until it gets here?"

"I'll have to," she replied. "Maybe you could see if you can find some water for him."

"I don't think there's any in here," he answered. "Maybe we should just leave him up here for now, and I'll see if I can find water anywhere in this God-forsaken place. I don't think this barn has been used in a long time, so I don't think we'll find any here."

"No, I suppose not."

"I may be gone for a while," he said. "If you hear anything at all, just cover yourself and Gaston up again with the hay and hope you won't be discovered."

She nodded, the familiar feeling of dread once again rising in her stomach.

59

It was the longest night of her life. Thérèse sat in the dark with Gaston, listening to his ragged breathing and knowing that his health was once again deteriorating. She prayed that he was up for the plane journey to England, followed by a possible ambulance ride to the nearest hospital. Injured people needed to rest and not be moved around constantly, but she knew there wasn't much hope of that.

She also kept an ear out for the sounds of returning German soldiers, but all was quiet during her vigil. She sent up silent prayers of thanks once again for their successful deliverance from the enemy and hoped that it would continue. How naïve she had been to think that she could go into an occupied country and rescue a wounded man without some kind of brush with the enemy.

Thérèse knew that her Resistance days were numbered. Her husband and children in England needed her, and she mustn't jeopardize her own safety like this again. She did some sober reflection during those hours while she waited for Racine to come back, yet somehow she couldn't get away from the intuitive feeling that she would return to her home without any more incidents. However, had her love of new experiences and desire to help others wherever possible blinded her to the risks that she was taking?

When she finally heard Racine coming back, she breathed a sigh of relief. She jumped up and went over to the edge of the loft, watching the torch light bouncing around in the dark as he walked. His facial features finally came into view, and she felt her fears slowly dissolving.

"I had to go back to the farm truck," he told her. "I found the canteen we left behind and filled it up at a water trough I noticed when we first came out of the woods."

No wonder it had taken him so long to get back! Thérèse once again marvelled to herself at the invaluable tracking and navigation skills of the man and felt that the Resistance was lucky to have him, as was she to have been assigned to him. She woke Gaston carefully from his deep sleep and was able to get him to swallow some water.

"You two stay here and I'll go outside and watch for signs of the plane arriving," Racine announced, once again climbing down the ladder of the loft and leaving the two of them alone. Thérèse couldn't help feeling a little disappointed, as Gaston had gone back to sleep once again and she was left with only her thoughts for company.

Thérèse had actually dozed off and was in the middle of a dream about soldiers dragging her screaming through the woods when her shoulder was once again shaken. For a moment, she thought she had been hearing one of them calling her by her code name while she begged for mercy.

"Rose, Rose . . . " Racine's voice was in her ear. She opened her eyes to see his face close to hers as he watched her with a concerned expression in the torchlight.

"Are you alright, *chérie?"* he asked.

She nodded and sat upright.

"I must have fallen asleep," she said. She turned and looked at Gaston, who was still in a deep sleep and not looking any better than he had. Thérèse frowned.

"The plane's coming," Racine told her tersely. "We need to wake our friend and somehow get him to the fields outside."

She leapt to her feet and bent over Gaston. Between the two of them, she and Racine managed to awaken him and get him to the edge of the loft, as he looked ahead groggily. Racine went halfway down the ladder and then, with a combination of pulling and pushing, they were able to get him down to the main floor of the barn. Thérèse was soon gasping for breath as her muscles strained to once again hold the weight of the man. Gaston moaned in pain on a couple of occasions but was mostly stoic about the whole operation. Then, leaning on both of them, he limped to the outside and into the cold night air.

Above, the sky was dark, and Thérèse could only see a few stars. The wind was blowing through the trees at the edge of the field and they looked like ghostly creatures swaying in a macabre dance. Thérèse shivered, then realized that what she had mistaken for the wind was actually the whirring sound of a plane engine stirring up the trees, just as she had heard in London when bombers flew overhead on their way to Europe.

Her stomach clenched with anticipation. The thing she had been praying for was almost here, and all of her prayers of the last few hours were being answered. She felt almost like a child at a birthday party, and excitement and relief coursed through her. She would soon be home, barring any unforeseen accidents in mid-air or being shot at by enemy planes. She banished those pessimistic thoughts and watched the plane's progress as it circled the fields several times.

It finally landed in a flurry of propellers and rushing air. Racine, who had been guiding the plane down to its landing, walked towards the door and waited while it was opened by the pilot. It was a small plane, but presumably had room for all of them. The pilot, wearing a helmet and dressed in full British military uniform, opened the door and attached a small ladder that reached the ground.

As they approached the plane with Gaston limping between them, Racine looked at Thérèse over his head.

"Well, *chère madame,* this is where I leave you," he announced. She nodded in acknowledgment.

At that moment, the pilot scaled down the ladder, then walked quickly towards them with an outstretched hand.

"Captain Richard Norton," he said, in clipped tones. He shook Racine's hand and turned to Thérèse.

"Let me help take the gentleman's weight, madam."

With relief, she stepped aside as the pilot took her place at Gaston's side. The pilot was a young man, with a snub nose and pleasant features. He probably wasn't much more than twenty years old, despite his rank.

"I'll come down and talk to you again, Rose," said Racine as he and Captain Norton started to help Gaston up the ladder.

"Alright," she answered him.

She waited on the ground for what seemed like an interminable time, clasping her arms around her waist in an effort to keep warm in the cold night air. Eventually, Racine appeared from the plane and climbed down the ladder.

"Your turn, *chérie,*" he told her.

Thérèse felt a little shiver go through her.

"I've never been in a plane before," she said solemnly.

"Well, you'll have something to tell your children about," he countered with an impish smile.

She smiled back, and he reached out and clasped one of her hands in his.

"Rose . . . Tropical Rose . . . , it's been a pleasure to have you along," he told her warmly. "This mission couldn't have been accomplished without you, and I congratulate you on your courage and willingness to help an Allied soldier in his time of need. The Free French movement is grateful for your help."

Thérèse was overcome with emotion and opened her mouth to speak, but Racine opened his arms and pulled her into a tight hug. He held her for a few moments, then kissed her on both cheeks in Gallic style.

"I hope we meet again," he said quietly.

She looked at that handsome face, committing it to memory. His high cheekbones and chiselled features would be forever imprinted in her mind, and she couldn't suppress a fleeting hope that she would one day see him again.

"It's doubtful, Racine," she replied. A thought occurred to her. "What's your real name? I promise I'll never reveal it."

"I really can't tell you," he answered reluctantly. "If things go horribly wrong and you get captured, I can't risk it being pried out of you."

"Fair enough," she said. Then, tentatively, "You don't think we'll be captured, do you?"

"I'm sure you won't," he hastened to assure her. "But we can't completely discount the possibility."

She nodded, then turned towards the ladder.

"You've been wonderful, Racine," she said. "You're a credit to the Resistance and to France, and I'm glad they have you and all of your great talents. The Allies will win the war with people like you on their side."

"God willing," he answered her. Thérèse would use that phrase for the rest of her life for whenever she felt she needed divine help with an earthly situation. They would be the last words she would hear from Racine and, sadly, she never did come across him again, although he came into her mind every so often and she would think wistfully of their adventure.

She began to climb the ladder, pausing to turn around and give him a little wave, feeling tears pricking her eyes. She didn't know if it was from the relief of being at the final stage of her mission, or regret from parting with Racine. Best not to think about that! She stepped inside the plane and Captain Norton closed the door after her.

60

Thérèse found the aeroplane journey exhilarating, although cold and bumpy. The feeling in her stomach as they climbed into the air set her pulses racing and, although she had never been fond of heights when it came to climbing up ladders and such, the sensation of going up into the air was very different. The sound of the plane engine was deafening in her ears, but she didn't mind that. Outside, blackness surrounded them as they flew through the night.

Every so often, she would turn around and check on Gaston, who was seated behind her. After the initial take-off, during which he gritted his teeth and looked as though he was experiencing a lot of pain, he had relapsed into what seemed to be a deep sleep, his face very still. She worried about him, but knew that help was not far off and that he would be in professional medical hands once they reached England.

Captain Norton flew with quiet expertise, turning around once in a while and asking her how she was faring. Knowing that her voice probably wouldn't carry much above the engine and the wind, she just nodded her head in acknowledgment.

Time went by uneventfully and, finally, Captain Norton turned to her again and pointed out the windshield of the plane in an easterly direction.

"Sun's rising," he called out, and Thérèse turned to look into the direction in which he was pointing.

Indeed, beautiful colours were visible from outside the window. Bright yellow, fiery red and deep orange hues layered on top of one another appeared in the lightening sky. It was a magnificent sight, and Thérèse continued to stare at it for a long time as the sun slowly and majestically rose from out of the clouds.

She turned to look at Gaston again to see whether he was awake and observing the miracle of sunrise as well, but he was still unconscious. She hoped it was due to sleep, and not because his condition had again worsened. She returned to watching the sunrise, and that occupied her time for quite a while.

As she was watching, she reflected on the last two days and what she had experienced. She knew that keeping her mission a secret from her family had been devious, but she still felt that she had done the right thing and was proud of her achievement. It had seemed like a fairly simple thing when she left England, to go into France and bring back a wounded man, but she had never seriously considered the possibility of being captured by the enemy. She knew she would not have returned home if that had happened, and was now hit by the gravity of this. Twice they had come close to being caught, and she silently thanked God for their escape.

She had wanted to do her part for the war effort and she had succeeded. Deep down, she knew that she had been very brave, if a little foolish and naïve, to have thought she could accomplish the rescue without any obstacles. A lot of the luck that they had experienced had been due to Racine's skills and experience and for that she would always remember him with gratitude.

The plane was finally flying over England and, with more and more light coming through the window beside her, she could catch glimpses of land below her. Trees and fields seemed to go by in slow motion, although she knew they were actually going very fast. Air transport was something Thérèse would always enjoy once civilian flights became readily available to the general public after the war. She would travel the world often throughout the rest of her life, from flying home to Mauritius to visit her family to travelling to Europe and parts of Africa to visit her various relatives, then finally flying as far as North America to see Vivienne, who had moved there in her middle years.

They landed in a field, guided by a man holding a baton. The landing was quite gruelling, jarring her body and making her feel as though her insides had risen into the air. Once things had settled, the plane sat for a few minutes on the field before Captain Norton turned off the engines. Pulling off his aviation mask, he turned once more to her.

"We're here," he announced. "How's the patient faring?"

Thérèse turned to Gaston and took a look at his face. It was still pallid, and his eyelashes lay along his cheeks in what looked like a deep sleep. She prayed that he wasn't in a coma.

"He doesn't look very well," she replied. "I'll take his pulse as soon as

I can. He's going to need to go to hospital as quickly as possible."

"I've radioed ahead for an ambulance," Captain Norton told her. They should be here fairly soon. Wait here until I get back."

She nodded and watched as he prepared to descend from the plane.

Once Captain Norton returned with two medical attendants and a stretcher, they lifted Gaston out of the plane and whisked him away into the semi-darkness of early dawn. The captain helped Thérèse out of the plane, then led her to an abandoned cottage not far from where they had landed.

"We're using this field as a temporary air strip," he explained to her. "If you can wait here for a little while, there's a car coming to take us back to London and you can make plans to travel home."

Thérèse nodded and thought how ironic it was that she had arrived close to London where her husband, blissfully oblivious as to what she had been doing for the last two days, had no idea that she wasn't in the north of England.

They sat and waited in the little house for a while without making much conversation, and then Thérèse heard a commotion outside.

"Where is she?" demanded a young female voice in English.

All of a sudden, Lucille burst through the main door of the cottage, followed by a male figure who Thérèse recognized as St. Tropez Harry.

"Thérèse!" Lucille exclaimed, running towards her and throwing her arms around her. She then switched to French. "My brave girl, I can't believe you did it! You rescued my brother! How can I ever thank you enough?"

"I didn't do it alone," replied Thérèse, returning her warm hug. "I had help from some wonderful people."

Lucille stood back and gazed at her face. There were tears in her eyes, and Thérèse thought she looked exhausted. Harry then stepped forward and shook Thérèse's hand.

"Well done, Tropical Rose," he said warmly, still gripping her hand. "The operatives on the other side said that you were admirable to work with. Congratulations on bringing back the subject of our mission."

"It was my honour," said Thérèse simply. "I hope they're taking him to hospital."

Lucille nodded in reply.

"They told me that I can visit him in the morning," she stated. "He's not looking well, but the ambulance attendants told me he'll be alright."

"What about you?" Thérèse asked her. "You look very tired."

"I've been travelling all night," she replied. "But enough about me. Are you well? Did you encounter any danger?"

"I'll tell you about that later," Thérèse answered. She then remembered the young man standing beside her. "I should introduce you to Captain Norton. I expect Harry here already knows him."

Harry nodded in acknowledgment.

"Ah, yes, the brave young pilot," said Lucille. "We've got a car here to take us all back to London."

"Lovely!" rejoined Thérèse. "I could do with a hot bath and a good, long sleep."

Lucille gave a little laugh, then held out her hand to Captain Norton as Thérèse quickly made the introduction. Harry indicated that they should go to the car that was waiting outside, and he would drive them back to London.

61

After they arrived back in London, they were driven to a hotel where they would all catch up on some sleep before going in their separate directions, Captain Norton to an air force base just outside the city, Lucille to the hospital where Gaston was staying, and Thérèse to her family in Southport. Harry, however, didn't say where he was going. She assumed he would have to check in with someone from MI6 about the rescue mission and report its success.

She shook hands with him once more, and he thanked her again for the part she had played in Gaston's rescue. He told her he would happily use her again for a mission if she ever indicated an interest in repeating the experience. She replied that she would have to think about that very seriously before committing to anything, then wished him goodnight and ascended the stairs to her room to fall into bed and sleep.

After she woke up the next morning, she spent a leisurely hour taking a bath in the big iron bathtub in her hotel room, then brushed her hair and once again dressed herself in the farmer's wife's dress. She frowned at her appearance in the full-length mirror in her room and vowed to stop at a dress shop before she returned to Emmett's cousin's house. Then she caught herself, remembering that she didn't have any money with her.

As she lay on the bed reading a magazine she had found on the bedside table, the telephone rang.

"Yes?" she answered, after lifting the receiver.

"Thérèse?" replied a voice she recognized. "Marie-Madeleine Fourcade here."

"Well, hello," Thérèse said happily. "How nice to hear from you."

"Congratulations, my dear," said the familiar voice enthusiastically. "Your mission was successful, and the patient will make a full recovery."

"Oh, that's good news!" breathed Thérèse. "He'll be alright?"

"Yes, they may do an operation on his leg, but they said it won't have to be amputated or anything like that. He has an infection in the wound."

"I tried to clear it up with iodine, but I think that hiding under some dirty straw certainly didn't help it."

"You had to hide under straw? Were you in danger of being found by the Germans?"

Thérèse then recounted the frightening story of their hiding place in the hayloft of the French farm building. When she was done, Mme Fourcade announced that she would like to take her out for lunch and discuss the whole mission in detail.

"That would be lovely," announced Thérèse. "But could I ask one favour before that?"

"Of course."

'Could we go to a dress shop and buy me an outfit? I look like a ragged French peasant right now, and I don't think I can go for lunch in a nice restaurant dressed like this!"

Mme Fourcade laughed her pleasant, tinkling laugh and agreed right away.

After the foray to the dress shop, in which Thérèse purchased a new dress and raincoat, they spent a very pleasant afternoon having lunch and drinking wine in an expensive restaurant that Mme Fourcade found. Thérèse told her the entire story of their mission, and her companion listened intently.

"Well, the mission was certainly not without danger," she commented when Thérèse had finished speaking. "You risked capture twice."

"Yes and, if it hadn't been for Racine, I don't think I'd be sitting here today," Thérèse replied. "He's a remarkable man."

"General de Gaulle has his eye on him," said Mme Fourcade. "The general knows the great things he's doing for France. He'll be informed of what you've done for us, as well," she added.

Thérèse blushed and shook her head.

"I did very little," she countered.

Mme Fourcade leaned forward and touched her hand.

"Never discount what you did, my dear," she said with a smile. "It took a lot of courage to go into France when it's under German rule and bring someone out of there, especially an injured man. It's why it took us such a long time to find someone who could do the job."

"I'm honoured to have done it," replied Thérèse warmly.

The two women continued their lunch, then Mme Fourcade called for the bill. Thérèse protested that she couldn't pay for herself since she didn't have any money with her, but her hostess dismissed her concerns. Thérèse suddenly remembered hearing from somewhere that Marie-Madeleine was an aristocrat who had given up her cosseted life to help her country during the war, and she thought perhaps that could be where she had seen her before. Perhaps at one of the Civil Service luncheons or formal dinners that she had attended?

As they left the restaurant, Mme Fourcade turned to her, holding out an envelope.

"You go back to the hotel and have another good sleep, Thérèse," she said. "Then, tomorrow morning, you can take a train back to Liverpool and go home to your family."

Thérèse opened the envelope and saw a train ticket and a twenty-pound note inside.

"Pay for your hotel room with this and use whatever's left over in the dining car," the other woman told her.

Thérèse thanked her effusively, then the two women exchanged kisses on both cheeks, as the French do. Murmuring "*Adieu*, Thérèse," Madame Fourcade turned and walked away. It would probably be the last time Thérèse would see her, although she read a lot about her in newspapers after the war. Mme Fourcade was actually captured by the Germans towards the end of the war, but managed to escape by climbing out a window of her prison and running throughout the night to safety.

The train ride seemed long, but Thérèse took the time to reflect once again on the last few days and to decide whether she would consider doing the same thing again. She regretted that she had not been able to visit Gaston in the military hospital to say goodbye, but she knew that Lucille would probably keep in touch with her, or the Women's Voluntary Service in Southport, and she would hear news of him.

After she arrived in Liverpool, she took a bus to Southport and felt anticipation growing again at the thought of seeing her sweet little daughter and her husband's cousins. As the bus drew closer to the little house, her excitement mounted and she could hardly wait for it to arrive at the stop just down the road from Eustace and Martha's house.

Finally, the bus pulled into the curb beside the bus stop on the street where they lived, and Thérèse descended from the vehicle with a rapidly beating heart.

She walked up the garden path and rang the doorbell. The door was opened after a few moments, and a rather harried-looking Martha peered out. As she recognized Thérèse, her expression gave way to one of delight and she pulled her into a tight hug.

"We've been so worried about tha!" The older woman exclaimed, pulling Thérèse back again to have a long look at her. "Where hast tha been?"

"I'll tell you all about it when I get in, Martha," said Thérèse. "Just let me in the house and we can have a chat."

"Yes, but . . . " Martha stammered, placing a hand on Thérèse's sleeve.

Thérèse brushed by her and into the house. She walked down the hallway to the living room, suddenly stopping dead. There, seated in one of the armchairs by the window, sat Emmett.

62

As she walked into the room, followed by Martha, Emmett stood up. Far from looking pleased to see her, he had an expression of extreme worry mixed with anger on his face. He came over to her and, rather than hugging her in relief, he stopped, his face close to hers.

"Thérèse!" he exclaimed. "Where have you been?"

"W - well . . . I was, . . . er, . . . I was in Liverpool!" she blurted out. This was not completely untrue. She had just come by bus from Liverpool, hadn't she?

"Liverpool??" His face darkened. "What on earth were you doing there? There are bombs being dropped every other day in Liverpool! I sent you here so you would be safe!"

She twisted her hands together, looking towards Eustace and Martha for support, but Martha stood regarding her uncomfortably and Eustace gazed at her with a stern face from his armchair.

"I - I . . . know," she stammered. "I had something to do there."

"What could you possibly have had to do?"

She stood there, facing him, all colour drained from her face. Was it worth telling more lies and getting herself embroiled in a tangled web she couldn't get out of? She had never seen Emmett so angry in their twenty-one years of marriage. Suddenly, she made the decision that it wasn't worth lying any more and took his hands in hers.

"Emmett . . . " she faltered.

"Tell me the truth, Thérèse," he demanded hotly.

She swallowed, then replied quietly. "I was in France."

"*France?* What were you doing in France?" He stared at her in outraged disbelief.

Then the whole story came tumbling out. Meeting Lucille and feeling sorry for the brother who had resisted the enemy and was injured by a gunshot, feeling she had to help him somehow, and making the decision to go over to France. She then recounted the rescue mission and her safe return, omitting the parts about being chased by the German soldiers and lying hidden in a stack of hay while the loft was being searched.

As she spoke, she saw that Emmett was slowly relaxing, his angry facial expression being replaced by one of admiration, almost awe. Eustace, too, and Martha were staring at her with open mouths, unable to believe that their cousin's little wife could go on such a daring expedition.

". . . and now Gaston is recuperating in an army hospital and . . . here I am!" she finished, wringing her hands together and waiting for Emmett's response.

He swallowed visibly, then placed his hands on her shoulders.

"Well, you're a very brave girl," he stated, then his expression changed again. "But also very foolish."

She threw her arms around his waist and pressed her face against his chest.

"I know, I know!" she exclaimed. "Please forgive me for lying to you, Emmett, and to your cousins!"

He lifted her face with his hands.

"And what about Vivienne? Didn't you think she'd worry about you?" he asked gently.

"No, she was fine here with Eustace and Martha. She loves being with them, and the dog."

"Well, she also worried about you. You've hardly ever been away from her, and she thought you were never coming back."

"I knew I was coming back," she stated with more bravado than she felt. "My intuition told me I'd be alright."

"Thérèse, you know I don't believe in that!" he rejoined, annoyed once again. "And you certainly shouldn't risk your life by going into an enemy-occupied country based on that."

She lowered her eyes.

"You're right," she said quietly. "I promise I won't do it again."

He looked at her, then kissed her lips by way of greeting.

Thérèse turned around and murmured something about "freshening up," then started up the stairs to her room. Martha followed her on the way up.

"I'm so sorry, Thérèse," she blurted out while Thérèse took off her coat and shoes and looked for something more comfortable to change into than the dress she was wearing.

"It's alright, Martha, I don't blame you," she replied.

"He rang up two days ago and asked where you were, so I made some excuses. Then he telephoned again and I tried to make more excuses, but he got suspicious. I couldn't think of any more reasons for you to be away, and he didn't believe the story about you having to sign some papers, so he said he was coming up here to find out for himself."

"Well, he always has been a worrier," Thérèse replied glumly. "That's probably where Vivienne gets it."

Martha nodded.

"I'm sorry you were put into the position of having to lie to him," added Thérèse. "I know it was a hare-brained scheme, but I feel really happy about being able to help that poor young man."

"Tha were so brave, Thérèse! I couldn't imagine doing such a thing," Martha said, an admiring expression on her face. "I've never been out of England, let alone travelling to France by myself to rescue someone."

"Well, I'll tell you all the details another time," Thérèse promised, patting Martha's hand.

"I can hardly wait!" said Martha, and she turned to go out of the room, leaving Thérèse to change her clothes.

After a happy reunion with Vivienne, who had tears in her eyes as she hugged her mother, followed by a rather strained tea meal with the whole family during which she felt that her escapade hung in the air like an elephant in the room, Thérèse offered to help her daughter with her homework. She then chatted for a few minutes with her and offered to tuck her into her bed.

"Goodnight, Mummy," said Vivienne, in a quiet voice. "Please don't go away like that again."

Thérèse felt a stab of guilt at the child's plea. People were being lost to the war every day, and she became aware that her daughter must have been terrified of losing her mother.

"Did you miss me?" she asked her daughter.

"Yes!" answered Vivienne. "I was afraid you were never coming back."

"I would never do that to you, darling" Thérèse replied firmly. "But I promise I won't do it again. Now you go to sleep and don't worry. I'll still be here in the morning."

She kissed the child's cheek and went downstairs, closing the door gently after her. Emmett was waiting for her in the living room.

"Let's go to our room, Thérèse," he said, taking her hand. "I want to talk to you."

She felt a quick clutch of dread in her stomach. She was afraid that Emmett had rethought his acceptance of her explanations from this afternoon and was now going to interrogate her about the entire truth.

They went into the spare bedroom that he had been occupying and he led her over to the bed, sitting down and patting the space beside him. She seated herself gingerly beside him.

He took her hand in his.

"Darling, you know I love you very much, don't you?" he said softly, looking directly into her eyes.

"Yes," she answered quickly.

"And do you love me?" His eyes were penetrating, almost looking into her very soul.

"Of course, Emmett," she replied sincerely. "I love you more than ever."

He smiled slightly, then took her chin in his hand.

"Then what on earth possessed you to do something so foolish?" He suddenly burst out, staring earnestly at her.

"I - I . . . wanted to do something more for the war effort than packing blankets," she explained in a defensive tone. "I had been into France once before and returned unscathed, and I just felt so sorry for poor Lucille, worrying about her brother and being afraid she'd never see him again . . . " her voice trailed off.

"Your feeling sorry for Lucille could have cost you your life!" he said, rather angrily. "Did you not think of the possible consequences of your actions?"

"Yes, I did," she told him firmly. "And I knew I'd be alright." She felt tears pricking her eyes and turned away from him for a moment. "Please don't ask me how I know about things, Emmett. I just do. I know you don't believe it, but I do have a special gift for knowing how things will turn out."

She turned back to him and put her arms around his neck, after wiping away the tears.

"I can't explain it," she continued. "It's just there. Sometimes it fails me for a few moments, especially if I'm scared, but it usually guides me in all of my decisions, including the one to marry you. That was the best decision of my life," she added, looking intently at him.

She saw his gaze soften. He touched her cheek, then kissed her tenderly on the forehead, wrapping his arms around her.

"Well, I'm glad you don't regret that," he replied. "And I know that you have extraordinary intuition, but I hope you won't endanger your life and make your family worry about you again."

"I won't," she affirmed. "I promise I will tell you if I ever have any inclination to do such a thing again."

"Well, that's good, then," he whispered against her ear, tightening his arms around her. "I want you to be safe. Please just stay in Southport for as long as this war continues, and I promise I'll come up to visit you and Vivienne as often as I can."

Thérèse melted against him. At that moment, she knew that she would keep her promise to Emmett, at least for a little while. However, she couldn't help but hear that voice in the back of her mind telling her that it might not be that easy should Mme Fourcade telephone her again. She returned her husband's kiss passionately and allowed him to hold her ever more tightly.

She felt safe and warm with him, and suddenly France and the war seemed very far away. This was where she wanted to stay. At least for now.

THE END

Epilogue

My grandmother, Cécile Marie Thérèse, did not go to France again during the war. However, she continued her work with the Women's Voluntary Service, and for all we know, she may have helped the Free French war effort by passing on messages between agents and emissaries from the Resistance movement. She stayed in England to finish raising her last child, my mother, who decided to become a nurse after finishing her schooling. My mother may have modelled herself after her mother and grandmother in wanting to take care of the sick. However, her father, Emmett, always forward-thinking when it came to the women in his family, urged her to become a doctor instead and she agreed to pursue medicine at the University of London.

Cécile continued to travel the world after the war, visiting her many French-speaking cousins across the globe, in places like South Africa, the Canary Islands, the island of Réunion (where her mother ended her days in the company of her youngest daughter) and several European countries. After my mother, Valerie (whom I called Vivienne) moved to Canada with her family, Cécile visited them many times. She was warmly welcomed by Valerie's family and their friends, as she was always a charming and intelligent woman. We loved her visits, and I also loved hearing the anecdotes about her life (especially about the many admirers she had!). And, yes, she really did have some kind of intuitive ability which allowed her to predict outcomes of situations, and to know things that nobody had told her anything about.

She sadly lost her husband when he was in his sixties but, with her usual determination and strength of character, she learned how to run her household affairs, to write cheques (something she had never done before) and to drive. I'll never forget her braving the London traffic and coming to visit us on many occasions after his death. She also tragically lost her only son in his early forties, but soldiered on as she always did with the many losses in her life.

After my mother died, my two brothers and I were clearing out her flat, and my sister-in-law came across a letter from General Charles de Gaulle (the mid- and post-war French president) thanking my grandmother for her "service to France." We don't know exactly what she did, and the letter didn't specify, but I felt that she must have done something quite extraordinary to receive a letter from de Gaulle himself, and this is what inspired me to write about her venturing twice into France to help other people come to England. (She really did have cousins who lived in France and came to live in England around that time.) We also know that she did in fact escape from France in a fishing boat, after a visit during the time when war broke out.

As for some of the other characters I've mentioned in the story, Adelaide was a neighbour who lived a few houses up the street from my grandmother and the family. Sadly, two of her four children were not well as infants and were later diagnosed with cystic fibrosis, a disease that affects the lungs and usually shortens the life of the sufferer. Her second child and her youngest both died early, one from the disease and one by suicide. Addie never really recovered from the loss of the younger one and turned once more to alcohol. She later died as the result of a tragic car accident.

Cécile's mother did indeed move to the Island of Réunion with her youngest daughter, and her father died in Mauritius. We don't know for sure whether it was a separation due to her mother's dismay at his philandering lifestyle, but there could be a very good case for it.

Marie-Madeleine Fourcade was a real person and was the head of the French Resistance at one time. She was a very brave and adventurous woman, an aristocrat who wanted to join the war effort in resisting the Nazis. At one time, she had to be smuggled out of France in a box on a cargo train, and spent several uncomfortable hours when the train was delayed for a long period on the tracks. Her story can be discovered in a recent publication about her life, "Madame Fourcade's War" , by Lynne Olson (Random House, 2019).

My grandmother was always an interesting and resilient woman, and I felt that she deserved to have her story told, even if it's been somewhat embellished. And who knows what she could have accomplished during her ninety-two years if she had been born at a later time, when most women were able to access higher levels of education and choose a career for themselves?

About the Author

Debbie was born in London, England, to scientific parents, but always preferred the arts, especially creative writing. At the age of 17, she moved with her family to Toronto and attended Trinity College, emerging with a degree in French and English. Being undecided on a profession, she became a bilingual secretary in a large corporation and met her future husband, Ed, not long after that. In 1980, they moved to his home province of Alberta, where they raised a family. She worked in many administrative jobs, and was involved in community theatre with her whole family. Debbie always wanted to write so, after the tragic loss of her second daughter, she wrote of the family's experience with mental illness in *A Moth to the Flame – Amy's Struggle with Borderline Personality Disorder* (2016). She thought she would try her hand at novel writing and hopes readers enjoy the adventures of her character, who is loosely based on her grandmother.